Chasing Newsroom Diversity

THE HISTORY OF COMMUNICATION

Robert W. McChesney and
John C. Nerone, editors

A list of books in the series appears at the end of this book.

Chasing Newsroom Diversity

From Jim Crow to Affirmative Action

GWYNETH MELLINGER

UNIVERSITY OF ILLINOIS PRESS
Urbana, Chicago, and Springfield

Manufactured in the United States of America
1 2 3 4 5 C P 5 4 3 2 1
∞ This book is printed on acid-free paper.

All photos and drawings courtesy of the American Society of Newspaper Editors.

Portions of chapter 2 previously appeared in "The ASNE and Desegregation: Maintaining the White Prerogative in the Face of Change," *Journalism History* 34, no. 3 (Fall 2008). Portions of chapter 3 previously appeared in "Rekindling the Fire: The Compromise that Opened Newsroom Doors," *American Journalism* 25, no. 3 (Summer 2008): 97–126. Portions of chapter 5 previously appeared in "Counting Color: Ambivalence and Contradiction in the American Society of Newspaper Editors' Discourse of Diversity," *Journal of Communication Inquiry* 27, no. 2 (April 2003): 129–51.

Library of Congress Cataloging-in-Publication Data
Mellinger, Gwyneth.
Chasing newsroom diversity : from Jim Crow to affirmative action / Gwyneth Mellinger.
p. cm. — (The history of communication)
Includes bibliographical references and index.
ISBN 978-0-252-03738-2 (cloth) —
ISBN 978-0-252-07894-1 (pbk.)
1. Minority journalists—United States. 2. African Americans in the newspaper industry. 3. Minorities in journalism—United States. 4. American newspapers—History—20th century. 5. Diversity in the workplace—United States. 6. Minorities—Employment—United States. I. Title.
PN4797.M48 2013
071'.3089—dc23 2012017777

To Mike and Cassady,
as always

Contents

Acknowledgments

A project of this scope, more than a decade in the making, benefits from the contributions and assistance of a number of people. Topping that list are members and staff of the American Society of Newspaper Editors, almost all of them journalism professionals more accustomed to applying scrutiny than being its subject. Their remarkable generosity in sharing archives and insight about newsroom diversity affirmed a commitment to the principles underlying their craft. As I labored to render this dimension of the ASNE's history, their voices never left my thoughts. It is my deepest hope that they find their treatment here to be fair and accurate, even if it is not always flattering.

ASNE members who granted interviews for this project are Gilbert Bailon, Creed Black, Linda Grist Cunningham, Gregory Favre, Pamela Fine, Albert Fitzpatrick, Loren Ghiglione, Charlotte Hall, Jay Harris, William Hilliard, J. Ford Huffman, Wanda Lloyd, Tim McGuire, Greg Moore, Rolfe Neill, Eugene Patterson, John Quinn, Rick Rodriguez, Sharon Rosenhause, Edward Seaton, John Seigenthaler Sr., Richard (Dick) Smyser, and William Woo. Members of the ASNE staff who assisted me are Scott Bosley, LaBarbara Bowman, Craig Branson, Richard Karpel, Diana Mitsu Klos, Christine Schmitt, Connie Southard, and, especially, Lee Stinnett.

In addition, this project benefited immeasurably from the perspectives of members of the newsroom diversity community who participated in ASNE discussions as nonmembers. They are Nancy Hicks Maynard, Pamela Strother, Walterene Swanston, and Keith Woods.

I also would like to extend a special thanks to Lucy Smyser Tashman, who continued to mail me early ASNE Minorities Committee files after the death of her father, Dick Smyser, who had trusted me to copy and return each batch he sent. The Smyser family has since donated those archives to the University of North Carolina's Southern History Collection. Thanks also to the executive staff of the National Lesbian and Gay Journalists Association, who gave me advance access to the papers of Leroy Aarons. Those materials are now part of the ONE National Gay and Lesbian Archives in Los Angeles.

Further, I wish to offer recognition to many strong mentors and fellow graduate students at the University of Kansas who offered guidance as the book took shape. I owe special thanks to Sherrie Tucker, William Tuttle, Norman Yetman, Cheryl Lester, Catherine Preston, William Staples, David Katzman, Barry Shank, David Anthony Tyeeme Clark, Anne Dotter, Maurice Bryan, Julia Good Fox, Ailecia Ruscin, Monique Laney, and Fabien Curie.

In addition, I am indebted to members of the American Journalism Historians Association, who provided a sounding board for this project as it evolved. In particular, Maurine Beasley, Michael Fuhlhage, Kimberley Mangun, David Sloan, Michael Sweeney, Douglas Ward, and Patrick Washburn deserve thanks.

Work on this book was supported in multiple ways by Baker University, which provided sabbatical leave and financial support for research and writing. I am indebted to Rand Ziegler and Jamie Comstock in this regard. In addition, several colleagues and former students encouraged and supported my work over a period of years: Joe Watson, Bruce Anderson, Rob and Kelly Flaherty, Patrick Lattin, Samuel Dester, and Andrew McGregor. The project also received invaluable staff assistance from Kathy Elliott, Sherri Wood, and Kaci Benjamin.

No critical inquiry would be complete without a devil's advocate, and Tom Eblen was mine. As a friend, he read every word and, as only he could, made sure I received alternative perspectives. Thanks also to Lynn Bonney for her sharp pencil and to Jeannie Mellinger and Alan Schueler, William Dobak, Andrew Nachison and Jenny Holah, Joanne and Gary Robinson, and John and Vera DeMott for small but important kindnesses along the way.

At the University of Illinois Press, I would like to thank Richard Wentworth, Daniel Nasset, Vijay Shah, Tad Ringo, Teresa Hudoba, and the series editors for their faith in this book.

Finally, this book would not have been possible without the unconditional support of my brother, Richard Mellinger, and the memory of our parents and stepfather, whose example of civic engagement is a daily inspiration. But my most heartfelt thanks go to Mike and Cassady, who lived and breathed this project with me and encouraged me every step of the way.

Chasing Newsroom Diversity

INTRODUCTION

The Black and White of Newspapers

The daily newspaper editors who met in Washington, D.C., in April 1948 should not have been surprised when James O. Eastland, a U.S. senator from Mississippi, used their convention podium to defend the South's social tradition and valorize its racial hierarchy. An outspoken segregationist, Eastland had been invited onto the American Society of Newspaper Editors' convention program as counterpoint to the civil rights reforms proposed by President Harry S. Truman, who sought to integrate the military, outlaw the poll tax, mandate fair employment, and make lynching a federal crime. In stating his case, Eastland implicated his white audience—particularly editors from Northern states who may have sympathized with racial reform—in the privilege whites enjoyed under segregation. Most important, Eastland construed the editors' nearly all-white newsrooms as a sign of kinship with those, like himself, who meant to continue de jure segregation in the South.[1] Eastland observed that the ASNE and its member newspapers practiced de facto segregation by not hiring journalists who worked for the black press, the network of black-owned weekly newspapers that served African American readers across the United States. "You are guilty of racial discrimination in the newspaper business," he said. "There are thousands of Negro reporters in this country, yet the newspapers do not draw 10 per cent of their reporters from that race. Ten per cent of your executives are not Negroes. You are not to be condemned. It is your civil right to associate with, employ and work with whomever you please. Liberty is dead in this country when you are deprived of that right."[2]

Eastland's attempt to sway the editors by pointing out their own hypocrisy could be dismissed as an artifact of America's racist past but for the broader context of his remarks. By raising the issue of "racial discrimination" in newsroom hiring, Eastland framed continued separation of the races as an exercise of individual freedom for editors whose professional calling was anchored in the Bill of Rights. Notably, Eastland posited the all-white newsroom as the product of the daily newspaper editors' conscious choice, not simply an incidental circumstance in a racially bifurcated society. Most significantly, however, Eastland emphasized the editors' whiteness, which had been taken for granted as a condition of employment by daily newspapers since before the ASNE's founding in 1922 and produced exclusions that leant impetus to the growth of the weekly black newspaper.[3] By juxtaposing the white editor with the black journalist and black news executive, Eastland demonstrated that whiteness was a norm that depended on racial discrimination for its existence.

In his references to "10 per cent," Eastland highlighted the portion of the U.S. population that comprised African Americans and suggested that nondiscriminatory hiring would have produced newsrooms with a racial composition just 90 percent white.[4] In other words, Eastland argued from the assumption that in an integrated newsroom, African Americans would be hired in proportion to their representation in the national demographic. While Eastland's invocation of a racial quota was a rhetorical ploy rather than a policy recommendation, he foreshadowed by exactly thirty years the key strategy that progressive reformers within the ASNE, many of them Southerners, would pursue in attempting to dismantle the daily newspaper industry's whites-only tradition in hiring. Eastland's speech would be long forgotten when the ASNE board voted in 1978 to adopt Goal 2000, an affirmative action initiative to achieve racially proportional employment in daily newspaper newsrooms by the end of the twentieth century.

As such, the senator's remarks offer a point of departure for this historical analysis, which first explores the ASNE's construction of a professional norm that marginalized journalists and editors who were not white, not male, and not heterosexual, and then traces the organization's subsequent attempts to democratize newsroom hiring. Despite passionate advocacy by a series of ASNE leaders and the expenditure of unprecedented industry resources, the organization's leadership would concede publicly in 1997—when nonwhites accounted for just 11.35 percent of the newsroom work force at daily newspapers compared to a nonwhite population of about 26 percent—that the parity hiring goal had been unattainable.[5] This analysis, which traces the ASNE's reckoning with inequality from the 1950s into the twenty-first century, demonstrates why an effort so promising failed so profoundly.

Indisputably, the ASNE's evolution in its understanding of race, as well as its later engagement of gender and sexual orientation, paralleled that of American society at large in the second half of the twentieth century. In the case of race, the ASNE registered the same tensions, hopes, fears, and regional conflicts as America's racial paradigm was unsettled and racial boundaries were redrawn by the U.S. Supreme Court and Congress in the decades following World War II. With the outlawing of school segregation and other manifestations of Jim Crow, the social and legal convention that had kept blacks in their place in many communities, particularly in the South, and the mandating of equal rights in such fundamental areas of society as voting, employment, and housing, the rules that governed American life were rewritten, even if the game was, to a large extent, still played the same. Daily newspaper editors were by no means above the fray or disinterested in its outcome. They were, after all, residents of communities across the United States; the disruption of the racial status quo, a breach of social tradition unparalleled in American history, was playing out in their cities and towns and on the pages of their newspapers.

While the tectonic shift in the legal standing of nonwhite Americans, which began in earnest with Truman's 1948 reform proposals,[6] would reorder the lives of blacks, it also would redefine white people's stake in race and produce a backlash that reasserted white investment in the traditional American racial hierarchy. Over the next several decades, as nonwhite Americans reevaluated the relationship between their own skin color and opportunity, many whites would believe that the privileges associated with Caucasian identity were in jeopardy. Although editors eventually would understand that accommodating change meant opening newsroom doors to those who not only looked different but often applied an unfamiliar sensibility to journalism, some would resist the new social order. But even for editors who supported racial progress, the egalitarian good intention engendered by the civil rights movement of the 1950s and 1960s often was trumped by a self-interest in preserving the racial status quo. For this reason, the story of the ASNE's reckoning with inequality is also America's story, replicated in schools and universities, professions, public accommodations, and throughout society.

The American Society of Newspaper Editors offers an important site for examining the ease with which identity-based professional norms become institutionalized and the difficulty of dismantling them after they have been embedded into a social, political, and cultural organization. The ASNE's significance in America's democratic evolution is grounded in its self-defined but generally acknowledged prominence, particularly for its roles in defending the rights of free speech and press and advancing the careers of its members. Moreover, the perceived influence of newspapers throughout much of the twentieth century persuaded ASNE members that their organization had the power to shape public discourse on a range of subjects. From its founding in 1922 forward, the ASNE injected itself into the most pressing political and cultural debates through the staging of its annual conventions, which offered an auspicious forum for national and world leaders. Every U.S. president since Herbert Hoover has addressed the ASNE.[7] Such American icons as Ann Landers, Rupert Murdoch, Bill Gates, and Gloria Steinem have spoken from its podium. The ASNE also has at times attempted to intervene in the international political conversation, as was the case in 1959, when the editors disregarded U.S. State Department concerns and hosted Cuban leader Fidel Castro. In more recent years, ASNE conventions, with their lineups of high-profile newsmakers and opinion leaders, have been considered so noteworthy that they have received nearly continuous televised coverage by C-SPAN. In short, the ASNE enjoyed unrivaled prestige among media associations during the twentieth century and, through such initiatives as advocacy for newsroom diversity, journalism ethics, and open government, was a leader in shaping the modern press.

As the civil rights movement confronted the intransigence of American racism, what scholar Gunnar Myrdal described in 1944 as "a caste system,"[8] the ASNE, which did not admit an African American member until 1965, was a microcosm and its history an analogy for the institutionalization of white privilege. Daily newspapers with all-white newsrooms primarily served a white readership, while weeklies owned and staffed by blacks published news for African Americans. So central to the structure of American racism was the segregated press that Myrdal devoted an entire chapter to this dimension of the democratic paradox in his groundbreaking study *American Dilemma: The Negro Problem and Modern Democracy.*[9] Although many places of professional employment—from universities to hospitals to funeral homes—remained segregated at midcentury, the color line in the American newspaper industry had a distinct set of implications. As a result of civil rights reforms in the 1950s and 1960s, the democratic ideal that manifested in the freedoms of speech and press gradually was reinterpreted to make journalism supremely accountable to the public as a whole, obligating white journalists to act out of a duty to the *entire* community, not just white readers. Second, because of the white press's historical role in shaping racial common sense, by portraying nonwhites as less than equal and perpetuating the assumption of white advantage, some ASNE members would believe, at least by the 1970s, that the daily newspaper industry, which had contributed to inequality and benefited from its legacy, had a moral obligation to participate in the remedy.

Thus, a primary curiosity of this book centers upon the evolution in many ASNE members' thinking about journalistic duty—particularly the gradual embrace by many white editors of an ethical imperative that advanced racial integration of newsrooms and eventually brought white women and, to some extent, nonheterosexuals into the diversity paradigm as well. Although ASNE members had to develop a sense of democratic stewardship that crossed boundaries of race and other identity-based differences, the organization had always viewed itself as the conscience of the journalism profession. Shortly after its founding in 1922, the ASNE published the Canons of Journalism, the code of ethics that served as the industry standard for decades. Even so, the ASNE initially squandered opportunities to lead in the emerging movement for social responsibility in the press, quite pointedly with a defensive condemnation of *A Free and Responsible Press,* the 1947 report of the Hutchins Commission, which emphasized the press's social duty.[10] The Hutchins report was followed in 1956 by Theodore Peterson's seminal essay articulating a social responsibility theory of the press, specifically that "freedom carries concomitant obligations; and the press, which enjoys a privileged position under our government, is obliged to be responsible to society for carrying out certain essential functions of mass communication in contemporary society."[11] Together, Peterson and the Hutchins Commission pointed the newspaper industry in a new direction, which the ASNE largely ignored. In addition, the ASNE paid scant attention to the 1968 report of the National Advisory Commission on Civil Disorders, known as the Kerner Commission, which devoted a full chapter to the press's perpetuation of a "black-white schism" in America by failing to integrate newsrooms and to report news for the entire community and from a multiracial perspective.[12] It would be another decade before ASNE leaders began to steer the organization and its industry toward egalitarian reform.

Yet once the 1978 ASNE board, led by Southerner Eugene Patterson of the *St. Petersburg Times,* embraced the notion that the Constitution's free press guarantee carried a reciprocal obligation to open newsroom doors to nonwhites, they enacted and championed the Goal 2000 demographic parity initiative. The ASNE board also designated as the central component of Goal 2000 an annual newsroom census to count the nonwhites working in daily newspaper newsrooms and decreed it to be the mechanism for ensuring root-and-branch change in the daily newspaper industry. It was immediately apparent, however, that Patterson and his prointegration allies may have wielded the authority to set ASNE policy, but they did not speak for a consensus of the organization's membership. Ultimately, this investigation highlights the struggle Patterson and other progressive ASNE leaders waged, from the 1970s forward, against a countervailing ambivalence among many white editors, which hindered ASNE-led reform of newsroom hiring practices. The ASNE and the industry it represented were part and parcel of the democratic paradox of American racial inequality; the legacy of racial segregation in journalism generated not only the impetus for the Goal 2000 hiring initiative but also the undertow that continually impeded its progress.

High but Exclusionary Principles

Understanding ASNE members' resistance to opening their newsrooms to the very civil rights reforms many of them advocated on their editorial pages requires an examination of ASNE history. In the 1920s the ASNE founders had envisioned their organization as an enclave of newsroom leaders, representing only "the great newspapers of the United States."[13] One of the organization's express purposes was the development of ethical and professional standards, to counter widespread public sentiment in the early decades of the twentieth century that journalists were little more than scoop-mongering scoundrels. Even so, the ASNE's early focus was shaped by a sense of destiny, a blind insistence that the profession's critics were wrong, and a belief that the work of the journalist, sanctioned as it was by the U.S. Constitution, was a calling situated above the plane of mortal employment. The ASNE's early members demonstrated their conviction that the organization occupied an extraordinary position in American culture with a hubris-laden decision, beginning with the second annual meeting in 1924, to preserve a full record of the discussion at their conventions. For eighty years, these gavel-to-gavel transcriptions were published in bound volumes that were distributed annually to members and, significantly, to university libraries across the country. In this way, the ASNE wrote the first draft of its own history and ensured itself an enduring place in the American media canon.

The elitism within the ASNE during its early decades manifested as journalistic exceptionalism, a sense of self-importance whose entitlements sometimes included exemptions from accountability to the public trust and other rules of the game. Journalistic exceptionalism, which lay at the heart of the ASNE's democratic paradox, helped editors to rationalize double standards.

For example, because journalistic exceptionalism posited journalists as extraordinary citizens, it allowed many ASNE members to exempt themselves from the obligation to integrate their organization and their newsrooms, even after equal opportunity employment was legislated through the Civil Rights Act of 1964. After the historic adoption of Goal 2000 in 1978, journalistic exceptionalism also excused editors' ambivalence about the initiative's objective to achieve proportional newsroom integration by the end of the twentieth century. It allowed white editors to indulge their fears about what would happen if nonwhites, whom they assumed to be less skilled and less prepared for the rigors of the profession, were allowed to report and edit news. Many members rationalized that maintaining the racial status quo in newsrooms was a reasonable and honorable course because it affirmed journalistic standards.[14]

Within the ASNE itself, journalistic exceptionalism normalized the double standard of restricted membership. While freedom of the press was to be revered as the bedrock of democracy, all presses were not created equal in the eyes of ASNE members. The ASNE was founded specifically as an elite organization whose mission was to promote "metropolitan" daily journalism over weekly newspapers and other publications. In his 1924 presidential address, founder Casper Yost of the *St. Louis Globe-Democrat* noted that the ASNE was intended to be an exclusive club and that he sensed "an increasing feeling that to be a member of this Society is a privilege, an opportunity and a distinction."[15] In one of its first acts of business, the ASNE erected exclusionary barriers around membership, reserving participation in the organization for the top editors of high-circulation, urban daily newspapers. Although the membership criteria were modified over the years, the initial proscription against inducting editors affiliated with other than daily newspapers remained until 2009.[16]

Although the ASNE never explicitly restricted membership based on race, the membership guidelines imposed racial barriers and complicated the organization's efforts to integrate its membership beginning in the 1960s, when the gains of the civil rights movement made inducting black members and demonstrating interracial goodwill politically expedient. Because of the daily newspaper industry's longstanding racial discrimination in newsroom hiring, the organization had difficulty finding nonwhite editors who had achieved sufficient rank at a daily newspaper to qualify for membership. The ASNE's ban on membership for editors of weekly newspapers meant that all but a few black editors employed by the black press were ineligible to join.[17] When John Sengstacke, editor of the *Chicago Defender,* was granted membership in 1965, he likely was one of just two African American editors who were eligible under the ASNE membership rules because their newspapers were published daily, not weekly.[18]

While the ASNE membership criteria reserved the organization for whites prior to the 1960s, the organization did not block white women from joining. White women who became editors or publishers of daily newspapers, often through marriage or inheritance, were few but were granted full voting privileges, even if some male editors were unenthusiastic about their induction and participation in ASNE meetings. In fact, the first woman member of ASNE, Zell Hart Deming of the *Warren Chronicle* in Ohio, joined in 1928. The record makes clear, however, that the men who dominated the organization saw the ASNE as a "fraternity" and some had reservations about memberships for women editors.[19] Moreover, the ASNE foreclosed the possibility that women members would be full participants in the organization prior to 1940 by holding meetings in the National Press Club, from which women were barred.[20] By 1948, just seven white women had been inducted into the ASNE.[21]

Just as the membership criteria limited participation of white women and nonwhites, the ASNE's strong advocacy for the accreditation of college-level journalism programs, which the organization treated as a priority from the 1920s forward, constructed and maintained a professional norm in journalism.[22] The ASNE's early interest in accreditation accompanied its leaders' vision that the journalist be an erudite man, an expert in many fields. This position, embraced even by such editors as ASNE founder Casper Yost, who did not have a college education, laid the groundwork for the ASNE's enduring interest in journalism accreditation and justified the organization's insistence on specific college curricula. "We believe," the ASNE's Committee on Schools of Journalism wrote in 1930, "that the boy entering newspaper life needs, prior to coming into the shop, more than all else a background of systematic study in the arts and sciences as extensive as his time, money and capabilities will permit." It continued, "This society knows it is far more vital to the welfare of mankind that the men who make its journals of public opinion be culturally superior than it is that the surgeon or the corporation lawyer be a man of manifold intellectual attainments."[23]

Accreditation injected elitism into the system for educating journalists, conferring value on some institutions of higher learning and devaluing others, all the while concentrating industry attention and resources on schools that met specific, and sometimes expensive, criteria. Not surprisingly, historically black colleges and other institutions that educated large numbers of nonwhite students were excluded under an accreditation process dominated by daily newspapers and the most prestigious and best-endowed college journalism programs. When the ASNE sought in the 1970s and 1980s to increase the number of nonwhite journalists working for daily newspapers, the organization confronted the reality that the journalism education model it had championed produced few journalists who were racial "minorities," in the parlance of the day.[24]

The ASNE membership criteria and the organization's ongoing intervention in journalism education are just two examples of how the ASNE institutionalized racial exclusion. Rather than by design, the white professional norm became embedded within the ASNE and its industry indirectly, through standards the editors imposed to improve their profession but which actually reserved professional privileges for people like themselves. While the ASNE's elitist membership restrictions and advocacy for accreditation had no explicitly racial motive, they were flagrant class maneuvers that proved later to have racial implications and to hinder the entry of nonwhites into daily newspaper newsrooms.

No one felt the impact of racial exclusion in the daily newspaper industry more profoundly than did Albert Fitzpatrick at the outset of his career. Fitzpatrick would compile an impressive résumé in journalism as he moved through the editors' chairs at the *Akron Beacon Journal* during the 1960s and 1970s. As news editor, Fitzpatrick would supervise the team that won a Pulitzer Prize in 1971 for coverage of the Kent State University shootings and then continue to rise through the ranks until he was appointed executive editor in 1977. A year later he would become the first African American editor of a white-controlled paper to be admitted to ASNE membership. Despite the steep trajectory of his career, racism proved a daunting obstacle in his early years in journalism.

As a 1956 journalism graduate of Kent State University, Fitzpatrick applied for jobs at about fifty newspapers, and the *Beacon Journal* was the only one to invite him for an interview. Once hired, he said, "I was the only African American in a building of 600 employees, and also the only person of color in that newsroom for ten years." For the first eighteen months of his employment, Fitzpatrick performed such tasks as writing obituaries and editing pages but was not given assignments that would bring him into contact with the public. Fitzpatrick finally confronted his editor and said, drawing a historical parallel, "Now, listen, I'm trained to be a reporter and I think it's time for you to take the chains off of me and let me go out and report." What happened next demonstrated the extent to which daily journalism was regarded as a white profession. Fitzpatrick recalled,

> So they finally sent me out, out to one of the suburbs, which was an all-white suburb, and I was covering a city council meeting. . . . This council clerk comes up to me, he must have been 85 years old, and he hobbles up to me, and . . . he says, "Can I help you?" And I said, "Yes, I'm a reporter from the *Akron Beacon Journal.*" And the gentleman looked at me, he says, "Porter? We don't need any porters here." So I told him, I said, "I didn't say 'porter,' I said 're-porter.'" . . . That was my first assignment.[25]

Whiteness as the Professional Norm

In the 1950s and early 1960s, the period in which our story begins, racial segregation was taken for granted in the profession of journalism, where the white and black presses functioned in parallel universes, with separate professional organizations, news services, and circulation auditing mechanisms. Traditionally, many white editors had even segregated "black news" within the pages of their daily newspapers; whether to run photos of African American brides alongside those of white brides remained a controversy in the South into the 1970s.[26] Compartmentalization of black and white news attested to the capacity of Jim Crow to segregate even words and images on newsprint. In such a framework—in which nonwhites are marginalized and frequently erased from view—whiteness functions as the norm. Within the newspaper industry, the white norm has been signaled and embedded through routine references to "the black press" and by labeling nonwhite journalists according to race: "black journalists," "Hispanic American journalists," and so forth. Conversely, the mainstream daily press and the white journalists it historically has employed require no racial qualifier to clarify meaning; they are "the press" and the "journalists" who work for it. Richard Dyer's observation is relevant here: "As long as race is something only applied to non-white people, as long as white people are not racially seen and named, they/we function as a human norm. Other people are raced, we are just people."[27]

Whiteness, which refers not only to pigment but also to the privilege that attaches to white identity, achieves and maintains its power largely through mechanisms of exclusion and the fraternity that obtains from membership in this club.[28] When Senator Eastland addressed the ASNE convention in 1948, he could assume that he and editors of various political stripe who hailed from all regions of the country had at least one thing in common. It was the unspoken bond of whiteness to which he appealed.

Because whiteness has represented a norm in American culture, it tends to be invisible much of the time and particularly to those who enjoy its privileges.[29] As Matthew Jacobson has noted, "The awesome power of race as an ideology resides precisely in its ability to pass as a feature of the natural landscape."[30] In addition, those who are in fact conscious of their racial motives often deny them. For these reasons, methodology becomes crucial in an analysis such as this one. ASNE texts, including convention transcripts and publications, member correspondence, and other archives, as well as interviews with ASNE members and newsroom diversity activists, provide the foundation for this study. Through a close examination of the record, this book traces the functioning of discourses that defined the ASNE's role—and stake—in maintaining imbalances of racialized power for a fifty-year period beginning in the mid-1950s.

This investigation examines competing discourses that circulated within the ASNE: those that conveyed journalistic exceptionalism and assumed an exclusionary professional norm as well as the more progressive discourses that rearticulated the ASNE's mission as a commitment to social justice and journalistic duty as a democratic endeavor. To bring such discourses into relief, this analysis focuses on the material effects they produced, not the conscious motives or stated intentions that became attached to them. Discourses can be tracked not only in language but also through their manifestations in institutions and their impacts on the lived reality of human beings, such as the policy decisions of the ASNE and outcomes of the diversity initiative. Of this analytical strategy, John Dorst has written, "Active discourses will 'find a way out,' showing themselves through the cracks in texts that seem to have entirely different agendas. It is often precisely in those subtle gestures that hardly seem worth mentioning that a discourse operates most effectively."[31] The measure, then, of the degree to which the ASNE perpetuated the white prerogative within daily newspaper journalism is not found in the organization's official positions or the sentiments expressed publicly by its members. We must look instead to the disparate experiences of the editors and journalists who enjoyed the privileges of whiteness and those who did not.

This approach is indebted to Michel Foucault, for whom discourse analysis is a "task that consists of not—of no longer—treating discourses as groups of signs (signifying elements referring to contents or representations) but as practices that asymmetrically form the objects of which they speak."[32] Foucault's redefinition of discourses as *practices,* not simply as language, is significant here. This analysis will be concerned not only with the stated intentions of ASNE members who discussed race during the organization's history but also with their actions, measured against the vision of social justice that evolved within the ASNE during the last three decades of the twentieth century. While patterns in the actions of ASNE members are significant, more revealing in many cases are contradictions between words and deeds, as well as omissions—inactions and silences—at key moments in the ASNE's racial history.[33] This can be seen, for example, in the ASNE's stonewalling on newsroom integration, through its ten-year delay in making a constructive response to the Kerner Commission's sharp critique of the social disservice of a segregated press. Viewed in the context of discourse analysis, the ASNE's failure to answer such a direct and significant criticism has greater consequence for this investigation than official statements of support for civil rights.

The challenge of racial integration and "diversity," as it later was called, occupied a considerable amount of the ASNE's time after the 1950s, but after 1978, even as the ASNE was broadly concerned with free press issues and industry trends, Goal 2000 dominated the organization's agenda and received more organizational resources than First Amendment issues.[34] Even so, this study's concentrated scrutiny of the ASNE's engagement of one issue should not leave the impression that newsroom integration was the only matter confronting the ASNE. To put this in perspective, an analysis of issues of the *ASNE Bulletin,* renamed the *American Editor* in 1995, suggests that Goal 2000 and newsroom diversity issues consumed only about 12 percent of the space in the organization's monthly publication. In framing this analysis, it also is important to note that Goal 2000, the ASNE's formal program to democratize newsroom hiring, was the direct result of the black movement for civil rights and focused exclusively on *racial* justice and primarily on the hiring and promotion of African Americans. Because this study traces the organization's effort to diversify newsrooms, the ASNE's disproportionate emphasis on black journalists is reflected in this analysis as well.

At the same time, this analysis considers the intersection of race with other signifiers. Inclusion and exclusion are never determined only by race, class, gender, sexual orientation, or nationality because subjects never embody just one identity. As the ASNE reckoned with the issue of race during the 1950s and 1960s, gender discrimination was accepted and even encouraged among its members. In the 1970s, however, a tension between race and gender was exacerbated when the category "women" was excluded from the Goal 2000 hiring criteria, which targeted four categories of race for the integration effort. Because nonwhite women were incorporated into the race-focused hiring initiative, white women were left on the sideline. As will be discussed throughout this book, the ASNE's severing of race from gender pitted white and nonwhite women against each other in a bid for ASNE resources and undermined the conciliatory objectives of Goal 2000.

Similarly, gay identity, which had been invisible, was actively marginalized during the 1990s within a newsroom diversity movement whose overriding vision of social justice continued to focus only on racial equality. Despite its transition into the more inclusive constructs of multiculturalism and diversity, the ASNE found itself caught in the crossfire of competing identity interests. In 1998, when the ASNE proposed an expansion of its newsroom hiring initiative to encompass women, gays and lesbians, and people with disabilities, the strongest opposition was voiced by nonwhite journalists. Although white women were incorporated into the annual newsroom census when the diversity goals were recalibrated in 1998, other nonracial identities remained excluded, primarily at the insistence of those who stood to benefit from the racial focus of the hiring initiative.

Not surprisingly, in the post-diversity era that dawned following the ASNE's formal concession in 1997 that the end-of-the-century parity goal lay out of reach, editors increasingly turned their attention to the faltering financial condition of their industry, and the newsroom hiring initiative, short on resources and enthusiasm, receded in priority. Despite the continued advocacy of ASNE leaders and a passionate few among the membership, many editors grew tired of unrelenting criticism for not achieving hiring targets that were generally understood to be unattainable. The organization's "diversity fatigue," as it was called, culminated in 2009, in a move fraught with symbolism, with the elimination of the full-time staff position devoted to diversity programming.

By raising the grain of identity politics throughout the ASNE narrative—from the Jim Crow years of the 1950s through the affirmative action efforts begun in the 1970s and the multiculturalism of the 1990s—discourse analysis makes possible a nuanced investigation of the competing stakes within the ASNE. This approach reveals the subtle tactics and maneuvers that continued to reaffirm a decidedly undemocratic professional norm in the ASNE's vision of daily newspaper journalism, even after organizational policy designated newsroom diversity as imperative for social justice.

A Time for Atonement

Even if the ASNE was instrumental in erecting racial barriers around the daily newspaper industry, it supplied many of the heroes of this story, who led the effort to integrate daily newspaper newsrooms. In the 1970s, Southern editors such as Norman Isaacs of the *Louisville Courier-Journal,* Eugene Patterson of the *St. Petersburg Times,* Richard Smyser of the *Oak Ridger* in Oak Ridge, Tennessee, and John Seigenthaler Sr. of the *Nashville Tennessean,* along with

John Quinn of Gannett Newspapers, took a conscious stand against discriminatory professional and social tradition and in favor of a democratic vision for newspaper journalism. Notably, however, the ASNE's early heroes were all white. Although such African American editors and journalists as Robert Maynard and Nancy Hicks Maynard, Albert Fitzpatrick, and Jay Harris were key organizers of the newsroom integration movement of the 1970s,[35] they agitated for adoption of Goal 2000 as nonmembers of the ASNE, which underscored the organization's us-them, insider-outsider construct, even on the issue of racial conciliation.

In the two decades following the hiring initiative's implementation, ASNE leaders would discover that remorse for the past—even when combined with passion, hard work, job fairs, and scholarships for nonwhite journalism students—was insufficient to dismantle the exclusionary norm that had become calcified into the organization and its members' newsrooms. When the Goal 2000 initiative was launched in 1978, the percentage of nonwhites in the professional work force in daily newspaper newsrooms stood at 3.95 percent, compared to a national nonwhite demographic of 17 percent. Year after year, ASNE leaders exhorted members to hire more nonwhite journalists and then nervously tracked progress through an annual census, which quantified the racial demographic in daily newspaper newsrooms. Year after year, the slow pace of growth in nonwhite hiring, combined with a more rapid increase in the U.S. nonwhite population, pushed the parity goal further out of reach. When the ASNE confronted the inadequacy of its good intention in 1998, the gap between newsroom employment and the U.S. nonwhite population had shrunk only about 1.5 percent, even though the portion of nonwhites in that workforce had risen about 7.5 percent. The organization developed a new target for the year 2025, along with intermediary benchmarks, but several ASNE leaders conceded that even the revised goal was overly ambitious and functioned as a source of inspiration rather than an attainable numerical outcome.[36]

Various demographic explanations contribute to an understanding of why the ASNE's Goal 2000 initiative failed. While some have argued that unanticipated growth in the nonwhite population posed an insurmountable obstacle for Goal 2000, others worried during the 1980s and 1990s that the size of the college-educated nonwhite population and gradual shrinkage in the number of newsroom jobs doomed the initiative.[37] Even taking note of demographic arguments and industry economic trends, the failure of Goal 2000 cannot be explained without also accounting for the institutionalized norms that transformed the ASNE and its members' newsrooms into venues in need of integration and posited the ideal professional journalist as white, heterosexual, probably male, and having a certain cultural and educational background. Opening the doors of daily newspaper newsrooms to nonwhites and others entailed a reconceptualization of *who could be a journalist*. In short, the norm on which twentieth-century journalism had been built had to be reenvisioned in order to enact social justice. While demographics and economics may have shaped the contours of Goal 2000's playing field, institutionalized discrimination within the ASNE and the daily newspaper industry dictated the rules of the game. That pattern of exclusion was entrenched even before President Truman proposed his civil rights reforms and Senator Eastland and his segregationist allies dug in for the coming fight.

In examining the promise and failure of Goal 2000, this book makes significant contributions to research on the press and workplace diversity. Although Goal 2000 is widely regarded as the prototypical affirmative action effort in the media professions, this is the first book-length history of the ASNE's newsroom integration initiative. Two previous books about the ASNE, both commissioned by the organization, have told its story more generally, but neither documents or provides critical insight into the organization's coming to terms with issues of race and other identity-based differences.[38] By providing a focused history of the evolution of the ASNE's affirmative action project, this narrative fills a clear void in historical scholarship on the twentieth-century press and augments studies narrowly focused on singular communities of journalists, such as Pamela Newkirk's *Within the Veil: Black Journalists, White Media* and Maurine Beasley and Sheila Gibbons's *Taking Their Place: A Documentary History of Women and Journalism*.[39]

Second, this book contributes to our understanding of how identity-based norms became embedded within a profession, how they become part of the structure of that profession, and the difficulty of leveling professional opportunity once inequity is recognized as a problem in need of a solution. As such, this book is most broadly a study of the social construction and institutionalization of race and other distinctions, an approach inaugurated most prominently by Michael Omi and Howard Winant's *Racial Formation in the United States: From the 1960s to the 1990s* and by Douglas Massey and Nancy Denton's *American Apartheid: Segregation and the Making of the Underclass*.[40] As discussed previously, this book also draws upon key concepts from whiteness studies, including the theoretical positions of David Roediger, Ruth Frankenburg, and George Lipsitz.[41] The book proceeds from an understanding that white identity is both a social construction and a normative advantage, requiring a certain degree of invisibility to maintain its power. As such, this book also is in conversation with a larger range of work that examines the role of colorblindness in perpetuating structures of inequality. Among the most important are Michael K. Brown et al.'s *White-Washing Race: The Myth of a Color-Blind Society* and Elizabeth Anderson's *The Imperative of Integration.*[42]

Finally, although this study is focused exclusively on the ASNE, its analysis of the Goal 2000 initiative contributes to a large and growing body of literature on workforce inequity and identity-based exclusions in employment, including William Julius Wilson's *When Work Disappears: The World of the New Urban Poor* and Deidre Royster's *Race and the Invisible Hand: How White Networks Exclude Black Men from Blue-Collar Jobs.* In its concern with the efficacy of affirmative action in the post-civil rights workplace, the book provides a comprehensive case study for an area of contentious public debate that has been dispassionately documented in Terry Anderson's *In Pursuit of Fairness: A History of Affirmative Action.*[43]

While this book analyzes competing discourses of social justice and identity-based exclusion, it does so through an accounting of the ASNE's journey from the era of Jim Crow to affirmative action and identity politics, and it does so through a chronologically unfolding, historical narrative. Chapter 1 opens in the mid-1950s, when ASNE members began registering the impact of the U.S. Supreme Court's *Brown v. Board of Education* school desegregation ruling and the specter of more sweeping civil rights reforms.[44] During the 1950s, the ASNE leadership was dominated by Southern editors and much of the organization's tension over civil rights was inflected with regionalism. Key moments in the decade examined by this chapter include the ASNE board's initial resistance to integrating the organization and the membership's discourteous reception of prominent civil rights leaders—the first African Americans invited to address the ASNE—at the 1964 convention.

Chapters 2 and 3, which cover the twenty-year period from release of the Kerner Commission's condemnation of segregated journalism in 1968, chronicle the ASNE leadership's shift from ambivalence about integrating daily newspaper newsrooms to evangelical support of the Goal 2000 demographic parity initiative in 1978. Chapter 3 also tracks the hiring effort's record through its first decade, when ASNE leaders began to realize that the organization's rank-and-file membership had not embraced the concept of affirmative action for their newsrooms to the degree necessary to achieve the end-of-the-century parity target and that a backlash against affirmative action would undermine efforts to integrate newsrooms. Analysis in the first three chapters also will examine the disparity in opportunities for women in the ASNE.

During the 1990s, the period that is the focus of chapter 4, the ASNE's Goal 2000 advocates contended with a shift in the way the broader diversity community envisioned social justice. As the more expansive concept of multiculturalism gained traction in American society, the racial integration model, on which Goal 2000 was premised, became outdated. The need for greater inclusiveness in the ASNE and its hiring initiative crystallized at the 1990 convention when an editor announced that he was gay, becoming the first gay ASNE member to be out within the organization. Chapter 4 examines the contentious identity politics that dominated the ASNE in the 1990s as professional organizations for nonwhite journalists gained and exercised greater power and many white editors grew weary of being continually scolded for not increasing the number of nonwhites working in their newsrooms.

Chapter 5 examines the crisis following the announcement in 1997 that the Goal 2000 target would not be met and the contentious negotiations to recommit the ASNE to the aims of newsroom diversity and to recalibrate the hiring target for the year 2025. Identity politics continued to complicate efforts to advance the cause of social justice as women were finally added to the hiring initiative, but gay and disabled journalists were not. The ASNE demonstrated that racial assumptions continued to be deeply ingrained when a racist comedy act at the 2001 convention touched off a nationwide controversy. Chapter 5 and the afterword also examine the devastating impact of the newspaper industry's declining fortunes on the cause of newsroom diversity during the first decade of the new millennium.

Any project that purports to explain systemic failure will isolate and find fault in the actions and motives of those who contributed directly and indirectly to that outcome. Although some in the ASNE certainly thwarted the organization's embrace of social responsibility—in some cases through active resistance but usually through recalcitrance—many of the ASNE protagonists in this story were sincerely committed to the cause of newsroom integration. Those who championed Goal 2000 certainly oversimplified the task before them, but overcoming naivete about the entrenched nature of identity-based norms is a necessary passage in any effort to achieve social justice. Giving fair account to such flawed heroes presents a special challenge to the historian. As Vron Ware and Les Back have observed, "Defining what counts as antiracism in earlier historical periods can be difficult, even with the benefit of hindsight. Sometimes actions that were intended to challenge racial attitudes and practices of the day can now provoke embarrassment and ridicule rather than posthumous respect."[45] Each chapter in this book introduces a new set of actors and situates them within a distinct period in the extended history of the ASNE's pursuit of newsroom diversity. While the attitudes and actions of some ASNE members will invite scorn, the efforts of those who embraced the cause of newsroom integration, no matter how imperfectly, should be judged in context.

With that, we turn our attention to the ASNE of the 1950s, where a sense of higher calling hung as resolutely over the organization as the smoky haze that filled the meeting rooms at each year's convention. There, daily newspaper editors communed with others like themselves, who had reached the top of a profession specially blessed by the U.S. Constitution, and rubbed shoulders with national and international leaders, the newsmakers whose words and deeds clattered each day from the wire service printers in their newsrooms. The majority in attendance were white men wearing the uniform of a top editor of a daily newspaper—business suit, white dress shirt, understated necktie—and the only dark complexions belonged to employees of the convention hotel, who served ASNE members their cocktails and bussed their tables. Most of the women at the conventions—with hats, gloves, and handbags—were editors' wives, who attended teas and fashion shows while their husbands got down to business. It is into this world that we now open the door.

1

Manning the Barricade

Maintaining the White Prerogative in the Face of Change, 1954–67

In 1957, members of the American Society of Newspaper Editors were invited to participate in a Civil War reenactment of sorts, a North-South tennis tournament to be played during the annual ASNE convention. The incoming ASNE president, Virginius Dabney, editor of the *Richmond Times-Dispatch,* and Grover C. Hall Jr., editor of the *Montgomery Advertiser,* issued the challenge. "It would give the Hall-Dabney Confederate . . . team exquisite pleasure to trounce the best combination the dam-yankees can put into the field," Dabney wrote in the *ASNE Bulletin,* the organization's newsletter.[1] Hall, who insisted "the Confederate Constitution was written in Montgomery, probably on an Advertiser letterhead,"[2] was in charge of scheduling the matches. A few months later, the outcome of the doubles tournament was loosely reported in the *Bulletin,* accompanied by a Chick Larsen cartoon showing a Confederate tennis player with his foot on the neck of his vanquished Northern foe. While the account of this first tournament was decidedly tongue-in-cheek—"it was not Pickett's charge, it was not Chancellorsville; it was not, at times, even good tennis"[3]—the tennis event became an assertion of Confederate identity that Southern editors repeated annually into the 1960s.[4]

That this tournament emerged at this moment in the ASNE's history is no coincidence. The impact of the Supreme Court's 1954 ruling in *Brown v. Board of Education* was not confined to school desegregation; its profound challenge to the racial status quo had extended into other areas of American life and, for the first time, members of the ASNE began to confront questions about the organization's identity as a racially homogenous and exclusionary professional enclave. Moreover, issues related to race began to appear on the ASNE's annual convention program, and members expressed a range of opinion during open sessions, from segregationist ranting to criticism of the all-white composition of the organization. In this respect, the ASNE replicated the fissures and shifts occurring in American culture. Ultimately, however, many ASNE members resisted change within the organization and, by extension, the daily newspaper industry. Although many editors conceded and even welcomed the inevitability of integration in American society at large, the ASNE would weather the 1950s with its all-white identity challenged but intact. Despite integration's growing support in the North throughout the 1950s, notably on the editorial pages of many daily newspapers, the ASNE accommodated the segregationists within its ranks and declined to integrate its own membership. Viewed in this context, the tennis tournament became both a metaphor for and a subtle validation of the segregation challenged by *Brown.*

In the 1950s, white identity was so much a part of the organization's fabric that it functioned as a norm and frequently escaped notice. Within the ASNE, racial inequality often was reaffirmed through supposedly race-neutral means that were ostensibly tied to merit or journalistic principles, such as objectivity and professionalism. For example, when the possibility of admitting African American members was broached during the 1950s, the ASNE could interpret its daily newspaper requirement—by then established as a threshold of professional merit—to exclude an editor of a black weekly and maintain an all-white membership. This rubric allowed ASNE members to blame the failure of nonwhites to meet professional standards, rather than a long-standing pattern of racial exclusivity, for the organization's all-white and predominantly male profile. This pretense of colorblindness not only institutionalized the white norm, but it allowed the white editors of the ASNE to construct themselves and their organization as racially neutral.

But the validation of racial difference during the 1950s relied not only on covert and systemic inequality but also, at times, on the prominent display of white supremacy. In the wake of the historic challenges to Jim Crow entailed by both the Truman Administration's civil rights initiatives and the *Brown* decision, the ASNE accommodated blatant expressions of racism in convention sessions during 1955 and 1956. In this important respect, racism within the ASNE was incarnated differently during the 1950s than it had been in the previous decade and would be in the future. Prior to the 1950s, when white superiority was a given, political, social, and economic barriers segregated American daily life and maintained a comfortable distance between white and nonwhite, and race was rarely mentioned during ASNE conventions and in its publications. But that changed when *Brown*'s perceived assault on the social order unsettled many white editors of the ASNE. As a few members began to suggest the integration of the ASNE, it became clear that desegregation was not a controversy that would play out only in public schools and on city buses. Sooner or later, the crumbling social barriers between the races would become an issue for the ASNE and the profession of journalism.[5]

ASNE members granted standing to the segregationist perspective, no matter how frankly it was articulated, by casting it as a requirement of journalistic objectivity. By treating the views of segregationists as one side of a news story that had to be told impartially and equitably, the ASNE granted these perspectives legitimacy, even as the culture at large was writing strident racism out of its social norm. Instead, overtly racist utterances were treated as matters of members' First Amendment rights, eclipsing the question of human rights. This neat bit of rationalization appeared to raise the all-white ASNE above the controversy, as will become clear in this chapter's analysis. Even without explicitly endorsing blatant racism, the ASNE facilitated it and granted it legitimacy.

This chapter brackets the period from 1954, when the ASNE was forced by the evolving legal status of nonwhites to engage the issue of civil rights, until just before the National Advisory Commission on Civil Disorders, also known as the Kerner Commission, excoriated the news media for their role in perpetuating racial inequality in the United States and for failing to integrate newsrooms.[6] Following the Supreme Court's decision in *Brown,* race emerged as a flashpoint for the ASNE, bringing attention to a North-South divide within the organization. This was an extraordinary moment in American history. Although the ASNE as a matter of policy did not take positions on issues outside the scope of the organization's journalistic mission, its members, whose newspapers were covering the race story directly or through the wire services, were immersed in the social uncertainty created by desegregation.

By 1955, the year after the school desegregation ruling and the point at which this analysis begins, Dr. Martin Luther King Jr. had been arrested for the first time in connection with his civil rights activism and the names of Rosa Parks, the Montgomery, Alabama, seamstress who refused to surrender her bus seat to a white man, and Emmett Till, the fourteen-year-old African American brutally lynched in Mississippi, had become icons of the civil rights movement. In the years that followed, newspapers chronicled confrontations over the integration of schools, voter registration efforts, and such civil rights marches and initiatives as the Freedom Rides to integrate interstate bus transportation and the lunch-counter sit-ins to integrate public accommodations. The violence that was a running theme during these years, punctuated by such atrocities as the bombing of the 16th Street Baptist Church in Birmingham, Alabama, in 1963, which killed four girls attending Sunday School, and the murders of three civil rights workers in Philadelphia, Mississippi, in 1964, ensured that race, the most compelling news story of the postwar era, remained a fixture on front pages across the country.

Eventually, the activism of the 1950s and early 1960s provided the momentum for passage of federal civil rights legislation. Congress passed the landmark Civil Rights Act in 1964, which outlawed, among other things, segregation in public schools, public accommodations, and federally assisted programs. It was followed a year later by the Voting Rights Act, which guaranteed all Americans the right to vote. Though members of ASNE did not realize it then, Title VII of the 1964 law, which prohibited discrimination in employment based on race and gender, had set the stage for the organization's own activism on behalf of equal opportunity. Nor did they recognize that riots in the Watts neighborhood in Los Angeles in 1965, as well as uprisings in other American cities, would set the ASNE on a circuitous path toward affirmative action. If Title VII provided a legal justification for Goal 2000, the riots, which triggered the 1968 Kerner Commission report chastising the press for its segregated newsrooms, offered up the moral imperative.

Policing the Boundaries in a New Era of Race

Prior to the 1950s, whiteness had been a taken-for-granted and usually unnoticed feature of the ASNE. Without specifically mentioning race in its official conversations about membership, the ASNE nonetheless had established itself as an organization for whites at the top of their profession. Through the exclusiveness of its membership structure, which limited participation to directing editors of daily newspapers deemed worthy of ASNE affiliation, the ASNE inadvertently ensured that nonwhite editors, almost all of whom worked for weekly newspapers, would remain ineligible for regular membership for years to come. Yet even as the ASNE continued to view the world from the vantage of the white professional norm, the *Brown* decision signaled for some members that the white prerogative was under challenge.

Although the integration controversy had dominated headlines both before and after the Supreme Court ruling in May 1954, ASNE members did not make the organization's all-white demographic a convention topic until 1955.

During a session titled "How Is the Press Reporting School Desegregation?" the discussion turned to whether coverage of desegregation was serving the needs of blacks as well as whites, yet no blacks were present to answer on their own behalf. A. M. Piper of the *Council Bluffs (Iowa) Nonpareil* noted, "I have been a member of the ASNE for about 15 years. I have not seen any Negroes at our conventions. Has there ever been an application from one? Perhaps we might make a beginning right here, to solve the problem."[7] In response, ASNE President James S. Pope of the *Louisville Courier-Journal* asserted that the daily publication requirement, not race, was a barrier to membership for African American editors. "To my knowledge there has never been an application," he said. "I believe most Negro newspapers are weeklies. There is a daily in Atlanta; I don't know what its circulation is. I'm not sure, but I don't believe there would be more than one Negro editor, or maybe two, in the country who would be eligible."[8] ASNE leaders would use this line of reasoning repeatedly over the years to justify marginalization of women and nonwhite men from membership and ASNE leadership. In this way, the ASNE could claim that the privilege of participation was tied to journalistic merit and attribute any exclusion to the perceived shortcomings of those who were not white and male.

This brief and rather nonchalant exchange followed a white supremacist screed by Frederick Sullens of the *Jackson (Miss.) Daily News,* who argued that "mixed schools mean mixed marriages and mixed marriages mean a mongrel race" and warned that "if an effort is made anywhere in Mississippi to put Negro children in white schools, it will mean bloodshed."[9] During the same discussion, members briefly debated whether photos of black brides should be published, and one editor, Wallace Carroll of the *Winston-Salem (N.C.) Journal & Sentinel,* announced that he had hired a black reporter.[10] It is significant that a single discussion at an ASNE convention could include such profoundly racist remarks as those offered by Sullens and leave them unchallenged alongside Carroll's disclosure that he had an African American on staff or Piper's simple inquiry about integrating the ASNE. In that moment, in which racism was both tolerated as well as questioned, the American social dilemma crystallized.

Race erupted as an issue again during the 1956 convention, in the context of another, more contentious plenary discussion about news coverage of *Brown*'s aftermath. During a protracted racist diatribe, Harry Ayers, editor of the *Anniston (Ala.) Star,* argued that "many Negroes are dirty, are unreliable, are liars," and were disproportionately afflicted with venereal disease. Moreover, Ayers harangued, it was "the consuming desire of every Negro to possess a white woman."[11] Just as it had been in 1955, the racist polemic was juxtaposed with a progressive point of view when James Wechsler of the *New York Post* again raised the issue of the ASNE's all white membership. He said, "I would think that a Society like ours ought to have in its ranks representatives of Negro newspapers so that we are not talking about these people as if they were the outcasts and second-class citizens of our society. I certainly hope before the next convention to sponsor the admission of at least some representatives of the Negro press."[12] In response, Talbot Patrick of the *Rock Hill (S.C.) Evening Herald* noted the dearth of nonwhite editors who would meet the ASNE's membership guidelines,[13] suggesting that the mono-racial composition of the ASNE resulted from circumstance, namely the failure of blacks to qualify, and was none of the organization's own doing.

Kenneth MacDonald of the *Des Moines Register,* the ASNE president, also invoked the membership guidelines. His detailed rationalization is worth considering at length.

> There is no policy of discrimination whatever in the Society's membership procedures and, so far as I know, there never has been. The Society has not had an application from a Negro editor, and this is easy to understand when you remember that the membership regulations require that a person be the editor of a daily paper.
>
> I am not certain I know the facts at the moment, but the last time I had any reason to check, there was not more than one daily in the country with a Negro editor, and I believe that may still be true. In the one case that I definitely know of, the man who is responsible for running the paper, I have been told, is primarily interested in the business side rather than the editorial side and, at any rate, has never applied for membership in the Society.
>
> I am sure that, if application were made, the Board of Directors would consider it very carefully. I feel confident there is no discrimination because of race or any other reason in selecting members of the Society. I do not think anybody here implied that there has been discrimination. But I would not want that misunderstanding to arise out of this discussion.[14]

Notably, MacDonald and Wechsler both assume the perpetuation of a segregated newspaper industry when they see black newspapers as the only potential sources of nonwhite members. The concept of integrating ASNE members' own newsrooms is not yet part of the conversation. Moreover, in this rationalization, MacDonald distances himself from the black press by expressing disinterest in specific details about black dailies, which he would not ordinarily have "any reason to check" and which would come to him only as secondhand information. However, amid the heat of the session on news coverage after *Brown,* the significance of the membership issue appears to have registered for only a small number of editors.

The Colonel's Last Stand

The Ayers incident at the 1956 convention sent the ASNE leadership scrambling for cover. While the Colonel—as Ayers was called, in acknowledgment of his World War I and National Guard service—had editorialized during the 1940s in favor of the right to vote and for improved education and employment opportunities for Alabama's blacks, he had been an intransigent supporter of segregation. In particular, Ayers had stridently editorialized about the threat of amalgamation, warning that integration of the schools would lead to race mixing and would place white women in harm's way.[15] While such comments may have been unremarkable in the Deep South of the 1950s, their utterance in mixed company—a national convention attended by editors from all regions of the country—amplified their impact.

As a result, the 1956 convention and the fallout from Harry Ayers's commentary about African Americans appeared to establish a line for the ASNE between what was an acceptable public discussion of race and what was not, although those who found Ayers's racist language objectionable were not necessarily persuaded of the injustice of segregation. Importantly, Ayers's comments were distinguished not only by their extremity but also by being reported in the Washington newspapers, to the supreme embarrassment of the ASNE. By comparison, Frederick Sullens's unreported and equally racist comments a year earlier had not drawn similar objections.[16] In its coverage of the 1956 convention, the *Washington Post and Times-Herald* offered a mild summation of Ayers's remarks.

> Harry M. Ayers of the Anniston (Ala.) Star said his state doesn't want school integration "because we're having enough trouble bringing our (white) schools up to the national average as it is."
>
> Then, in a language that had some of his audience literally shuddering, he declared that Negroes are inferior people and insisted they don't want to mix with others anyway. One editor in the audience rose and asked the moderator, Erwin D. Canham of the Christian Science Monitor, to invoke a time limit to halt Ayers' comments. But Ayers said he was finished.[17]

Significantly, the editor who asked the moderator to call time on Ayers appears to have been a fellow Southerner, Reed Sarratt of the *Winston-Salem*

Journal & Sentinel, who opposed both court-ordered desegregation and resistance to it.[18]

Despite Ayers's long-standing position on segregation, which he had expressed in both his editorials and correspondence with other editors, some ASNE members who were well-acquainted with Ayers expressed surprise at the tenor and content of his contribution to the convention panel. In fact, *Richmond Times-Dispatch* editor Virginius Dabney, who was consulted on the composition of the panel, had recommended Ayers as a "middle roader" and placed him in the same category as Lenoir Chambers of the *Virginian-Pilot,* who would editorialize against massive resistance to school integration in Norfolk in 1958.[19] Although Dabney had been familiar with Ayers's opinions on race because the two exchanged editorials and corresponded from time to time, he wrote ASNE President Kenneth MacDonald after the convention to express his shock at Ayers's remarks. "I still am mystified by the totally contrasting views as to what he might have been expected to say on that panel," Dabney wrote of Ayers.[20] While Dabney appears to have been naive in claiming ignorance of what Ayers might contribute to the panel, his expression of surprise offers insight into where he himself stood on the issue of race as he prepared to assume the ASNE presidency in 1957. Although Dabney had editorialized for many civil rights reforms—an end to the poll tax, passage of antilynching legislation, integration of public transportation—he remained a segregationist. He may have objected to the delivery of Ayers's remarks and regretted the backlash they created, but on many political questions Ayers's views intersected many of his own.

One theory that circulated following the 1956 convention suggested that Ayers had been invited onto the panel precisely because he would make provocative remarks. In a letter to the editor of the *Bulletin,* George Clapp of the *New London (Conn.) Daily,* speculated that Ayers, "a real Southern hot-head on the segregation issue," was invited to liven up the discussion.[21] It appears, however, that Southern editors were working from a conflicting set of ideological definitions when they set up the panel. A week before the convention, program chairman Jenkin Lloyd Jones of the *Tulsa Tribune* wrote to Ayers, apparently after consultation with Dabney, that he had invited speakers who could "keep this on a high plane without descending to the nigger-lovin' and nigger-beatin' level which produces nothing but heat, lightning and thunder." He asserted that the Supreme Court had usurped states' rights and that school desegregation was an issue of national importance, which the ASNE should not ignore. "We thought a frank discussion of the problem by able and intelligent men might ease the situation a little," Jones wrote.[22] In addition to Chambers and Ayers, panelists included Herbert Brucker of the *Hartford Courant,* who spoke of integrating coverage in his paper, and John Q. Mahaffey of the *Texarkana Gazette,* an outspoken segregationist who was admonished during his remarks for employing off-color humor about both blacks and women.[23] Clearly, Jones, who was about to succeed MacDonald as ASNE president, had strong feelings of his own on the segregation issue, which may have influenced his decision to include such a panel on the convention program and to staff it as he did.

In the wake of Ayers's remarks and the negative publicity they had drawn to the ASNE, the organization's leaders embarked on a campaign of damage control. For the May 1956 issue of the *Bulletin,* Frederick and Alice Fox Pitts, who were the organization's administrative staff, assembled a sampling of more moderate opinion from members of Ayers's audience. In a memo to Dabney, Alice Fox Pitts expressed satisfaction with the balance these perspectives would provide. "The Bulletin comments . . . are so sound that, on reading them in connection with Ayers, I don't think even Thurgood Marshall would object to the over-all picture!" she wrote, referring to the African American attorney who represented the plaintiffs in *Brown.*[24] She also persuaded MacDonald, the ASNE president, to allow her to add the member comments to the published convention transcript, even though they were not in fact part of the proceedings.[25] Mindful of the archival value of the bound *Proceedings,* which were distributed to libraries and universities across the country, Pitts argued that doing so would allow the ASNE to distance itself from Ayers.

While the audience comments were deployed as a public relations tool, they contribute a deeper insight into the perspectives of rank-and-file ASNE members. By several accounts, some members of the ASNE audience did not sit quietly through Ayers's rant, but grumbled and occasionally shouted disapproval.[26] James Saxon Childers of the *Atlanta Journal*—who also questioned the wisdom of putting Ayers on the panel, given his well-documented views on race—was among the Southerners who condemned Ayers's remarks as "an echo of an imagined past and a distortion of present realities." He wrote, "There were men in Mr. Ayers' audience who support segregation, both as a legal right and a present social necessity, who drew back in regional disapproval and personal embarrassment, from the harangue. Apart from, totally dissociated from, the issue of segregation, numerous Southern editors were among those who shuddered."[27]

Among those who commented for the *ASNE Bulletin*'s follow-up coverage, some defended Ayers's remarks on First Amendment grounds and as having made a contribution to their general understanding of the segregation controversy. For example, Basil Walters of Knight Newspapers said he appreciated the variety of perspectives expressed by the panel and then unwittingly added a touch of irony, given the unegalitarian spirit of Ayers's remarks. "This is democracy at work," Walters said. "It's rugged but it's the way we solve our problems in America, always moving forward in the development of a better way of life for all our citizens."[28] In addition, Clapp, the editor from New London, wrote in the *Bulletin* that he appreciated the dire warning about blacks provided by Ayers. "I submit the ASNE must be able to stand the shock of hearing him out, . . ." he wrote. "Are ASNE editors afraid to listen to a speaker who obviously represents a disturbingly large segment of Southerners of the die-hard variety, who *know* the Negro 'jungles' of their cities, and the staggering job of raising the levels of living, individual self-respect and responsibility, etc.?"[29]

Dabney, who was a year away from the ASNE presidency, also worried whether Ayers should be given an opportunity in the May *Bulletin* to ameliorate the public humiliation he had brought upon himself. In a note to Alice Fox Pitts, Dabney expressed deep sympathy for Ayers. "The poor guy was feeling so awful Saturday night that I felt sorry for him. It may be too late to get his apologia into the Bulletin, and maybe you've got one in there already. I can't help hoping such is the case, and that if it isn't scheduled, you will see if he wants to be heard."[30] Pitts's response to Dabney makes clear her opposition to the idea as well as that of her husband and Miles Wolff of the *Greensboro (N.C.) Daily News,* who had just become chair of the Bulletin Committee. The exchange emphasizes the disconnect between Dabney's sentimentality for segregationists like Ayers and the pragmatism of those of more moderate disposition. Regardless of their feelings about integration, Wolff and the Pittses understood the public relations liability that expressions of overt racism entailed for an organization like ASNE. In turning aside Dabney's concern, Alice Fox Pitts exhibited an unusual degree of candor in addressing an ASNE officer.

> You mean Harry Ayers is contrite? That really amazes me, because from opinions he has expressed before (though going further this time) I thought he'd stick to his guns.
>
> No, there's nothing from him in the May Bulletin. . . . Of course he can write a piece in June, if he wants to. But it seems to us that he has to submit it, rather than someone asking him to do so, for a couple of reasons.

1) You can't ask a man to apologize, can you? That has to be of his own free will.
2) If Freddy or Miles asked for it, they'd have to print it as is. And how do we know if it is printable? Suppose he said "I didn't mean that what I said applied to all Negroes—only to most of them." We're really scared that, even though well-intentioned, his apologia might only mess things up worse. So, Freddy and Miles would need a free hand in editing it if he submitted something that seemed unsuitable. [*sic*][31]

The significance of Ayers's comments lay not in their tone or content, although both were stunning, but in what the planning for his participation on the panel and the reaction during the aftermath reveal about the stance of ASNE leaders and members on race relations. As the racial status quo was being renegotiated in American society at large, editors' attitudes ranged from progressive enthusiasm for integration to white supremacist defenses of segregation. Most ASNE members foundered somewhere in between. Notably, none of the editors who responded to Ayers on the record offered a moral condemnation of the segregationist perspective, other than to say it was outdated. At this point in the ASNE's history, most members still appeared unable or unwilling to conceptualize racial inequality as social injustice proscribed by the U.S. Constitution, and those who did were not yet inclined to force the issue within the ASNE. Instead, many editors rationalized Ayers's views as archaic, unpleasantly informative, or an exercise of free speech.

On the other hand, Childers, the embarrassed Atlanta editor, thought censorship after the fact was called for, and asked President Kenneth MacDonald to expunge Ayers's remarks from the convention transcript. At issue was not only whether to preserve an accurate transcription of the convention for posterity but, ironically, given the ASNE's commitment to freedom of information, whether to release the verbatim record to members of the press who were clamoring for it as word of Ayers's comments spread. In her history of the organization's first fifty years, Alice Fox Pitts recounted the furor that erupted after Ayers's remarks and MacDonald's quandary about whether to edit the transcript. Pitts recalled that David Lawrence of *U.S. News & World Report* was so intent upon obtaining a copy of the transcript before MacDonald decided to release it that she feared Lawrence might break into her convention hotel room to get it. For safekeeping, she stashed the transcript in her laundry bag, "certain that Dave was too gentlemanly to root through a lady's dirty lingerie."[32]

After polling members of the board and mulling whether the remarks could be edited on grounds of obscenity, MacDonald decided a couple of weeks after the convention to leave Ayers's statements intact.[33] It appears that a few Southern editors, including James Pope of the Louisville papers, took a progressive stance in discussing the matter with MacDonald. In explaining his decision to Dabney, who had initially thought the *Proceedings* should be censored, MacDonald wrote, "It is unfortunate that the incident happened. But there is no way we could have anticipated it. Jimmie Pope and one or two others have tried to convince me that in the long run we have served a useful purpose by exposing that type of thinking to public view. Perhaps we have."[34]

Closing Ranks

A significant postscript to the 1956 convention discussion was added eighteen months later. At its fall meeting in 1958, the ASNE board of directors appears to have given lie to President MacDonald's assertion that its membership was open to African Americans. The application of Louis Martin, who had been editor-in-chief of the *Chicago Defender* since 1947, was rejected, the only one of twelve from editors of papers with circulations below 20,000 to be denied by the board that year, and the minutes of the meeting explain the board's reasoning: "Discussion of Mr. Martin's eligibility hinged on the definition of a daily newspaper (The Defender publishes daily four times a week and has a weekly edition in addition) and on whether it is a newspaper of general circulation with 'adequate journalistic standards' as required by the by-laws, when, in fact, it is not available on newsstands throughout the city and its appeal is specialized rather than general."[35]

The board's rejection of Martin's application was significant, as it exceeded the recommendation of the Membership Committee. In correspondence prior to the board vote, Wallace Lemoe of the *Milwaukee Journal*, the membership chair, indicated that Martin, "our first negro applicant," had been sponsored by James Wechsler of the *New York Post* and Irving Dillard of the *St. Louis Post-Dispatch*.[36] In a letter to the ASNE board, Lemoe itemized circulation figures for the *Defender*, addressing the requirement that an editor represent a five-day daily with a circulation of more than 20,000 to be eligible to join the ASNE in the regular membership category. Lemoe's analysis of the *Defender*'s status as a daily newspaper focused on the circulation of the four daily editions, which was under 20,000, and ignored the circulation of a Saturday edition, whose circulation was reported to be more than 77,000, because that issue of the paper was designated on its front page as a weekly. For his part, Lemoe told the board that the Membership Committee would recommend only that Martin's paper be classified in the under-20,000 category and that the application be held over for later consideration.[37]

It is significant that at the same board meeting at which Louis Martin was denied membership, the ASNE board of directors tightened the restriction on memberships for the editors of low-circulation dailies. Thereafter, the board said, election to membership by editors at papers with circulations below 20,000 "shall be considered recognition of merit," meaning that papers in this category were in fact suspect and that an applicant would be required to present evidence of awards and copies of his paper—"for gauging its quality."[38] Similar assessments were not performed on applications in other categories.

The board's vote to reject Martin's application, in part because of his newspaper's "specialized" content, is revealing. The black press had long been disparaged by white editors for its advocacy on behalf of civil rights, even though newspapers that editorialized in favor of segregation did not come in for parallel criticism. In fact, a chief detractor of the black press had been Virginius Dabney.[39] By labeling the *Defender*'s audience as "specialized rather than general," the ASNE board used the pretense of journalistic objectivity to disqualify Louis Martin from ASNE membership. For this maneuver to succeed, white-run daily newspapers had to be understood as the norm, as being unraced, and as being immune to ideology. The *Chicago Daily Defender,* in the view of the ASNE board, existed to serve the interests of the black community and to advocate on behalf of civil rights. The irony of an all-white organization of editors criticizing a black paper whose "appeal is specialized rather than general" speaks to how narrowly the white editors of the ASNE viewed their own stake in race. Specifically, by invoking the requirement that members' papers exhibit "adequate journalistic standards" in conjunction with the complaint that the *Defender* targeted a "specialized" audience, the ASNE labeled the black press's engagement with issues of race as bias and as evidence of unprofessionalism.

As a practical matter, the board's rationale for rejecting Martin is problematic in light of the presence on the ASNE rolls of members from the *Wall Street Journal,* another paper whose appeal could be described as "specialized rather than general." With its weekly edition plus the four daily issues, the *Defender* published five issues a week, which matched the output of the *Wall Street Journal,* as well as the *Christian Science Monitor* and numerous small dailies across the country. Moreover, from its inception the ASNE had arbitrarily bent the membership rules to admit editors who were not directing editors of daily newspapers but whose affiliation might bring a certain social capital to the organization. Examples of such exceptions were David Lawrence of the weekly magazine *U.S. News & World Report,* who even served as an ASNE director and treasurer, and the columnist Walter Lippmann. Clearly, the ASNE membership restrictions were at times interpreted literally to maintain a boundary or relaxed to bring desirable applicants into the fold.[40] In either case, by denying membership to Martin, the racial exclusivity of the organization was preserved—for the time being.

Coincidentally, Eugene Patterson of the *Atlanta Constitution* was among editors granted ASNE membership in 1958, even as Martin's application was rejected. Twenty years later, Patterson, as ASNE president, would champion the cause of newsroom integration by leading the ASNE board to adopt Goal 2000, the initiative to bring the number of nonwhites working in daily newspaper newsrooms into parity with the nonwhite demographic in the population at large.

The issues of race and membership did not reappear together in the ASNE's formal record for several years; however, given the social and political pressures from outside and members' evolving sensibilities inside the organization, the racial integration of the ASNE was inevitable. Once social attitudes had shifted sufficiently in the 1960s, many ASNE members recognized the political expedience of admitting a black member and welcomed the prospect. In 1965, two years before the release of the Kerner Commission report, the ASNE admitted John Sengstacke of the *Chicago Daily Defender* as its first African American member. Significantly, Sengstacke had been the founder in 1942 of the Negro Newspaper Publishers Association, which, along with the Negro Press Association, had been organized to counter the racial exclusion of white press organizations such as the ASNE, American Newspaper Publishers Association, and the Associated Press.

In contrast to Martin's experience in 1958, Sengstacke's application was subjected to no more scrutiny than that of other potential members.[41] In the seven years since Martin's application was rejected, the civil rights movement had changed the racial landscape in the United States. A high-profile organization like the ASNE, which did not have a nonwhite member, now was a target for criticism and the board dared not quibble about circulation and the "specialized" nature of the *Defender*'s content. Sengstacke would remain the only African American member of ASNE until 1973, when the board revisited its decision to deny membership to Martin. The ASNE's daily newspaper requirement would prevent the ASNE from admitting a black directing editor from a white-run paper until 1978.[42]

Dancing Along the Mason-Dixon Line

The Civil War metaphor embodied in the North-South tennis tournaments extended throughout the later 1950s as Southern editors grappled with the implications of court-ordered desegregation and used regionalism as a cover for racial anxiety. Within the ASNE, Southern identity became a symbol of renewed defiance, an indication that even editors less intractable on the issue of integration saw themselves as losers in the new social order augured by the Supreme Court ruling. In the post-*Brown* years, knowing references to the Confederacy and inside jokes about the North were sprinkled throughout the ASNE *Bulletin,* owing largely to the prominence within the organization of several Southern editors who had been vocal on matters related to *Brown.* Among them were tennis aficionados Grover C. Hall Jr. of the *Montgomery Advertiser,* who contributed frequently to the *Bulletin,* and Virginius Dabney, editor of the *Richmond Times-Dispatch,* who became ASNE president in 1957. Dabney was succeeded in that office by segregationist George Healy of the *New Orleans Times-Picayune,* who was even caricatured in the *Bulletin* wearing a Confederate uniform.[43] For such editors, united by what W. J. Cash in *The Mind of the South* called the "mysterious bonds" of a shared Southern past, it was important to be known as Southerners and as proud stewards of their region's social traditions.[44]

Even many moderate ASNE members from the South who editorialized against resistance to school desegregation and became known for opposing mob violence were gradualists who supported social segregation to varying degrees and objected to the imposition of federal will represented by the *Brown* ruling, preferring that the South be allowed to evolve without intervention. These editors included Dabney, Reed Sarratt of the *Winston-Salem Journal Sentinel,* C. A. McKnight of the *Charlotte Observer,* and Ralph McGill of the *Atlanta Constitution.*[45] It is worth considering Southern editors within the context of their communities. As John Egerton has argued, many residents of the South viewed the integration of public schools as an assault on the social order and even many of the moderate Southern editors, who witnessed visceral opposition to the Supreme Court's order among their readership, struggled to maintain a voice for the middle ground.[46] While much of the country was reeling from the implications of *Brown,* many of the Southern editors who were active in the ASNE during this period were from communities literally in turmoil or, at the very least, experiencing some degree of anxiety over the end of what commonly was called "the Southern way of life."

The bond of Southernness grew stronger during this period as prominent Southern editors in the ASNE united in regional defensiveness. During the mid-1950s many Southern daily newspaper editors grew resentful of the Northern press, which had taken a deep interest in the white South's reaction to *Brown* and the burgeoning civil rights movement. The cadre of newspaper journalists routinely covering the activism of Dr. Martin Luther King Jr. and such racial violence as the Emmett Till murder included reporters for the *New York Times* and other metropolitan dailies, whose editors also were ASNE members, and the Associated Press wire service, which fed news to many member newspapers in the North. Many Southern editors believed the Northern press's unrelenting scrutiny, which focused on racism only in the South, to be sensationalized and hypocritical. One of the most persistent advocates of this perspective was Grover Hall Jr. of the *Montgomery Advertiser,* who became an impassioned critic of his Northern peers. "Northern editors," he wrote in the *ASNE Bulletin,* "have not in their thinking come to grips with the sorrowful but evident fact that wherever the Negro migrates in significant numbers, he encounters resistance."[47] Hall urged Northern editors to cover the race story in their own communities before worrying about the transgressions of the South. "What the national press has done so far is to turn out bubbly stereo plates about that part of the race problem under the magnolia," he said.[48]

Significantly, during the 1950s Southern editors achieved a stature within ASNE that they had not held before. This occurred with the consent of a majority of ASNE members, as they elected five presidents from Southern and border states during the decade. In addition to Dabney and Healy, these presidents were Wright Bryan of the *Atlanta Journal* (1952–53); James Pope of the *Louisville Courier-Journal and Times* (1954–55); and Jenkin Lloyd Jones of the *Tulsa Tribune* (1956–57). Because presidents appointed the chairmen who controlled such important committees as those overseeing membership, board nominations, the *Bulletin,* and convention programs, many key positions within the ASNE also were held by Southern editors, some of whom had strident views about race. A case in point is John Q. Mahaffey of the *Texarkana Gazette*, who was admonished during the 1956 convention for his remarks about women and blacks. Even so, Dabney appointed him as membership chair in 1957. Neither before nor since have Southerners had such a lock on the ASNE leadership.[49] The fact that a succession of Southern editors, some of whom routinely expressed racist views, were elevated to the ASNE's most prestigious posts at precisely this moment in the history of both the organization and the U.S. racial struggle suggests that a cross-section of members empathized with their Southern peers or did not see their views on *Brown* as professionally relevant.

While Southern editors discussed segregation frankly in private, they were more circumspect in public. During this period, humor allowed Southern editors to flaunt their regional identity and telegraph their opposition to the Supreme Court ruling without engaging the subject directly. Take, for instance, a *Bulletin* item about Grover Hall Jr., which appeared the month following the 1956 convention and reported that he had "left early to make a speech, Saturday evening, before the Huckleberry Indians, a social group of the New York Athletic Club. At that banquet the club received a copy of the Constitution of the Confederate States of America, appropriately bound and inscribed in gold, carried through enemy lines by Confederate Agent Hall."[50] *Bulletin* reports of the C.S.A.-G.A.R. tennis tournaments also served this purpose. For example, Dabney, who partnered with Hall and lost in the 1960 tournament, reported, "Gen. Hall's dipsy-doodle service had been as effective as Stuart's ride around McClellan, but like his partner, he could not in the end manage to dodge Yellow Tavern and Appomattox."[51] In this way, these Southern editors were able to keep their opposition to *Brown* in front of the ASNE membership without mentioning the desegregation ruling.

Naming and Framing Race

In the post-*Brown* period of the ASNE, discussion of race coverage focused not only on resistance to integration but also on whether African American news subjects should be identified as such. Editors who did not embrace integration purported to view these issues through the lens of journalistic objectivity. For his part, Hall, the editor from Montgomery, contorted the argument and complained that if Northern papers failed to label blacks in stories about crime and living conditions, as requested by the National Association for the Advancement of Colored People, they would be downplaying the effect of racial discrimination in the North.[52] Fellow Alabamian Harry Ayers put a First Amendment spin on his objection to eliminating racial identifiers for criminal defendants. He wrote, "There seems to be a policy of studied and unwarranted favoritism toward the Negro race, which is exercising a censorship over the American press that is without precedent within my knowledge."[53] Even for some Northern editors, a person's race had news value. Kansan John P. Harris of the *Hutchinson News-Herald* asked, "Is it possible that such a pointed omission of a basic news fact as this is a subconscious journalistic penance for past sins?"[54] Similarly, John T. O'Rourke of the

Washington Daily News portrayed the use of racial identifiers as an exercise of editorial independence. He said, "The Washington Daily News never has acceded to the demand of Negro pressure groups that race be deleted from news stories. On the contrary, The News is the only Washington paper that has consistently insisted that race be included in its stories, because it is an essential part of the social scene about which it reports."[55] By insisting on the news value of a racial signifier, the editors who supported labeling for blacks but presumably not for whites—this possibility is never mentioned—were reinforcing the white norm.

At the same time, the ASNE also was open to the occasional argument from an editor who favored integration, infrequent though it was. For example, E. T. Stone, managing editor of the *Seattle Post-Intelligencer,* wrote in a 1955 issue of the *Bulletin* that his paper "believes whole-heartedly in desegregation," perhaps the only statement of support for *Brown* to appear in the *Bulletin* in the decision's immediate aftermath. Stone noted that "even on our enlightened newspaper there was one inner sanctum that remained locked and barred. That was the section devoted to the doings of women, a sort of double segregation, sexual and racial." The *Post-Intelligencer* integrated its society pages, running photographs of black brides next to white, to only minor reader objection, and Stone urged others to follow suit: "I wonder how many of the editors who thunder loftily in behalf of the downtrodden minorities have examined the beam in their own eye while calling attention to the mote elsewhere. How many have gone the whole route and eliminated racial distinctions from their women's sections—their so-called society pages?"[56]

The opportunity for direct expressions of support for or opposition to civil rights diminished as time went on, as race virtually disappeared as a convention topic until the 1960s and contributors to the *Bulletin* generally avoided any discussion of race until civil rights legislation began making its way through Congress in 1964. An exception, and one that ASNE members of the time may not have recognized as commentary on race or gender, appeared in a 1961 *Bulletin* item in which Jenkin Lloyd Jones of the *Tulsa Tribune* mocked the bare-chested women in a photo taken on an ASNE-sponsored excursion to Africa. The photo was published in the *Bulletin* with the following caption: "In spite of its depressing effect on circulation, The Tulsa Tribune is proud that it remains a FAMILY NEWSPAPER. This photo of shameless hussies near Ft. Lamy, Chad, was taken by Tribune Editor Jenk Jones. It was, of course, withheld from tender Oklahoma eyes but copies were sent privately to other members of the party. Arizona Daily Star editor Bill Matthews boldly included it in his articles."[57] In this caption, Jones describes the African women as objects of disdain and ridicule but also as being so sexually illicit that the photo should be circulated "privately." It is hard to imagine the *Bulletin* publishing a photo of a partially nude white woman whom editors encountered in their foreign travels. In addition, framing the commentary as humor allowed editors to defend it as just a joke about foreigners rather than a disparagement of black people.

Another editor who found indirect means to express contempt for African Americans was Mahaffey, the editor of the *Texarkana Gazette*. Mahaffey had been a member of the infamous 1956 convention panel on which Harry Ayers had ignited controversy with his racist diatribe, and while Mahaffey's remarks were anything but pro-integration, his contributions on that occasion were subdued by comparison to Ayers's.[58] In a submission to the *Bulletin* two years later, however, Mahaffey included a description of the black newsroom porter who worked at his paper, poking fun at his dialect and mannerisms.[59] But his most pointed discussion of race came in his report in 1967 about a community banquet honoring professional football player Willie Davis, whose hometown was Texarkana, Arkansas.

While Mahaffey's piece, titled "The Night Texarkana 'Turned the Corner,'" purported to demonstrate his community's newfound commitment to equality, it in fact was wholly derisive of Davis, who was reduced to a buffoon for the benefit of white Texarkansans—and members of the ASNE. Mahaffey wrote, "You've got to accentuate the positive and eliminate the negative if you want to have good race relations in your city. . . . That's why we viewed Willie Davis, the great defensive end of the Green Bay Packers, as manna from heaven and parlayed him into a smashing demonstration of racial harmony that we believe will enable our people to turn the corner into this new way of life that is still very strange indeed." Mahaffey recounted Davis's local history and even included the disingenuous claim that Davis "had been a personal friend of mine since the days when he was a bartender and waiter at the Texarkana Country Club." Mahaffey then condescendingly described Davis's gratitude for a banquet held in his honor, as if an African American's debasement could contribute to racial harmony. Mahaffey wrote, "With tears streaming down his face, this great big black boy who can be mean as hell on the football field, said [the banquet] was the 'super-bowl' of his life."[60]

Mahaffey's characterization of Davis is racially condescending, yet the episode demonstrates the change in the ASNE's public rhetoric about racial difference since the 1956 convention. Just as Mahaffey had described the alleged corner-turning in Texarkana, many editors, even some who resented desegregation, felt obliged to disclose their efforts to defuse racial tensions or engender racial harmony. This was a theme in many editor profiles that appeared in the *ASNE Bulletin* during this period, as well as first-person accounts of newsroom policy changes on segregated society pages and other content issues.[61] Locking step with society at large, the editors generally followed evolving standards for discussing race, which appeared to be more socially conscious than those that held sway prior to *Brown.* At the same time, some editors carried on a different and more candid conversation in private, where they did not attempt to dress up their remarks for broader consumption. This becomes poignantly evident in the nonpublic usage of the slur "nigger" and the tolerance of it by editors thought to be progressive on the issue of racial equality.

Again, Mahaffey provides an example, this time through a note he sent a couple of weeks before the 1965 ASNE convention, which was scheduled in Washington, D.C., to Georgia editor Louis Harris, executive editor of the *Augusta Herald,* and copied to Sylvan Meyer, the editor of the *Gainesville Daily Times.* Interestingly, Meyer had chaired the Georgia Advisory Commission to the U.S. Civil Rights Commission. Harris had written Mahaffey seeking support for Meyer's candidacy for the ASNE board, and Mahaffey concluded his response, saying, "Ruth and I look forward to seeing you and our other Deep South friends in Washington. Don't let 'them' 'niggers' get you down. I'm so sick of blackfaces, I could erp. (or is it urp)?"[62] Mahaffey's message of racial hatred is unsettling, but these few lines from a memo circulated among professional acquaintances also reveal the degree to which racism was tolerated among ASNE insiders during the 1960s. To speak with such candor to editors he probably saw just once a year at the ASNE convention, Mahaffey must have felt certain that his audience was sympathetic. Perhaps most significant, however, is Mahaffey's conceptualization of the upcoming ASNE convention as a refuge from African Americans for an integration-weary editor like himself. Clearly, Mahaffey was looking forward to spending time within the white enclave that the ASNE had come to represent.

Ironically, the convention Mahaffey is anticipating would be the last prior to John Sengstacke's election to membership. While Sengstacke's induction would not make the ASNE any less a bastion of whiteness, in future years Mahaffey would run the risk of encountering at least one "blackface" during the convention.

A Melting Pot of Contradiction

As landmark civil rights legislation moved through Congress in 1964, the ASNE began occasionally to slate race issues for discussion at a general session of the annual convention. U.S. Attorney General Robert Kennedy had touched lightly on the topic of civil rights during a convention speech in 1961, but for all intents and purposes race had been off the convention agenda since the 1956 white supremacist rant of Harry Ayers and the public relations debacle that followed. The 1964 program featured another appearance by Kennedy, this time with Assistant Attorney General Burke Marshall, who spoke on the topic "After the Civil Rights Bill, What?" and discussed the implications of the legislation designed to guarantee, among other things, protection from racial discrimination in employment. During the question-and-answer session, John Knight of Knight Newspapers, who generally was regarded as racially progressive, said he had "taken exception to Title VII," which specifically mandated equal opportunity in the workplace, and pressed a concern about quotas and whether promotions, pay increases, and firings would result from increased scrutiny under the new law. Marshall reassured him that the civil rights law did not establish quotas but in fact "would forbid them because it forbids discrimination on the grounds of race," which would foreclose reverse discrimination against whites.[63] While editors' attitudes about workplace discrimination would evolve in coming years, this conversation offers a baseline against which to measure the task that confronted the founders of the ASNE newsroom integration initiative in 1978, when they sought to persuade their peers to hold themselves accountable for the numerical target in the plan. Knight's comment also is noteworthy as the Knight-Ridder newspaper chain would, along with Gannett newspapers, become a leader in the newsroom integration movement.

The 1964 convention was significant as well because it was the first time the ASNE had invited African Americans to speak on the issue of civil rights.[64] The ASNE scheduled a panel of the most prominent civil rights leaders, including not only Dr. Martin Luther King Jr. but also Roy Wilkins, executive secretary of the National Association for the Advancement of Colored People; John Lewis, chairman of the Southern Christian Leadership Conference; James Farmer, national director of the Congress of Racial Equality; and Whitney Young Jr., executive director of the National Urban League.[65] At the same time that the ASNE placed these speakers on the convention program, however, the organization also marginalized them through a series of slights that effectively undercut the impact of their message.

For starters, although all of these civil rights leaders advocated nonviolence, their convention session was titled "Civil Rights Combatants." This choice of language, which underscored the oppositional nature of the civil right movement, also seemed to place the panelists at odds with their audience. This sense of disconnect was amplified in the *Bulletin*'s coverage of the panel the following month. The article began,

> Four of the nation's top Negro leaders starred on the Thursday afternoon panel. And nobody asked them:
>
> "How would you like to have your daughter marry Governor Wallace?"
>
> In fact, not a single anti-civil rights or hostile question was asked.[66]

The author of this article clearly assumed his readers would be surprised that the civil rights panel did not encounter hostility from the all-white ASNE audience. In his assessment of a friendly reception, however, the author ignored a barbed question posed by Georgia editor Sylvan Meyer of the *Gainesville Daily Times* about "irresponsible Negro leadership," believed by many white Americans to be the cause of confrontations over civil rights.[67]

The ASNE's interaction with the civil rights leaders was much more revealing than this, however. Because of a decision that morning to reschedule the afternoon sessions, the ASNE made it impossible for King, who had another engagement that day, to appear and reduced the time allotted to the panel such that each speaker received just five minutes to make his case for civil rights. As the panel's moderator explained, editors had learned in that morning's *Washington Post* that they had been invited to attend a Lyndon Johnson press conference at the State Department late that afternoon. Although the White House had not bothered to give the ASNE timely and direct notification, which might have allowed the program committee to accord the civil rights panel its full time and avoid a conflict for King, ASNE members voted not to maintain their previous commitment to the invited civil rights speakers but to move up the afternoon schedule to accommodate editors who wished to attend the press conference at 4:30. The slight to the civil rights leaders seems all the more unnecessary because ASNE members had another opportunity to interact with President Johnson at a White House reception the following evening.[68]

Not only were the civil rights leaders, who presumably had prepared remarks for the occasion, forced to ad lib a shortened version and to proceed without King, but they also had to continue speaking while a large portion of their audience walked out. For editors to arrive at the State Department on time, they had to leave in the middle of the civil rights panel, and many did.[69] This rude treatment of nonwhite speakers on the convention program was not an anomaly. Over the decades to come, ASNE members who supported newsroom integration would complain that convention audiences often got up and left when presentations by African Americans and sessions on diversity began. In the context of the pivotal historical period surrounding the 1964 convention, the ASNE's dismissive posture toward the civil rights leadership was fraught with significance.

Despite clear indications that many ASNE members were not prepared to embrace civil rights as a moral absolute, the mid-1960s also saw the emergence within ASNE of a strain of activism that had not been evident before. Even as some editors still wrestled with such issues as whether to segregate obituaries and wedding write-ups in their papers,[70] others were beginning to advocate prominently on behalf of racial justice. In 1964, Donald Baldwin of the *St. Petersburg Times and Independent* submitted an item to the *Bulletin* asking fellow editors to lend support—moral and financial—to Hazel Brannon Smith, a white woman who was on the verge of losing her weekly newspaper in Mississippi because of segregationist boycotts.[71] Smith, who won the 1964 Pulitzer Prize for editorials, had long stood up to the racist law enforcement and judicial systems in the South, and now found herself and her paper, the *Lexington Advertiser,* on the brink of being put out of business. Baldwin's article was followed a year later by a similar plea from Hodding Carter, editor of the *Delta Democrat Times* in Greenville, Mississippi, and Edward Barrett, dean of Columbia University's School of Journalism, who were formally raising money to aid Smith.[72] It is unlikely that such vigorous support for any editor—much less a Southern woman—who sought social justice for African Americans would have found space in the *Bulletin* a decade earlier.

During the mid-1960s, those who would guide the newsroom integration initiative in its early years were finding their voice on the issue of racial equality, chief among them Eugene Patterson, editor of the *Atlanta Constitution.* Patterson would be ASNE president in 1978, when the newsroom integration initiative was launched, as well as a lifelong advocate of newsroom inclusion. Although the thought of hiring African Americans to work as journalists at white-run daily newspapers did not occur to most ASNE members, Patterson later recalled that he and Ralph McGill, his publisher and mentor, had "spent a great deal of time sort of worrying ourselves as to what we were going to do about this" and indeed hired the *Atlanta Constitution*'s first black reporter in 1964.[73]

Another future ASNE diversity leader who developed an activist bent during the 1960s was John Seigenthaler Sr., editor of the *Nashville Tennessean.* Seigenthaler, who had taken a leave from the paper to work for Attorney General Robert Kennedy in the Department of Justice, was beaten by a white mob when the Freedom Riders stopped in Montgomery, Alabama, in 1961. When he returned to the *Tennessean* in 1962, Seigenthaler began working to hire African Americans onto his news staff. Despite his relatively forward-thinking approach, during an interview four decades later Seigenthaler offered a self-effacing anecdote that illustrates the obstacles that the common sense of segregation posed even for editors who were beginning to see the necessity of integrated newsrooms. Seigenthaler recalled an eye-opening experience during a talk he gave at Fisk University, a historically black institution.

> Shortly after going back as editor, I went out to Fisk one day and made a speech. You know, I'm sure I was spouting profundities about the state of the world affairs and thought, what a downright, upright editor I was, until this young woman got up and said, "Sir, can you tell me why it is that when I get married in two months you won't run the picture of my engagement or the announcement of my engagement?" And, of course, I said, "Well, of course I will," and broke the policy of the paper's lifetime. And you tell me, why the hell had I not paid attention to that situation before I went out there? I'd probably been editor a year or two. It was my first speech at one of the black universities. And you know, it's hard to recognize how blind we were, even with some experience and some sense of awareness. I mean, from '54—*Brown v. Board of Education*—and in 1963 I'm just now finding out that I'd better start paying attention to what all the sections of the paper are doing on this subject of race.[74]

Like Patterson at the *Atlanta Constitution,* who had a front-row seat for the nonviolent protests led by Martin Luther King, Seigenthaler had developed an awareness that the normative value of whiteness was constructed on a weak foundation, one that crumbled as soon as it was removed from the context in which its dominance was accepted uncritically and assumed to be reasonable. Standing before an audience of African American students at a historically black college, itself a monument to America's history of racial segregation, Seigenthaler's whiteness and the injustice it represented were obvious not only to the woman who addressed him but also to himself. In this instant, the idea of whiteness as a norm appeared painfully absurd.

Burying the Gender Story

While editors were beginning to devise new ways of talking about and relating to race in their newsrooms, few showed the same concern about the status of white women in their profession. In fact, some editors showed an open hostility toward white women during the 1950s and 1960s that was striking, given the tact most editors were developing in discussing race. After the civil rights movement, this entrenched misogyny would open a second front in the ASNE's identity battles, creating a tension between race and gender and demonstrating the limits of Goal 2000's democratic mission. The ASNE's relative disregard of gender equity would remain problematic through the end of the century, as white women would be excluded for twenty years from the newsroom census and newsroom hiring mission that was adopted in 1978. This stunning omission had deep roots, however. Time and again during the ASNE's first fifty years, white women were openly derided and denigrated; yet such comments drew no significant protest. The scorn heaped on white women in such public forums as the *Bulletin* and ASNE conventions sometimes matched the tone of Ayers's 1956 rant about race mixing, but never drew the same degree of public censure, if any.

Typical of the ASNE's treatment of women is the cover of the January 1956 *Bulletin,* which featured a package of stories about women in journalism, illustrated by a photo of a pretty young reporter sitting at a typewriter and staring dreamily into space, the antithesis of the earnest, scoop-seeking male journalist. While articles in the section included testimonials from editors who had found women reporters competent for the job, most women were stuck in entry-level positions—unless, as in the case of *Newsday* publisher Alicia Patterson, they owned the paper.[75] A profile of *Newsday,* where women who had been employed during World War II were let go to make room for returning male veterans, reported that just fifteen of the editorial department's 107 employees were women, with nine more relegated to the women's department. Patterson, who noted that just seventy-six women were editors at the 1,700 daily newspapers publishing at the time and just seven of those were at papers with a circulation greater than 20,000, said a double standard applied even to her. "There is a kind of invisible conspiracy among males of watchful waiting to witness the little lady fall on her face," she said.[76] In employing the term "watchful waiting," which was often used to described the South's posture immediately after the *Brown* decision, Patterson aligned the plight of women journalists with the civil rights movement for African Americans.

While the 1956 package offered some room for optimism that women were beginning to be taken just a bit more seriously by the ASNE, even if stereotypes lingered, the situation appeared less promising ten years later in another package of stories labeled "Females in the Newsroom." Prompted by the implementation of Title VII of the Civil Rights Act of 1964, which outlawed employment discrimination based on gender as well as race, C. A. McKnight of the *Charlotte Observer,* the *Bulletin* chairman, asked an assortment of editors to discuss their experiences with women employees. Not only were the remarks largely negative, but they were pointedly so. One of the most acerbic comments came from Robert Atwood of the *Anchorage Daily Times,* who complained that women employees were unpredictable: "We think our troubles with women stem from the fact that they are always in one of four stages: premenstrual, menstrual, post-menstrual or pregnant. We call it 'moon phases.' We think emotional peaks and depressions affect women's work as they move from stage to stage. Moon changes make production lag or copy dull. On the other hand, the copy sometimes becomes brilliant and very prompt! Dispositions vary from charming to snarling."[77]

In a related piece, Ken Tooill of the *Toledo Times* proudly announced that no women were employed on his paper's editorial staff—not including the women's department, which generally was not considered part of a paper's news operation. Tooill wrote, "We get our quota of interns for a few weeks in the summer, but these lovelies are gone before our men, those young enough to be interested in such things, have a chance to ask them what time they get off and what they are doing this evening. At this season, all that lingers is the fragrance of their perfume, and a memory of the damnedest syntax you ever saw. Our sister paper, The Blade, on the other hand, is thoroughly integrated sexually. I suppose they have a problem. Where there are women, there are problems."[78] These sentiments would appear to substantiate the claim of an unidentified female journalist who spoke in 1963 of the need "to eliminate the prejudice against women that is still rampant throughout the profession."[79]

While some editors complained of higher turnover among women employees, who often quit when they married or had children, Atwood did concede that in the previous five years, eleven women had stayed at his paper an average of forty months, while seventeen men had an average tenure of thirty months.[80] Another editor, Vern Croop of the *Rochester (N.Y.) Times-Union,* said newspapers, not women, were at a disadvantage. "We do not discriminate against women in hiring, they discriminate against us," Croop complained. "In these critical times, why can't we have a law passed (everybody else seems to) and stop women from this crass discrimination in favor of boys, babies and whims."[81] What was more, the women he hired did not want to work on women's pages.

Even as social change left its mark on American culture and politics, the ASNE glided through the 1960s with its exclusionary traditions virtually intact. In 1955, just six women were among the 562 members of the organization, and just one woman had served on the organization's board of directors.[82] By 1972, even as the organization's membership topped 700, the number of women members had risen to just seven. Meanwhile, the ASNE had admitted just one African American to its membership by the end of the 1960s.

While few editors openly opposed social integration by the end of the decade, few openly supported the integration of their newsrooms. Although many would argue that the U.S. Constitution mandated equal rights for all Americans, a surprising number of editors drew the line at the newsroom door. This would become clear through the ASNE's nonresponse to the 1968 report of the National Advisory Commission on Civil Disorders, also known as the Kerner Commission, which lambasted the press for its history of racial discrimination. Newspapers themselves may have been empowered by the Constitution, but many of their editors still resisted the notion that they had a democratic responsibility to report the news for all readers and to include diverse perspectives in their reporting. This sense of journalistic exceptionalism, which set newsrooms above other places of employment in editors' minds, allowed them, individually and collectively through the ASNE, to exempt themselves from the democratic mandates that applied elsewhere. This double standard and the inability of many editors to appreciate its irony would become important themes as the ASNE inched closer to the board's 1978 vote to support newsroom integration.

2

Seeking Justice in a Climate of Irony

The Hiring Initiative's Uneasy Prelude, 1968–76

During his career in journalism and academia, Norman Isaacs grew accustomed to playing the odd man out in professional controversies. A thoughtful, idealistic editor with a crusader's distaste for ambiguity, Isaacs always began from the premise that the editor's covenant required him to serve as a moral compass for his community. Dismayed by the widespread ethical failings of journalism, Isaacs tried unsuccessfully as ASNE president in 1969–70 to interest the organization in starting an ethics enforcement procedure. At the end of his term, Isaacs left the *Louisville Courier-Journal* and joined the faculty of Columbia University, where he took up the cause of the National Press Council, a noble though ill-fated attempt to hold news media accountable for their conduct.[1] In this way, Isaacs frequently cast himself as a nagging conscience that many of his fellow editors preferred to ignore. Given his habit of going against the grain, it seems fitting that Isaacs also inaugurated the ASNE's campaign for newsroom integration.

After months of work through the ASNE's first Minority Employment Committee, Isaacs stood before the 1972 convention to report that non-whites accounted for just three-quarters of 1 percent of the professional employees in daily newspaper newsrooms. "It supports the assertion that we have, indeed, been racist in our employment practices throughout our years in the calling," Isaacs told his fellow editors.[2] For the most part, Isaacs's audience greeted the news with indifference, his enthusiasm for a remedy failed to catch on, and this initial effort to promote newsroom integration sputtered to a halt. With little to show for its labor and the number of non-whites working in daily newsrooms virtually static, the Minority Employment Committee disbanded two years later. "It is the committee's feeling that after three years of repeated checking [on the number of nonwhite journalists], it has served its purpose for the time being," Isaacs reported in 1974.[3]

The work of Isaacs's Minority Employment Committee was the ASNE's first significant response to the rebuke delivered in 1968 by the National Advisory Commission on Civil Disorders, more commonly known as the Kerner Commission. The presidential commission, which investigated the causes of the urban uprisings from 1964 through 1967, devoted a chapter of its report to exploring the news media's role in perpetuating the "black-white schism" in American society that had precipitated violence in the cities.[4] In both tone and message, chapter 15 was a scathing and unprecedented indictment of the news media's failure "to analyze and report adequately on racial problems in the United States and . . . to meet the Negro's legitimate expectations in journalism." The report continued,

> By and large, news organizations have failed to communicate to both their black and white audiences a sense of the problems America faces and sources of potential solutions. The media report and write from the standpoint of a white man's world. The ills of the ghetto, the difficulties of life there, the Negro's burning sense of grievance, are seldom conveyed. Slights and indignities are part of the Negro's daily life, and many of them come from what he now calls "the white press"—a press that repeatedly, if unconsciously, reflects the biases, the paternalism, the indifference of white America. This may be understandable, but it is not excusable in an institution that has the mission to inform and educate the whole of our society.[5]

Chapter 15's most significant contributions were not only its emphasis on the need for more inclusive news coverage but also its insistence on integrated hiring in journalism. The Kerner Commission did not mince words on this point, framing newsroom integration as a democratic mandate and insisting that nonwhites be among newsroom decision-makers who shaped news content.

> The scarcity of Negroes in responsible news jobs intensifies the difficulties of communicating the reality of the contemporary American city to white newspaper and television audiences. The special viewpoint of the Negro who has lived through these problems and bears their marks upon him is . . . notably absent from what is, on the whole, a white press. But full integration of Negroes into the journalistic profession is imperative in its own right. It is unacceptable that the press, itself the special beneficiary of fundamental

> constitutional protections, should lag so far behind other fields in giving effect to the fundamental human right to equal opportunity.[6]

The forcefulness of this recommendation caught many editors off-guard. The idea that nonwhites should be promoted into newsroom management positions may have been the point on which the Kerner report met the greatest resistance from editors, even if this resistance was not always articulated directly.

Within the context of its time, the Kerner Commission's chapter 15 was revolutionary. In effect, the Kerner Commission suggested that an objective view of U.S. race relations was not to be found in the self-interested and narrow perspective offered by the white press. In addition to its call for integrating white newsrooms and the assimilation of nonwhites into these professional environments, the Kerner Commission validated the black press, suggesting that representatives of the black press were real journalists who should be used as resources in covering the race story.[7] This was an important challenge to the notion that the professional template of white daily journalism was the only one that mattered. In this way, the Kerner report also contradicted the argument, which had begun to develop currency among white editors, that "qualified" nonwhite journalists were not available for hire.

Not since the Hutchins Commission's report in 1947 had the press received such an unequivocal broadside from a source with comparable public credibility, yet the Kerner report arguably represented an even more significant dressing-down, given the politically diverse composition of the commission and the historical context in which the commission worked.[8] While the Hutchins Commission had addressed general complaints and philosophical differences about press performance, the Kerner report was a direct response to burning cities, loss of life, and racial panic resulting from riots in U.S. cities, and it made a specific and detailed case that the white news media—specifically through their failure to integrate newsrooms and to produce racially sensitive news coverage—bore significant, if indirect, responsibility for the meltdown. Moreover, the commission's claims received wide circulation and the Kerner report, which was quickly published in both hardcover and paperback, shot to the top of the *New York Times* best-seller list and remained there for sixteen weeks.[9]

The ASNE, however, treated the release of the Kerner report as a nonevent and did not spare even the terse and testy response it had offered the Hutchins Commission in 1947.[10] If they mentioned the report at all, speakers during the 1968 convention acknowledged it only in passing.[11] Allowing for the report's publication in March, one might blame timing for the ASNE's failure to incorporate it into the April convention program in a meaningful way; however, that would not explain the failure of ASNE members to examine the topic in some depth in the pages of the *Bulletin* during the months to come. The *Bulletin* managed a single story in its April 1968 issue, buried well inside the publication—in which, ironically, Ben Gilbert of the *Washington Post* accurately assessed the historical significance of the commission's recommendations. His brief analysis should have piqued interest, if not for what it said about the press' performance on race, then for the specter it raised of government scrutiny of the news media, which is an affront to journalistic exceptionalism and traditionally had been an ASNE hot button. Gilbert wrote, "The indictment was extraordinary. It is most unusual for any government agency—even a Presidential commission—to take a searching look at the press in the United States."[12] And then the *Bulletin* let the subject drop, offering none of the postmortem analysis the editors might have given any other development of comparable import and relevance to their profession.

Notably, the *Bulletin* and convention programs carried far more discussion of issues aligned with Kerner's chapter 15 during the three years before the report's release than during the three years afterward.[13] The ASNE's interest in the subject of race and the press before the Kerner Commission released its findings paralleled the conversation that was taking place outside the ASNE. For example, in 1965, the University of Missouri School of Journalism had used its annual Freedom of Information Conference to explore the issue of "The Racial Crisis and the News Media," and in 1967 the Foreign Journalism Award Program at the University of California, Los Angeles, had sponsored a symposium on "The Black American and the Press."[14]

While such pre-Kerner conferences were held on academic turf, participants included working journalists and editors. This was also true of conferences held shortly after the report's release, which meant the audience for these discussions was not confined to the academy. In May 1968, just two months after the Kerner report's publication, the University of Chicago's Center for Policy Studies hosted a conference on "The Media and the Cities." A month later the University of Washington sponsored a similar program. The fact that academics could organize extensive discussions on short notice—a book even was published from the Chicago conference that year—and the ASNE could not, or would not, address the report in a timely way did not go unnoticed. Edwin O. Guthman, national news editor of the *Los Angeles Times*, told the Chicago conference, "When the American Society of Newspaper Editors can meet, as it did in mid-April 1968, in Washington, D.C., and fail to take up Chapter XV or discuss the ways the press might do better in accurately reporting riots and ghetto problems, does it not raise a question of whether we are not even capable of communicating the urgency of the racial situation to ourselves?"[15]

Because the topic of hiring nonwhites had been part of the official ASNE conversation before the report's publication, its disappearance becomes all the more curious considering that the Kerner Commission characterized the press' failings as a crisis of civic and journalistic responsibility. The commission was speaking directly and forcefully to media managers, including the editors of daily newspapers, about the core mission of journalism, and the ASNE turned its back on the report. The ASNE's silent disengagement from newsroom integration issues during the three years between the Kerner report's release and the appointment of Norman Isaacs's Minority Employment Committee in 1971 is significant, particularly given the conversation taking place elsewhere in the profession. In addition to the conferences in Chicago and elsewhere, another professional association, the Associated Press Managing Editors, quickly issued a report responding to the Kerner Commission.[16] The *Columbia Journalism Review,* which had established itself as the news media's watchdog, also devoted twenty-four pages of its fall 1968 issue to discussion of the Kerner report's ramification for the profession. Through its initial silence, however, the ASNE affirmed the white professional norm that had been woven into the culture of the organization and its members' newsrooms. While the ASNE's resistance to the Kerner Commission's message may have been tacit, the organization's silence betrayed an ambivalence that would pose one of the most significant obstacles to newsroom integration in the years to come.

Undergirding the ASNE's nonresponse to the Kerner report was a renewed and defiant sense of journalistic exceptionalism, which allowed many editors to ignore the constitutional double standard created by their own insistence on a free press and their continuing historical denial of equal rights to nonwhites and white women. But it also would be a period of awakening to the evolving ethical precepts of journalism, most notably its own need for accountability, which had been treated as platitudes by some editors. The accentuation of journalistic exceptionalism was in some measure a defensive reaction to widespread public and political attacks on the media, most publicly by Vice President Spiro T. Agnew, who delivered a series of speeches in November 1969 in which he derided members of the media for their arrogance and suggested using federal licensure to regulate television news reports about the Nixon Administration.[17] While some editors may have seen Agnew's critique as an affront to the free press, Philip Geyelin of the *Washington Post* noted that the press was widely regarded as arrogant and indifferent to criticism. "The hard fact of the matter," he wrote, "is that not one kind, but all kinds of people do not trust us."[18] While some editors dug in their heels, positioning themselves as above the criticism, Isaacs and others tried to persuade their peers of the importance of journalism ethics and public accountability for the news media. In 1970, with Isaacs as president, the ASNE board appointed its first Ethics Committee, which remained a standing component of the organization into the twenty-first century.[19]

From the conflicting currents within the ASNE emerged a heightened awareness of the corrosive effect of public perceptions of impropriety, which would forever alter the ASNE's conversation about ethics. Even as editors worried about what the New Journalism of Tom Wolfe and *New York Magazine* meant for the ideal of objectivity,[20] the new concern about public credibility, a corollary to both accuracy and ethical performance, demonstrated that editors were beginning to view themselves and their role in the world differently than they had in the past. At this point in the ASNE's trajectory, however, the issue of newsroom integration was not linked to the broader concern for journalism ethics.

So it was that the ASNE found itself in the crucible of historic political and social turmoil, its profession convincingly indicted for breaking faith with its democratic imperative and its ethical traditions in disarray. Facing a choice between revalidating its indisputably exclusionary pattern of conduct or working toward a more egalitarian future, the ASNE initially cast its lot with the past and followed its short-term self-interest. Despite clear signs that the ASNE was beginning to reenvision its mission and self-interest in conjunction with more exacting ethical standards, the conversation did not yet encompass the notion that journalism's democratic values, which were rooted in the U.S. Constitution, might require equal employment opportunities for nonwhites in traditionally white newsrooms. Isaacs and a few other ASNE advocates for this position clearly stood outside the organization's mainstream and did not have the numbers to do more than raise the issue. The years immediately following the Kerner Commission were, therefore, a time of transition, when the *idea* of integrating newsrooms and the ASNE had appeared on the horizon and many editors had begun contemplating its distant inevitability. This was not, however, a time of concrete change in the membership's collective thinking about race. During the late 1960s and 1970s, many editors were suspicious of the equal employment mandates contained in the Civil Rights Act and were sympathetic to white Americans who opposed such affirmative action measures as school busing.

Nor did the ASNE eagerly extend equal opportunities to white women, who became an increasingly vocal constituency within newspaper journalism during the 1970s. The movement for women's liberation, as it was known, gained ground during this period, as a national discussion of the Equal Rights Amendment, the U.S. Supreme Court's 1973 ruling guaranteeing safe and legal abortion, and Title IX, the 1972 amendment to the Civil Rights Act that mandated gender equity in education, all focused attention on women's social, political, and economic equality. This chapter will explore the ASNE's response to "women's lib" and begin a discussion of how the ASNE's responses to the concerns of nonwhites and white women, which the organization treated as separate matters, exacerbated the division between race and gender, producing tension between the marginalized constituencies and a disparity in the resources accorded to each.

"Starry-eyed Visionaries"

A racial moderate during the desegregation battles of the 1950s, C. A. "Pete" McKnight of the *Charlotte Observer* may have seemed an unlikely person to help Norman Isaacs open the door for the ASNE's newsroom integration debate; however, like many Southern editors who had stuck to the safe middle ground after the Supreme Court's ruling in *Brown v. Board of Education,* McKnight evolved into a full-fledged advocate for equal opportunity and civil rights for all Americans. By the mid-1960s, McKnight was forcing the *Bulletin* to discuss newsroom integration and attempting to develop awareness of the need for proactive recruitment of nonwhite journalists.[21] When he assumed the ASNE presidency in April 1971, one of his first acts was to appoint a special Minority Employment Committee, chaired by Isaacs, who argued that editors who made personnel decisions were culpable for racial segregation in journalism. "We on newspapers are responsible for the present state of affairs," Isaacs said. "We had a closed-door policy toward all minority groups up until the recent past. . . . The publishers are not your problem. . . . It is the editors and managing editors, and once their disposition is correct, proper, right, and they want to get it done, they will get some hiring done."[22] Isaacs had suggested the next ASNE president appoint a committee to study newsroom integration, and McKnight complied as soon as he assumed the post.[23]

Over the next year, leading up to the 1972 convention and Isaacs's inconsequential attempt to sell the ASNE membership on newsroom integration, the Minority Employment Committee, which comprised Isaacs and six other members, worked diligently to quantify newsroom segregation through a survey of members at daily newspapers with circulations greater than 75,000, where the most interest in and previous experience with hiring nonwhite journalists was assumed to reside. From the beginning, however, members' resistance to newsroom integration undercut the effectiveness of the effort. In addition, while Isaacs and McKnight's general philosophical commitment to the project is indisputable, the rhetoric they employed in presenting the concept of newsroom integration to ASNE members betrays an expectation of resistance and led them, at times, to appear to waffle in their conviction.

From the beginning they made their advocacy for nonwhite hiring contingent upon the supply of *qualified* nonwhite journalists. In doing so, they gave white editors who wanted one a ready excuse for maintaining a white newsroom, such that responsibility for the effort's failure would be blamed on nonwhites who allegedly failed to meet the professional standards of journalism. As one editor wrote, "We have bent our standards pretty drastically to give an unqualified, but promising minority applicant a chance. But this has never worked out and I am convinced such lenience serves no good purpose, either for the individual, or for us."[24]

By summer 1971, members of Isaacs's Minority Employment Committee were sending personal letters to ASNE members, soliciting answers to a series of questions about the number of nonwhites they had hired, their positions and pay, and how the editors felt about having nonwhites on the news staff.[25] The slant of the committee's questions reflected Isaacs's emphasis on obtaining "qualitative appraisals of the work of minority staffers" and his fear that nonwhites' lack of journalism ability would cause "a good deal more trouble in the years to come."[26] In contrast with his passionate advocacy for nonwhite hiring, such equivocation sent mixed signals about the direction Isaacs was setting for the project. In addition, the use of personal correspondence to a limited sample of editors, rather than uniform surveys of the entire membership, and the emphasis on anecdotal responses, complicated the effort to gather information that would shed light on the status of newsroom integration. This loose methodology would not have been deemed acceptable when the ASNE began gathering hard data for the Goal 2000 newsroom census in 1978.[27]

The concern about qualifications was in fact a defense and reaffirmation of the racial hierarchy of professional journalism, which posited the white journalist as the norm and as being uniquely capable of objectivity, of exercising sound news judgment, and of producing accurate news stories while abiding by certain conventions of written English. The qualifications on which white editors insisted had been cemented through the ASNE's effort, spanning five decades, to mold professional standards through journalism prizes, accreditation, and the like, and had maintained the exclusivity of newsroom employment. These were standards by and for white journalists, and they sought to invalidate the sort of noncompliant journalism practiced by the black press and other newspapers on the fringes. While white editors frequently raided the newsrooms of black newspapers to achieve token integration, these black hires were the primary subject of the complaints about qualifications.

Second, while qualifications and professional standards clearly are social constructions, in this context they hint at tired ideas about innate ability and the myth of race as biological difference.[28] In this way, the argument that nonwhites did not meet the standards of journalism, particularly in the areas of writing and critical thinking skills, implied that the shortcoming was natural and, therefore, insurmountable. This position rested on the assumption that white journalists represented the norm against which nonwhite journalists would be judged and invariably would come up short. This assumption also was the prerequisite for white journalists' claims that they alone could be objective, that their reporting was a gauge of truth, while the journalism of nonwhites was tainted by bias and self-interest.

And finally, the issue of qualifications offered white editors who did not want to integrate their newsrooms a socially acceptable, and even noble, reason for not doing so. After all, they were not practicing racial discrimination, they were maintaining the integrity of journalism. As one Western editor told the Minority Employment Committee, "We think that yielding to any pressure to adopt a quota system, or adopting any criteria except ability would damage our product."[29] More was at stake here than "damag[ing] our product," however. If editors had granted legitimacy to nonwhite journalists and nonwhite presses, it would have been tantamount to acknowledging that *all* journalists had a stake in race and that even the white daily press was incapable, by virtue of its subject position, of anything approaching neutrality or objectivity.

But the issue of standards did not work in isolation, as the concern about qualifications was linked to a running complaint from many ASNE members about the unavailability of nonwhite journalists. "The big trouble isn't with the editors now," Isaacs wrote to McKnight in August 1971. "They (most of 'em, anyway) are ready and willing. The supply just ain't."[30] Under this rubric, segregated newsrooms were an unfortunate development over which white editors had no control. As with the claim that nonwhites who wanted to work in daily newsrooms were not qualified, the supply excuse not only let editors off the hook but went a step further and implied that any criticism of editors who had failed to integrate their newsrooms was misplaced and unfair. According to this reasoning, accountability for segregation in journalism lay squarely with nonwhites who were either unwilling or unqualified to take the jobs that suddenly were said to be readily available. Former journalist James Aronson exposed the folly of the supply argument in the March 1972 *Bulletin.* "One thing [editors] could do is abandon the 'qualification' standard which is rarely raised when a bright, talented, untutored *white* youngster comes along and they are challenged to take a chance," he wrote. The low level of nonwhite interest in journalism jobs, he said, could be directly traced to "the distrust among young blacks about careers in the white media. The reason is not difficult to determine: it stems from the persistent disappointment and rejection experienced by black job applicants not only in journalism but in most areas of professional life."[31]

As it went about its work of collecting information, the Minority Employment Committee sought to avoid alarming editors who might perceive the committee as encroaching on editors' autonomy or threatening their conception of racial hierarchy. In his final report, Isaacs acknowledged that the committee had met with some "denunciations for meddling and trouble-making; personal slurs; some patent evasions. Fortunately, the overwhelming number of responses can be reported as serious, thoughtful and often painfully soul-searching."[32] It appears, however, that the committee catered to some extent to those who resisted the idea of newsroom integration and the ASNE's involvement in the effort. In the case of the questionnaire sent by at least one committee member, Larry Jinks of the *Miami Herald,* the text contained the assurance that the committee was not really seeking to change the racial imbalance in newsrooms. "Let me emphasize," Jinks wrote, "that facts (and a few opinions) are all we're after now. We're not in the placement business, and we're not exhorting anyone to do anything."[33] While Isaacs and his committee members clearly were sincere in their recognition of newsroom segregation as a grave injustice, these conciliatory gestures toward editors who presided over monoracial newsrooms worked against the egalitarian aims of the committee's work. This pattern of soft-pedaling newsroom integration would be repeated during the next thirty years and would play out as ambivalence toward social justice, as the ASNE routinely undercut its own diversity efforts in a series of contradictions between objectives and outcomes.

The supply and qualifications issues were emphasized in the committee's final report, largely the result of a strategic decision by Isaacs to supplement the work of his Minority Employment Committee with information-gathering by the Education in Journalism Committee. To the latter committee fell the task of reporting on the number of nonwhite students in journalism schools, the quality of the programs in historically black institutions, and the extent to which the newspaper industry was regarded as "a closed-door calling" by nonwhite high school students and their guidance counselors.[34] This collaboration resulted from Isaacs's assessment in fall 1971, after his committee had received data and opinions from ASNE members, that "the problem goes beyond the powers of our [Minority Employment] committee," and that supply and qualifications were the primary issues a newsroom integration effort should address. In a letter to Sylvan Meyer, the Gainesville, Georgia, editor who chaired the education committee, Isaacs summarized the survey's preliminary findings as follows:

> 1. The attitude of most editors is good. Not all, of course, but easily 70%. These men are aware of the problem, feel newspaper journalism was slow to get going, and that the door is now open for any reasonably qualified candidate, but . . .
> 2. The shortage of such candidates is nationwide, and applies to all minorities: Black, Mexican-American, Indian, what-have-you.
> 3. Repeatedly, these editors say that the schools they check are woefully short on such minority students.[35]

By the end of the year, the education committee had amassed considerable support for Isaacs's thesis, and Meyer concurred that a "limited supply of prospects with [a] reasonable chance of success in the first place" was "the key log in the jam."[36]

The final joint report of the two committees, which was presented at the 1972 convention, diplomatically noted "a great variance in the replies to the questions about the quality of work produced by minority staff members. Many editors reported satisfactory experiences; others reported unhappiness."[37] Even so, the report's emphasis on qualifications and supply was unmistakable. An appendix to the report offered more than six pages of comments from unnamed editors on these topics, as well as such issues as the philosophical necessity, or a lack of one, for hiring nonwhites. In the body of the report, the concern about qualifications and supply received the most prominent play.

Even editors who supported the idea of newsroom integration portrayed themselves as hamstrung by the shortcomings of nonwhites. An East Coast editor is quoted as saying, "The quality of work produced by our minority staff members has been consistently inferior to the general body of work produced by their nonminority colleagues. I regret to say that the usefulness of minority professionals has been confined largely to a very selective sense: minority coverage. In that field they have sometimes given us insights and stories we would not have had otherwise. We have not been able to hire, ever, a minority professional where we did not have better nonminority candidates available."[38] Ironically, the argument that nonwhites were suited only for "minority coverage" performs a resegregation of the tentatively integrated newsroom. If nonwhites' perspectives were valuable in ensuring comprehensive coverage of nonwhite communities, it stands to reason that nonwhite perspectives also would have improved the objectivity and balance of coverage about whites. In many newsrooms, however, the pigeonholing of nonwhite journalists was in fact an affirmation of a racial status quo in which white journalists occupied the norm.

Although some editors reported positive experiences with nonwhite employees, the thrust of the report was that the nonwhites who were available for hire were, by and large, inferior journalists: "The expressions of interest being what they are, the Committees believe that from 50 to 100 minority professionals could be placed on newspaper staffs overnight. There is one proviso—the disputed word '*qualified*.' The Committees have been compelled to conclude that there is no such pool of adequately *qualified* minority professionals presently available."[39] For this, the committees blamed the colleges and universities that supplied journalism personnel. At the same time, however, the ASNE was not availing itself of opportunities to resolve the supply problem. In February 1972, an ASNE representative declined a request by Lionel Barrow, an African American faculty member from the University of Wisconsin, to help distribute mailings from his job placement bureau, which assembled listings of black candidates for journalism jobs.[40]

Adding another variable to the supply-and-demand equation was the specter of litigation—raised in 1972 by an equal opportunity complaint filed by seven black employees of the *Washington Post*.[41] In mentioning it within this report, the ASNE suggested that legal consequences might follow if white editors did not hire and promote nonwhite journalists.[42] Rather than concentrating on developing editors' awareness of the ethical necessity of integrated newsrooms, the report hinted that editors should voluntarily hire nonwhites to fend off the legal compulsion to do so.

Anticlimax and Ambivalence

Despite the ASNE's tendency to divert blame for unintegrated newsrooms onto nonwhites and to scapegoat the schools that educated them, Isaacs insisted that the final report would be sufficiently compelling to open the eyes of recalcitrant editors to the need for newsroom integration. As early as August 1971, as survey responses began coming in, Isaacs envisioned his committee's work making a splash at the 1972 convention with a panel staffed by an array of speakers. He wrote Pete McKnight, "Too early to be jumping to the Big assumptions, but it ought to be a damned provocative report, come April. Maybe, Pedro, even a high level Program item. The new boss man of the Urban League? Some big shot from the USofA to say what's in the government's collective mind, some editorial genius who isn't afraid to take the rocks for saying what he thinks, and some young black or Chicano newsman to tell how he sees it all?"[43] [*sic*]

When the 1972 convention arrived, however, the minority employment segment of the program would fail to match Isaacs's grand expectations. Isaacs would be joined on the program by allies Charles Kilpatrick, white editor of the *San Antonio Express,* and Robert Maynard of the *Washington Post,* an African American journalist who was a leader of a minority training institute at Columbia University. As the convention neared, however, Isaacs wrote McKnight to express concern that he was continuing "to struggle with the problem of luring an honest doubter onto our platform. . . . I most certainly understand the delicacy, but we do ourselves no honor and offer no enlightenment if we cannot talk—even gently—of some of the touchy areas affecting minority staffing."[44] Ultimately, sixteen editors who had reservations about newsroom integration—including Sylvan Meyer, the education committee chair who presumably coauthored the joint report—declined Isaacs's invitation to appear on the program.[45]

Isaacs's effort to have skeptics air their misgivings about newsroom integration was a throwback to the past. While Isaacs was interested in resolving editors' concerns, his attempt to put opponents on the program harkens to the ASNE of the 1950s, when outspoken racists were included in post-*Brown* convention sessions to tell the segregationists' side of the story. Isaacs's characterization of newsroom integration's opponents as "honest doubters" appears to forgive their intolerance in much the same way that ASNE members of the 1950s had excused the ranting of white supremacist editors as being informative. Moreover, had any opponents of newsroom integration taken Isaacs up on the invitation, their comments likely would have validated racial intolerance rather than ameliorated such sentiments within the organization. Their views, expressed in that public forum, would have given credence to the idea that newspaper journalism was "a closed-door calling." As with the 1956 convention, a "balanced" program almost certainly would have been a public relations disaster.

As it was, the one-sided program did not fare much better. Richard Cohen, a *Washington Post* reporter who attended the 1972 convention and wrote a convention diary that was published in the *Bulletin,* reported that the "Newspapers and Minority Employment" panel was "the worst-attended session yet. It begins late and backs into the trip to the White House. The women are upstairs [in the hotel] getting ready. The men, too, have to get ready."[46] In a situation reminiscent of the 1964 convention, when many ASNE members walked out on prominent civil rights leaders to attend a presidential press conference, Isaacs and his fellow panelists found themselves talking about racial equality to a sparse and not entirely receptive crowd.

As Isaacs was being introduced, Domingo Nick Reyes, executive director of the Mexican American Anti-Defamation Committee, interrupted to read the following statement: "By excluding Chicanos as writers, editors, management or as people worth noting, the American Society of Newspaper Editors exposes the racial-cultural prejudice that only blacks and whites are worth writing about or involving in the mass media."[47] As Reyes spoke, Cohen reported, "Some editors laugh. One within earshot says, 'I don't see why we have to listen to this.' Norman Isaacs, the moderator, is smooth, unruffled. He lets Reyes finish, disarms him through courtesy and then launches into the findings of a survey."[48] While the ASNE did tend to view race as a black-white dyad, Isaacs's program was, ironically, one instance when this did not hold true. Kilpatrick of the *San Antonio Express* argued that for his paper, which served a city in which more than half the population spoke Spanish, hiring Mexican Americans was essential to the journalistic mission.[49]

Isaacs, Kilpatrick, and Maynard made a powerful case for the ethical imperative of newsroom integration. In arguing that his committee's major finding, that just three-quarters of 1 percent of daily newsroom employees were nonwhite, was evidence of racial exclusion in the profession, Isaacs held himself up as a repentant sinner. His address to the ASNE offered a compelling testimonial of his transformation from an editor who saw whiteness as the professional norm and as a requirement for objectivity to an editor who recognized his own stake in race.

> Even though my credentials as a crusader for civil liberties and for the equality of opportunity for all races were honorable in motivation through my first 25 years as an editor, I came to recognize that I was practicing a double standard. I thoroughly believed my contention that I was in truth colorblind. Yet while I took many a long shot on white reporters, deskmen and photographers, I somehow always thought it necessary to exercise the greatest of care when it came to hiring minority staffers. . . . Even some of us whom many of you regard as starry-eyed visionaries were much less visionary than we should have been—and as a result contributed to holding back journalism.[50]

For his part, Kilpatrick insisted the idea that qualified nonwhites were unavailable for hire was a myth and laid the blame for slow hiring on the attitudes of the middle managers in newsrooms. In underscoring the urgency of the situation, Kilpatrick portrayed newsroom integration as a matter of newspaper credibility. He asked, "How can the newspaper industry take moral positions on any subject concerning freedom of opportunity so long as it is very much like Ivory soap—99.something lily-white?"[51]

Maynard's contribution to the program was a frank and powerful statement of black discontent that stunned even Cohen, his empathetic white coworker at the *Washington Post.* Cohen wrote in his convention diary for the *Bulletin,* "I know Bob. I have worked with him, partied with him. He says, 'I want to invite you to see how the newsroom looks to a black.' What he sees is racism in the raw. It is clear that I really don't know Maynard at all."[52] Like Kilpatrick, Maynard emphasized the theme of newsroom integration as an ethical issue and noted the irony of editors defending their First Amendment rights from the platform of all-white newsrooms. Maynard argued that the racial composition of newsrooms had a direct bearing on the quality and credibility of newspapers and on their ability to carry out their democratic mission. "The picture of America as seen through the lens of the mass media is badly distorted," he said. "In a society racked by the problems of race, white voices dominate and white hands control the final outcome of the product. That is not just unfair to blacks and other minorities, it is unfair to whites as well, because they are not getting their money's worth when they pay for a paper. It is this, I think, that hinders ultimately, the fulfillment of democracy itself."[53] Like Kilpatrick, Maynard strongly disputed the notion that the supply of qualified nonwhite journalists was low. Notably, this assertion from the convention podium directly contradicted the joint committee report.

The evidence suggests the panelists' ethical appeal failed to produce much effect. A year later, in 1973, the Minority Employment Committee said it could find no direct indication that the hiring push had produced a backlash but that only a minimal increase in the number of nonwhite journalists could be discerned at daily newspapers. But for the addition of forty-four nonwhite journalists in the newsrooms of the Knight Newspapers chain, which was actively seeking nonwhite employees, the number would have been flat. "Matching the lessened ardor of the public at large, recruitment activity among minorities by newspapers has diminished considerably," the committee reported.[54] In 1974, the committee found editors so disengaged from the project that it was unable to obtain a sufficient number of responses to requests for information to allow the calculation of an employment total. By then, the committee surmised, nonwhites may have accounted for 1 percent of the professional employees in newsrooms. In sharing the news about editor indifference to newsroom integration, the committee indicated that concerns about nonwhites' qualifications had become thoroughly entrenched. "Many editors focus on the tension between their determination to maintain their newspapers' editorial standards and their eagerness to hire blacks, many of whom have sharply weaker credentials than average white applicants," the committee's final report said.[55]

This lack of enthusiasm for integrating the profession was reflected in the convention programming and *Bulletin* content during 1973 and 1974. Following the 1973 annual meeting, the *Bulletin* included a scalding commentary by satirist Leonard Lewin in its roundup of views about the convention. Lewin wrote, "The sparse representation of women and black members was a visible reminder that newspaper editors too have a hell of a long way to go before they can erase the stigma (yes) of being as much a white-male dominated and biased (yes) professional power group as any other. That's the way it looks. It's not hard to understand why it takes so agonizingly long to make qualitative changes in this area—assuming you want to make them—but an A for effort still isn't worth as much as a C for results. And that's the way it is."[56] Lewin also noted the small audience for the panel "Women in the Newsroom: Trends and Attitudes." He wrote, "The majority who stayed away apparently just didn't want to hear any more about the woman question."[57] Notably, the 1973 convention included no sessions on race or nonwhite employment in journalism. In fact, with the exception of Isaacs's report the previous year, the ASNE conventions had never featured a session specifically on the interrelationship between nonwhite hiring and journalism.

The Minority Employment Committee's disheartening experience in attempting to interest editors in newsroom integration suggests that the issue of racial equality was not resonating in a meaningful way with many ASNE members. By this point, the pattern of nonresponsiveness and rationalization on the issue of newsroom integration, which became noticeable after the Kerner report's publication in 1968, had become embedded as the ASNE's primary mechanism for resistance to minority employment concerns. This is apparent both in members' disinterest in the subject and in its neglect by the ASNE leaders who set the organization's agenda. Overt resistance entailing the kind of blatant racism espoused in conventions of the 1950s would no longer have been tolerated in the ASNE's open forums, and silence became one of the primary tactics of resistance in the post-civil rights era. At the same time, however, there were signs that some members were engaging the subject constructively. Not only had a core group of editors, including some of those on Isaacs's committee, taken an activist approach to newsroom integration, but the 1974 annual meeting generated a belated though necessary Membership Committee recommendation to emphasize women and minorities in the recruiting of new members.[58] Such disparate and contradictory sentiments contributed to a deepening sense within the ASNE of ambivalence about race and equality, and this lack of unity hobbled efforts to move the organization toward viewing newsroom integration as a moral absolute. Nowhere are such impulses more evident than in the ASNE's uneven treatment of John Sengstacke, the organization's first African American member and director.

A Tentative Welcome

Sengstacke's election in 1965 as the first African American member of the ASNE was significant enough to warrant mention in a noted history of the black press.[59] As the editor of the *Chicago Daily Defender,* which had published a daily edition since 1956, Sengstacke was deemed eligible for membership when the ASNE became motivated to admit a black member. As described in chapter 1, the *Defender* had not met the ASNE membership criteria in 1958, when managing editor Louis Martin's application was rejected because, under the logic employed at the time, the paper fell outside the ASNE's guidelines for a daily paper of general circulation and sufficient quality. In the mid-1960s, however, when the civil rights movement brought pressure to bear and the ASNE became obligated to integrate its membership, the organization was unable to find any black editor but Sengstacke to whom it could extend membership under the existing daily newspaper criteria. White-run daily newspapers simply did not have nonwhite directing editors and most black-owned papers were weeklies—with the exception of the *Chicago Defender* and the *Atlanta World,* whose editor never became interested in joining ASNE.[60] And so it was by default that Sengstacke became the first black member of ASNE, and the only one until 1973, when Martin was allowed to join as well.[61]

Sengstacke's relationship to the ASNE appeared to be an uneasy one, at least in the early years of his membership. In their dealings with Sengstacke, but more particularly in the way they talked about him outside his presence, several prominent figures within the ASNE leadership circle did a poor job of concealing their disdain for him. Sengstacke, who died in 1997, was silent on his views of ASNE during these years,[62] and we do not know whether he recognized his membership as a gesture of tokenism that had only recently become politically expedient, which it certainly was. At the same time, membership in ASNE may have represented a triumph for Sengstacke, as his professional trajectory had been shaped to a considerable degree by the racial exclusion that had defined the newspaper industry. As publisher of the *Defender* since 1940, Sengstacke had been a major leader in the black press as it battled Jim Crow during the 1940s and 1950s and endured the criticism during World War II of ASNE stalwart Virginius Dabney and other prominent white journalists, who believed the black press' complaints about segregation in the military were unpatriotic.[63] Sengstacke also had been a founder and the first president of the Negro Newspaper Publishers Association, which was a direct response to the exclusionary framework that now wanted to embrace him.[64] As such, it would have been reasonable for Sengstacke to harbor deeply mixed feelings about membership in the ASNE, just as some in ASNE appeared to have been ambivalent about him.

Sengstacke was elected to membership in 1965 and then elevated to the board of directors in 1970, a distinction usually reserved for members who had made exceedingly strong contributions to the organization through committee work. In fact, from 1966 to 1971 Sengstacke is not listed on any of the committee rosters published in the annual convention proceedings. Even so, Sengstacke breezed onto the board with substantial member support for his ascension. After the Nominating Committee voted on its 1970 board slate, Sengstacke advanced to the April elections as the third-highest vote-getter in the final committee balloting.[65] Clearly, ASNE members wanted a black man on their board of directors.

Given this enthusiastic support of Sengstacke during the election process, it is curious that within a year he apparently had developed a somewhat prickly relationship with certain ASNE leaders, including newsroom integration advocates C. A. McKnight and Norman Isaacs. The friction resulted from their expectation that Sengstacke assist with the recruiting of black ASNE members and with the extent of his contribution to the early "minority" hiring effort.

From the beginning, Sengstacke was pigeonholed and his name was mentioned in conjunction with tasks having to do with race rather than those that might benefit the organization or the profession generally. For example, he was suggested for membership on the Education in Journalism Committee in 1969, when the idea of doing outreach to nonwhite high school students first was discussed.[66] He agreed to serve on the Minority Employment Committee in 1971 and was offered an appointment to the Program Committee, where his role also would have been defined by his race. Just before his election to the ASNE presidency, C. A. McKnight wrote to Gene Giancarlo, the organization's executive director, "I had asked John Sengstacke to serve on Warren Phillips' program committee, thinking he might be useful if blacks figure in the 1972 program. He declined because of other commitments but I suspect we will be able to call on him if needed."[67] At the same time that his utility as a recruiter of black convention speakers was being discussed, Sengstacke also had been assigned the job of trying to find black editors who would be eligible for ASNE membership, even though he was not on the Membership Committee.[68] Given the constraints of the ASNE membership criteria, finding black members was an impossible job, yet ASNE leaders assigned it to Sengstacke and expected him to produce results.[69] In this way, ASNE leaders limited Sengstacke's participation in the organization to roles related to race and circumscribed his effectiveness as a director.

The ASNE leadership's dissatisfaction with Sengstacke became heightened over the subject of the fall board meeting in 1971, at which Norman Isaacs's Minority Employment Committee was to give an interim report on its efforts to assess the level of nonwhite employment in newsrooms as well as attitudes about newsroom integration. Isaacs was scheduled to be out of the country in October when the board was to hold its midyear meeting, and he expected Sengstacke to present the report to the board in his stead. In late summer, Isaacs became annoyed when he was unable to contact Sengstacke to discuss the assignment. In a letter to McKnight, Isaacs lodged a barbed complaint that suggested Sengstacke's commitment to the ASNE Minority Employment Committee was less than Isaacs would have liked. He wrote, "I'm having the customary troubles with Brother Sengstacke. I've phoned him twice. He's reported 'out.' I'm due in Chicago next week again and will bird-dog the be-Jesus out of him."[70] Eventually, Isaacs secured Sengstacke's commitment to present the report, yet this episode raises a question about Isaacs's goal. If Sengstacke was not interested in presenting Isaacs's Minority Employment Committee report to the board, why not simply have someone else read it? Why was it so important to force Sengstacke's compliance? The task, after all, was merely to read a report, which any member of the committee could do.

Sengstacke also was at the center of a behind-the-scenes controversy involving the fall 1971 board meeting, which arose from McKnight's decision to hold the gathering at a North Carolina resort. While the ASNE's spring board meeting was held during the annual convention, the fall meeting typically convened at a location chosen by the president, frequently in the president's home state. A year before the meeting was to be held, McKnight began making arrangements with the management of the Grandfather Golf and

Country Club in Linville, North Carolina, to bring the board there, and this included negotiations for Sengstacke's attendance. Even though Jim Crow was no longer the law of the land, integration had not yet arrived at many U.S. resorts and country clubs, and certainly not those in North Carolina. Correspondence between McKnight and the Grandfather management makes clear that if not for the clout of the ASNE, a black person likely would not have been welcomed as a guest. At this time, however, the club's developer, Hugh Morton, was more interested in gaining exposure with an upscale crowd that would include such luminaries as Vermont Royster of the *Wall Street Journal* than in preserving racial tradition. In a letter to the club's president, urging him to allow the ASNE meeting to be held there, Morton wrote,

> There is no resort in the country that is open to increasing its membership or property sales that would not go all-out to land this select meeting. We are fortunate that Pete is in line to be President, and that he thought enough of us to investigate. . . .
>
> The only fly in the ointment is that one of the Board members is the Editor of the Chicago Defender and a Negro. Pete McKnight assures me that he is a gentleman of the highest order, and that there has been no difficulty created by his attending meetings at Palm Springs and Maine in the last two years. I feel that most of our people recognize that we live in a day that matters like this must be taken in stride, but wanted to pass it along to you for a decision.[71]

While one might credit McKnight with forcing a North Carolina golf resort to allow an African American guest, the choice of meeting location raises questions about the ASNE's sensitivity to the politics of being a black visitor to a Southern country club in 1970. McKnight promised Morton he would not disclose their discussions about Sengstacke's race, and in all likelihood he maintained the confidence, yet Sengstacke would have known that his presence at the Grandfather Golf and Country Club was an exception to racial tradition. While it is entirely possible that the idea of breaking the color barrier at the Southern resort brought Sengstacke satisfaction, it is reasonable to wonder, given the lack of enthusiasm for participating in the meeting that he demonstrated to Isaacs, whether Sengstacke faced the trip to North Carolina with unease. This appears more probable when the Grandfather meeting is juxtaposed with the initial findings of the Minority Employment Committee. The preliminary report Isaacs insisted Sengstacke read to the board asserted that black journalists were substandard and not worthy of daily journalism. This disparagement was directed not only at African Americans in general but also to those affiliated with the black press.

Sengstacke was reelected to the board in 1973, rotated off after he had served the maximum two terms, and remained a member of ASNE until 1995. For whatever Sengstacke and Louis Martin, who was elected to membership in 1973, brought to the ASNE through their symbolic integration of the organization, they ultimately did not win universal respect. In 1977, when James Powell, the Nominating Committee chair, asked if he should be trying to recruit a woman or black editor to the board slate, he received this response from Gene Giancarlo, the ASNE's executive director: "There are presently only two black editors in the Society, one of whom, John Sengstacke, was a director for six years. During that time his contribution to the board and to the Society was almost zero." Then Giancarlo characterized Martin in a patronizing way and cast doubts on his professional abilities: "The other man, Louis Martin, works for John and, I believe, is on the verge of retirement. Louis is a very affable and, probably, capable newspaperman."[72] Even if the ASNE's jury was still out on Martin's journalistic abilities, he had received an honorary doctorate from Harvard University and was earning sufficient distinction as an adviser to U.S. presidents to persuade the Library of Congress to add his papers to its permanent collection.[73]

The problem that Powell and his Nominating Committee encountered in proposing nonwhite editors for membership was, of course, the result of the membership criteria, which required that an ASNE member be a directing editor of a daily newspaper. Despite professing concern that Sengstacke was the only African American member of ASNE, the organization was unwilling to change the daily newspaper requirement for membership, which would have made it easier for nonwhite editors to join. In August 1971, McKnight received word that John Woodford, editor of *Muhummad Speaks,* was interested in ASNE membership. With a circulation of 600,000, Woodford's paper, published by the Nation of Islam, was the largest black-owned paper in the 1970s.[74] As a weekly, *Muhammad Speaks* clearly was at odds with the daily newspaper criterion, but even if it had been a daily, it is hard to imagine the ASNE board admitting an editor whose paper advocated militant positions on race. It is important to note, however, that even when viewing the situation from a post-civil rights movement perspective, McKnight defended the membership restrictions and rationalized a black editor's ineligibility much as his predecessors had in the 1950s. In correspondence on the matter, he wrote,

> The ASNE Constitution provides that: "Persons of suitable qualifications who are directing editors having immediate charge of editorial or news policies of

> *daily* newspapers which, in the opinion of the directors, shall have attained adequate journalistic standards, are eligible to membership."
>
> That's why John Sengstacke of the Chicago Defender is the only black editor in the Society. His is the only black daily.
>
> Moreover, in recent years, we have not had any applications from black directing editors of other U.S. dailies; perhaps because there are none.
>
> This is bothersome.
>
> I have appointed a special committee to review the ASNE Constitution—all sections of it—to see what revisions are needed.[75]

Although McKnight acknowledged that the membership criteria contributed to a "bothersome" situation, he deferred to the special committee on this matter; however, McKnight's records of that committee's work contain no indication that revising the membership rules to make the ASNE more inclusive was seriously discussed, and none of the proposed amendments generated by the special committee addressed the membership definition.[76] Not only did the eligibility criteria remain intact, but the ASNE's administrative disposition toward nonwhite membership affirmed the exclusionary structure of the organization, even as it professed a new openness. Guidelines for the Membership Committee, which were updated in 1976, said that while there was no urgent need to expand the number of members, "the membership committee should be alert, however, to invite applications . . . from members of minority groups who are *eligible*"[77] [emphasis added]. Once again, the membership criteria, functioning as a mechanism of exclusion, would continue to police the boundaries of the ASNE—but race was not the only identity that figured into the professional norm.

The White Woman's Decade

As women's issues moved to the foreground in American society during the 1970s, primarily through public debate over the Equal Rights Amendment and access to abortion, the ASNE was forced to contend with the growing sense of injustice experienced by white women in journalism, who were omitted from the race-focused discussion of newsroom hiring and promotion. Although workplace discrimination against women had been illegal since passage of Title VII of the Civil Rights Act in 1964, those who entered the profession found opportunities for advancement restricted, as evident in the ASNE's own roster, which included just four active and three retired women members in 1972—virtually unchanged from the membership levels in the 1950s. Many white women journalists grew increasingly impatient with sexism in the news coverage of women and with the misogynistic attitudes of the male editors who managed the profession.

Typical of such treatment was a piece in the *ASNE Bulletin,* in which the author, a past ASNE president, emphasized the physical appearance of women from the University of California–Berkeley, including "a long-legged blonde lawyer in a micro-knit,"[78] who had met with editors during their 1970 convention in San Francisco. In an article for the *Bulletin* later that year, Maggie Savoy, women's editor of the *Los Angeles Times* and *Arizona Republic,* wrote, in Tom Wolfe-ish prose, that women "deeply resent the front page masculine-edited and/or written put-downs, off-the-track smirky reportage from defensive ego-weightlifting male reporters who claim objectivity while their pants are on fire."[79] A year later, Jean S. Taylor of the *Los Angeles Times* complained of sexist reporting and sexist comments in newsrooms and lambasted the ASNE as "a male country club" that "resents any discussion above a B-cup level."[80] She also recounted the treatment another woman, presumably a reference to Savoy, received in dealing with the previous editor of the *ASNE Bulletin.* Taylor wrote that the woman who authored "last year's Bulletin thesis on discrimination against women on newspapers received, along with the assignment, a note in which the then-editor stated that he thought a good-looking girl had made it in journalism."[81]

White women's complaints about misogyny in the ASNE and in newsrooms did not go unnoticed. In 1972, ASNE President-Elect J. Edward Murray of the *Arizona Republic* notified the board of directors that he intended to appoint an ad hoc committee "to find out why there aren't more women in ASNE and to recommend what, if anything, we should do about it." He wanted the committee to have a man and a woman as cochairs—apparently the ASNE was not yet ready for a female committee chair—and an even number of men and women on the committee. Murray anticipated some resistance to the project and asked board members to keep the plan under wraps "until it is ripe for official disclosure. Otherwise, we could stir up unnecessary arguments, bleed the whole thing to death before it has a chance, or even complicate selection of the committee."[82] When the lid came off and formation of the Women's Rights Committee was announced, the idea of cochairs had been lost in the shuffle. Clayton Kirkpatrick of the *Chicago Tribune* headed the committee and Judith Weld Brown of the *New Britain (Conn.) Herald* was "vice chairlady." Six of the committee's twelve members were women, but because the organization had so few female members, the chair was forced to appoint nonmembers to the group.[83]

During the mid-1970s, the emergence of women's issues in ASNE identity discourse brought overdue attention to the subordination and disparagement of white women in journalism; however, the omission of nonwhite women from discussions of gender made it impossible for marginalized groups to form alliances to work toward a common goal of inclusion for all journalists. Although this chafing of race and gender was a defining characteristic of the ASNE of the early 1970s, it replicated a well-established pattern. Of this phenomenon, scholar bell hooks has written, "No other group in America has so had their identity socialized out of existence as have black women. We are rarely recognized as a group separate and distinct from black men, or as part of the larger group 'women' in this culture. When black people are talked about, sexism militates against a recognition of black female interests. When black people are talked about, the focus tends to be on black *men;* and when women are talked about the focus tends to be on white *women.*"[84] For this reason, an analysis of equal opportunity movements within the ASNE must not lose sight of the opposition of race and gender.

As the ASNE's Women's Rights Committee set about its work, it discovered that women editors who might qualify for ASNE membership were not only few in number but concentrated on papers with circulations of less than 20,000. The committee found that fifty-nine women would be eligible for ASNE membership, and all but seven of them were at papers in the smallest circulation category. Just as the membership criteria obstructed efforts to increase the number of nonwhite members, the guidelines also made it impractical for the ASNE to recruit any but the seven members at papers with circulations greater than 20,000. This was because ASNE bylaws limited the smallest papers to just one member; no more than twenty members total could be accepted from papers in the under-20,000 category in a given year. While the board instructed the Membership Committee to draft a constitutional amendment that would relax the restrictions to allow more women to join, it would be three years before the change was made.[85] In spring 1973, at the end of the committee's first year, Kirkpatrick and Brown reported that the ASNE now had just seven women members, two of them retired, among a total membership of 749.[86] After considerable effort to attract additional women members, the board minutes characterized the initiative as "one of history's most unproductive ventures."[87]

The committee's 1973 report emphasized that opportunities for women were scarcest at larger papers, where few women editors were employed. Kirkpatrick and Brown wrote that "most of the women who had found opportunity on smaller papers regarded it as a function of discrimination."[88]

Owners of smaller papers were not more enlightened but more pragmatic, they concluded, noting that talented women cost less than talented men and were, therefore, the better value for papers of limited means. Most of the women who responded to the survey reported receiving less pay than men doing the same job, although many perceived that opportunities were expanding. For the most part, however, male editors indicated acceptance of the idea that women could be newsroom managers.

For the Women's Rights Committee's second year, Brown finally would be deemed worthy of being the chair and white women achieved a much higher profile on the convention program and through articles in the *Bulletin*.[89] At the same time, the ASNE displayed ambivalence about white women's participation in the organization during contentious negotiations over the membership rules. At their 1974 spring meeting, when the number of active women members had risen to nine, the ASNE directors approved a constitutional amendment to allow papers with circulations above 20,000 that already had met their membership limits to enroll an additional member above the limit for their size, if at least one member was a woman.[90] A year later, the membership ratified the amendment. Notably, the amendment relaxed the restrictions for women editors only at newspapers with circulations above 20,000, not at smaller papers where most women, according to the 1972–73 survey results, were actually employed. In addition, the amendment was worded such that any newspaper with a female member could add a member, which technically allowed a paper to add a male member if the other member was a woman. Quite predictably, no newly eligible women were among the 1975 applicants for membership, even though the anticipated change had been widely publicized within the ASNE.[91] While the board appeared to have opened the door wider for the admission of women members, the change actually maintained the former restrictions.

This exclusion of women at newspapers with circulations under 20,000 did not escape the notice of Loren Ghiglione, a Massachusetts editor whose *Southbridge Evening News* belonged to that circulation category. As the proposed amendment worked its way through the approval process, Ghiglione lobbied the Membership Committee to extend the change to the smallest papers as well. His efforts initially were rebuffed in a series of correspondence among members of the Membership Committee, which began shortly after the 1975 convention, at which the amendment for the over-20,000 category was ratified. The committee chairman, Charles Rowe of the *Fredericksburg Free-Lance Star* in Virginia, initially predicted the expanded proposal would not garner sufficient support because of sentiment against increasing the number of members from the smallest papers.[92] He noted as well, "as a practical matter, to include the smaller papers in the amendment might make very little difference, since I imagine few of them would be able to pay the expenses [dues and convention costs] of two members."[93]

Membership Committee member Robert Chandler, editor of the *Bend Bulletin,* an Oregon newspaper in the under-20,000 category, said he was "somewhat sympathetic to Loren Ghiglione's proposal. What he really wants to do, of course, is to get a membership for his wife." Chandler said he would like to get a membership for a female relative as well and continued, "What I am saying is that I think that in most cases extension of the additional membership to newspapers our size would result in another member of the family being granted Society membership, and I am not sure that is what was intended."[94] Reflecting on this issue almost three decades later, Ghiglione expressed amusement that anyone had thought his goal in pressing the matter was to get his wife, who was uninterested in the organization, an ASNE membership.[95] But even if that had been Ghiglione's motive, why should it have mattered to anyone in ASNE?

American newspapers often have been family businesses, and the smaller the paper, the more likely this has been the case. Many women have worked at their family's newspaper, although the jobs of editor in chief and publisher usually have been reserved for male family members. In many cases, women who held the top positions did so only after the death of a spouse or male relative. In this way, the traditional model of the patriarchal household was imposed on family-owned papers. Chandler's concern that Ghiglione merely wanted a membership for his wife suggested that this particular variety of female member, namely a newspaperman's wife, was not who the ASNE envisioned in launching its drive for women members. The argument that a wife should not be an ASNE member devalued the women who participated in family newspapers and positioned them as something other than bona fide editors. Significantly, ASNE members did not raise similar concerns at any point about granting memberships to more than one male relative from the same family-owned newspaper.

In a letter to Ghiglione just three weeks before the fall board meeting in 1975, Membership Chair Rowe rejected the proposal. "After testing Membership Committee sentiment . . . I felt it would be best to let the matter rest for awhile," Rowe wrote. "The members of the committee felt that ASNE should go slow on any further amendments to its membership bylaws at the present time. . . . With the amendment permitting increased female membership having just been approved, they thought we should wait and see how the changes work out in practice."[96] Rowe suggested that Ghiglione contact the ASNE president directly if he wanted to pursue the matter. Between the time of that letter and the meeting of the board, however, Ghiglione's idea had gained traction and the Membership Committee had reversed its position, perhaps as a result of Ghiglione's lobbying of ASNE officers. The board endorsed a constitutional amendment to increase the number of women members by including newspapers in the under-20,000 category. The membership ratified the change at the next convention in April 1976.[97]

While white women appeared to be winning more of the ASNE's attention during these years, they still had trouble increasing their direct influence within the organization. By 1978, the ASNE had eighteen active women members, but a glass ceiling clearly was in place that maintained the board of directors as a masculine domain. Not since Oveta Culp Hobby of the *Houston Post* was elected to a single term in 1947 had a woman served on the ASNE board.[98] In 1975, Meg Greenfield of the *Washington Post* ran for the board and lost.[99] The obvious gender discrimination in the composition of the board was pointed out by Christy Bulkeley of the *Saratoga Springs (N.Y.) Saratogian,* who noted that the ASNE "has relaxed membership limits to let more women in and committee chairs seem to be making a good effort to include women on committees. But the nominations committee says women need years of ASNE experience and the visibility experience brings to be considered for office. That, my friends, is the same kind of excuse that was used for years to keep women in limited roles within newspapers and out of the mainstream, regardless of ability and interest."[100] In 1976, even after her high-profile effort to increase the number of woman members, Judith Brown came in eighth in the board elections and did not win a seat.[101] She finally was elected the following year, coming in fifth.[102]

Attitudes expressed in the *Bulletin* during the 1970s about women and their roles included the condescending annual discussion of convention activities for editors' wives, which often included teas and fashion shows, and, in a debate over whether women journalists belonged in male sports teams' locker rooms, the disparagement that "a consistently sound woman sports journalist has yet to surface."[103] In 1973, Myra McPherson, a *Washington Post* reporter who had appeared on an ASNE program, complained about the "underlying hostility to women" from editors at the convention, which registered in the tone of questions from the floor and references to the appearance of women speakers.[104]

During this period of extremely slow change in thinking about gender, ASNE discourse registered tensions between men and women over women's increased demand for inclusion in newsrooms and the ASNE. In a *Bulletin* article, Tom Collins, media specialist for *Newsday,* reported on the effort to organize women journalists and the threat it posed to a professional norm that envisioned journalists as males, white, and heterosexual. Collins, who observed the National Conference on Women and the Media that four hundred women attended in May 1975, assumed the persona in the article of an eavesdropper reporting to a male audience the concerns women discuss only among themselves. He wrote, "There's really no way of gauging how militant the movement is becoming. It is clear, however, that in newsrooms across the country there are growing numbers of women who feel cheated, distrustful and in some cases bitter toward their male colleagues whom they see in better jobs at better pay."[105] Collins also suggested that recent challenges in courts and before the Equal Employment Opportunity Commission by women journalists at *Newsday,* the *St. Louis Post-Dispatch,* the *Long Island Daily Press,* and the *Washington Post* may have been a harbinger. He noted that women who attended the conference received advice on how to sue under Title VII of the 1964 civil rights law. "It is my solemn and onerous duty," he wrote, "to report that it looks as if the good times are over. The day is coming, if it is not already here, when it may be impossible for a hiring editor to look at a chick just out of journalism school and only see a pair of boobs."[106]

White women were clearly at a professional disadvantage during the early 1970s. Like nonwhites, white women succeeded during this period only in making an initial case for greater inclusion in the ASNE and newsrooms, as most editors remained deaf to pleas for social justice within journalism. The significance of this early advocacy lay in the pattern it established for separate and parallel demands for democratic reforms in journalism rather than a unified movement for social justice. As subsequent chapters will demonstrate, white women and nonwhites would continue to advocate separately for greater opportunity and the ASNE would continue to treat their claims as distinct. Ultimately, this bifurcation weakened the movement for change and, ultimately, strengthened the exclusionary professional norm in journalism.

3

"A Sensitive and Difficult Task"

Establishing a Framework for Newsroom Integration, 1977–89

On April 8, 1978, Richard Smyser, editor of the Oak Ridge, Tennessee, *Oak Ridger,* asked the American Society of Newspaper Editors to take responsibility for integrating the newsrooms of U.S. daily newspapers. The Minorities Committee, which Smyser chaired, proposed that the ASNE board lead an effort to raise, by the end of the century, the percentage of nonwhite journalists at daily papers to match the U.S. minority population, then the distance between 3.95 percent and 17 percent.[1] Moreover, to encourage nonwhite hiring, monitor progress, and hold editors accountable, Smyser's committee wanted the ASNE to conduct an annual census of the nonwhites working in daily newsrooms.[2] Although the movement to hire nonwhite journalists had begun to coalesce during the 1970s, it also had provoked discernible resistance, and Smyser, who had been a lightning rod for the effort, was not certain the board would receive the proposal favorably. "I was very hesitant, and I was sort of in fear and trembling and feeling that the board would reject it," Smyser recalled of his presentation to the directors that day. "Much to my surprise, they not only endorsed it, they said it should be made a little bit stronger."[3] Indeed, in an uncharacteristic display of social activism and, it turned out, unfounded optimism, the board amended the Minorities Committee proposal to add these words: "It will be the objective of ASNE to achieve this goal earlier than the year 2000."[4]

After the vote, in a gesture that encapsulated the segregation still afflicting the newspaper industry a decade after the Kerner report, Smyser left the all-white ASNE board of directors, which was meeting in Washington, D.C., at the J.W. Marriott Hotel, and headed to the Capital Hilton ten blocks away, where nonwhite journalists were gathered at the National Conference on Minorities and the News, discussing how to improve their employment opportunities and the quality of news coverage about nonwhites. Smyser recalled that he "walked in and announced to great applause that . . . the board of directors at ASNE had adopted this goal. . . . It was a big moment."[5] The news was particularly welcome for Bob Maynard and Nancy Hicks Maynard, the newsroom integration activists who had organized the minorities conference and intentionally scheduled it in Washington to coincide with the ASNE convention, in hopes of producing a "conversation" with ASNE members.[6] The Maynards had formally put the concept of demographic parity into play in September 1977. "Realizing that desegregation is a sensitive and difficult task," Hicks Maynard had written to Smyser, "we would like to set the turn of the century—the year 2000—as the target for newspapers to have minority reporters and photographers and editors and publishers in some rough approximation to the nation's minority population."[7]

Smyser had reason to fret the outcome of the board vote, the culmination of his sometimes unwelcome efforts over the previous decade to enlighten fellow editors about the need for integrated newsrooms. A former president of the Associated Press Managing Editors, Smyser had established himself as a newsroom integration advocate in 1968, when he authored "In Black and White," an APME report responding to the Kerner Commission.[8] After Smyser became active in ASNE, however, his attempts to interest its leadership in picking up where APME left off initially had been rebuffed.[9] His worry about the board's response to the committee's proposal also followed a series of meetings, including two at Northwestern University in September 1977 and Oak Ridge, Tennessee, in February 1978, at which editors had been far from consensus on both the need for integrated newsrooms and the propriety of ASNE involvement in the process. Some ASNE members viewed the social and political activism entailed in a hiring initiative as a breach of journalistic objectivity that would transform daily newspapers from impartial documenters of trends and events into makers of news. "All of those meetings were about as lively and controversial as any ASNE meeting that I can remember," recalled ASNE board member John Quinn of Gannett Newspapers.[10] As an advocate for the hiring initiative, Quinn urged editors attending the Oak Ridge meeting to recapture the optimism and high purpose of the civil rights movement, emphasizing that the need for integrated newsrooms trumped other concerns. "In the matter of hiring minorities, of covering minorities, we have found a lot of excuses to do something else," he argued. "We must find a way to recreate the feeling that there is a moral reason to do the right thing—to get ourselves fired up to right a wrong in the same way we get fired up to right a wrong we have uncovered at city hall."[11]

Nancy Hicks Maynard, who was present for several of the discussions, said many reluctant editors also remained convinced that nonwhite journalists lacked the necessary qualifications. "There was a belief that we just weren't smart enough or well-trained enough to do this work," she said. " . . . There was an inherent belief that to get involved in an organized way in changing the face, if you will, of the newspaper industry was going to harm it in some basic way."[12] Smyser said some editors also couched their reservations in assertions of editorial autonomy, which invoked First Amendment principles and positioned newsroom integration as a threat to a core value of journalism.[13] "Occasionally you would sense some really open hostility to what you were trying to do, but it wasn't very often expressed because, I guess, even then there was a sensitivity," he said. "Even among, we could imagine, the most racist of our members, there was a certain sensitivity to, you know, being labeled a racist or something like that. But I think there was an equal amount of 'this is nobody's business but our own paper's and nobody should be trying to tell us who we should hire or what.'"[14]

Smyser also was aware that just six months earlier, the all-white ASNE board of directors had declined Hicks Maynard's invitation to cosponsor the National Conference on Minorities and the News. In a fence-straddling maneuver, the board had sent ASNE members a contradictory memo in February 1978, informing them that the conference would be held in Washington immediately prior to the ASNE convention to discuss issues of newsroom integration but clearly withholding a formal endorsement. The memo stated, "The subject is timely and worthwhile and the ASNE board and members of the Minorities Committee suggest members might profit by participation. It should be emphasized, however, that this is not an official part of the ASNE program."[15]

Out of this political and cultural protoplasm—a strange mix of optimism and righteousness, indifference and fearful self-interest—the ASNE newsroom integration initiative came into being. While the movement for social and political equality in journalism had attracted passionate advocates by 1978, progress would be complicated by the intransigence of white privilege and assumptions of white merit and nonwhite deficiency. In addition, resistance to newsroom integration found a rationalization in journalistic exceptionalism, which staked out the profession as uniquely exempt from the requirement to be inclusive that applied, at least in principle, to other American institutions and industries. Even so, the heroic dimension of the ASNE hiring initiative cannot be ignored. By tapping into historical circumstance, a small group of editors who embraced social justice sought to reconcile the reality of American journalism with the democratic principles that empowered it and to erase the glaring racial double standard that mocked the ASNE's insistence that journalism's calling was one of service to a broadly defined public.

As with any human endeavor, the way was not always clear and straight nor the motives always pure, but there can be little doubt that the common and sincere objective of the white and nonwhite people who committed themselves to founding the newsroom integration initiative in April 1978 was to right an egregious wrong. There also can be little question that the most influential variable in all of the newsroom integration discussions was whiteness, whose unacknowledged self-interest made it an ideological wild card that often trumped good intention and reaffirmed the racial exclusivity within the ASNE and, by extension, its members' newsrooms. Significantly, most white editors never fully acknowledged the normative function of whiteness, which had made race a professional standard in journalism and imposed an ongoing obstacle to the social justice aims of the initiative.

This chapter, which covers the period of greatest racial instability within ASNE, roughly 1977 through the 1980s, will explore the hiring initiative as a historically, politically, and socially contingent event. During the 1970s, public consciousness about lingering discrimination was heightened, as were a sense of racial and ethnic pride among nonwhites, and feminism among women. It is no coincidence that during this period many American universities inaugurated ethnic and women's studies departments. Parallel to such developments, the Equal Employment Opportunity Commission increased scrutiny of differentials in hiring, promotions, and pay, which institutionalized the provisions of the Civil Rights Act of 1964. But the rising momentum of such pro-equality efforts was checked by political cross-current. Many white Americans of the late 1970s, even if they believed opportunities for nonwhites were unjustly unequal, objected to the use of quotas to enforce equality, and the frequency of the term "reverse discrimination," which referred to the denial of opportunities for whites to compensate nonwhites for past injustice, attested to the growth of an anti-affirmative action backlash.[16]

While such social and political forces influenced the thinking of many ASNE members, they do not explain why Goal 2000 was doomed from its inception. This chapter will isolate components of the integration initiative that were conceived as progressive mechanisms for reform but ultimately undercut the effectiveness of the effort and reaffirmed the white professional norm. These included the contradictory attempt to sell the integration initiative as a business imperative as well as a moral necessity, the ongoing objectification and racialization of nonwhite journalists through the annual newsroom census and related conversations, and the continuing tension between perceptions about nonwhites' qualifications and the ASNE's ongoing zeal for standards in journalism education. In addition, the ASNE's prioritizing of race over gender, which neglected white women, structured the hiring initiative as exclusionary rather than democratic, exacerbating identity politics and circumscribing alliances among all marginalized journalists.

Fanning the Flame

Dick Smyser was the workhorse behind the 1978 newsroom integration proposal, but Eugene Patterson was the spiritual leader who converted nonbelievers and brought the ASNE board of directors into line. Patterson, who had been editor of the *St. Petersburg Times* since 1972, had the credentials to hold sway with ASNE directors on matters of journalism values and race. As editor of the *Atlanta Constitution* from 1960 to 1968, Patterson had been deeply influenced by Martin Luther King Jr. and had established himself as one of the emblematic liberal voices of Southern journalism, through a continual appeal to his white readers' sense of virtue.[17] In 1967 Patterson had won the Pulitzer Prize for editorial writing for his advocacy on behalf of African American Julian Bond's right to be seated in the Georgia Legislature, despite Bond's outspoken opposition to the Vietnam War. From 1968 to 1971, Patterson had been managing editor of the *Washington Post,* presiding over the newsroom during publication of the Pentagon Papers and the ensuing litigation before the U.S. Supreme Court. Under his leadership, the *St. Petersburg Times* was becoming regarded as one of the exemplary American daily newspapers in matters of reporting, ethics, and design.[18]

Patterson's esteem among his fellow editors and his persuasive skill made him the ideal advocate for social justice within the context of the newsroom integration discussions.[19] Deep in his bones, he felt that newsroom segregation was "a great failing that had crippled us";[20] left unchecked, it would continue to taint the soul of journalism and impede newspapers in their constitutional and ethical mandate to serve the entire public. And Patterson, who had weathered the civil rights battles in Atlanta during the 1960s, was undaunted by opposition from the editors who wanted to preserve the racial status quo in their newsrooms. "We can't cover the news as well if we don't have them there," Patterson said of nonwhite journalists. "That's where you start, and so I recognized from the beginning that there would be some contention and some hesitation on the part of some of the more conservative editors of our Society against the rather activist approach that we adopted in 1978. But, so? That's the way that progress works."[21]

Patterson and Smyser's chief ally on the ASNE board was John Quinn, a top executive with Gannett Newspapers. During the 1970s, Gannett's corporate leadership had begun tying the compensation of newsroom managers to the diversity of their staffs and news content, so Quinn already was part of an institutional effort to integrate newspaper newsrooms. Quinn, who would be a lifelong newsroom integration advocate, had developed a deep sense of the injustice and ineffectiveness of segregated newsrooms during the 1960s, when he was editor of Gannett's papers in Rochester, New York, a city divided by racial tensions. He had been a primary liaison between the organizers of the National Conference on Minorities and the News and the corporate leadership at Gannett, which had supplied funding for the event when the ASNE had not.[22]

Another ASNE member who played a significant role in the ongoing discussions leading up to the 1978 board vote was John Seigenthaler Sr., editor of the *Nashville Tennessean,* who had been beaten by a white supremacist mob in 1961 in Montgomery, Alabama.[23] Although he was not yet a member of the ASNE board, Seigenthaler would be a key newsroom integration advocate during the 1980s. Like Patterson before them, Smyser, Quinn, and Seigenthaler would become ASNE presidents, and their service to the ASNE would become associated in institutional memory with Goal 2000.

While the efforts of the ASNE insiders were indispensable, the newsroom integration initiative was very much the result of activism by four African American journalists who exerted influence on the ASNE. Albert Fitzpatrick, managing editor of the *Akron Beacon Journal,* had participated in the Northwestern and Oak Ridge meetings and had begun what would be a long and distinguished second career as a newsroom integration advocate. Notably, Fitzpatrick, who in the 1950s had been the first African American journalist hired at the Akron newspaper, would create a minority affairs department for Knight Ridder Newspapers and would help found the National Association of Minority Media Executives.

In addition, Jay Harris, associate director of the Gannett Urban Journalism Center at the Medill School of Journalism at Northwestern University, was assigned to assist the ASNE newsroom integration push in 1977 and remained in charge of collecting and analyzing the ASNE's annual census data until 1983. Harris's influence extended beyond preparation of the numbers, however, and Smyser in particular considered him an important adviser who showed great patience in educating white editors about the issues at stake for nonwhites.[24] Harris would leave Medill and eventually become executive editor of the *Philadelphia Inquirer,* publisher of the *San Jose Mercury News,* and dean of the Annenberg School of Journalism at the University of Southern California.

Robert Maynard and Nancy Hicks Maynard had done the most focused, long-term work on newsroom integration of anyone in the newspaper industry. Through their summer minority journalism training project, started in 1968, and later through the Institute for Journalism Education, both of which taught journalism to nonwhites, the couple created a response to the supply-and-demand excuses of white editors who claimed that qualified nonwhite journalists were not available for hire.[25] Both were journalists of some accomplishment, Hicks Maynard having worked at the *New York Times* from 1968 to 1977, much of that time in the Washington bureau, and Maynard having been a business writer, columnist, and ombudsman at the *Washington Post,* where he had worked with Gene Patterson. In 1977 Maynard brought the issue of newsroom segregation into focus with a riveting speech titled "This Far by Fear," which he delivered to Kerner Plus 10: Conference on Minorities and the News, at the University of Michigan. In his remarks, Maynard invoked the image of the mobile unit of Los Angeles television station KNXT, which had been tipped on its side and ignited during the Watts uprising twelve years earlier in Los Angeles. As the Kerner report had noted, all-white news staffs had been incapable of providing comprehensive coverage of urban violence during the 1960s. The vandalism to the KNXT van, Maynard said, was the "precise moment in time—August 11, 1965, to which virtually every working black journalist in America owes his or her employment. It was that frightful scene in south central Los Angeles that made most editors across the country aware for the first time that there might be an imperative for even the token desegregation of their newsrooms."[26] Through such appearances and direct advocacy to industry leaders, Maynard had cemented himself as the primary spokesman for the newsroom integration effort.

Significantly, although Fitzpatrick, Harris, and Bob Maynard all would become eligible to join ASNE over the next several years, at the time of the negotiations leading up to the integration initiative, none of them had been admitted to membership.[27] While this division underscored the racial exclusivity of the ASNE, it also compounded the oppositional nature of the early integration discussions. The advocacy by nonwhite nonmembers highlighted the conversation as an us-them, insider-outsider construct in which the white members of ASNE were in sole control of the outcome. The Maynards had targeted the ASNE as the site at which to effect change because it was the most central power base in the newspaper industry. Nancy Hicks Maynard said the integration advocates believed "if you were going to have a real change, you would have to do it through some existing mechanism. Otherwise it would be much harder to do it and take a much bigger effort to get it going."[28] At the same time, this was a tactical maneuver that would work only to the degree that ASNE members would allow it to work, because they still controlled the rules of the game and newsroom resources.

For these reasons, the agitation by those who sought change, working inside and outside the ASNE, entailed negotiation, concession, and a willingness to accept incremental progress, belated though it was. Such was the case with the compromise that arose from a well-intentioned agreement that John Quinn described as the "Urinal Manifesto," which effectively made the April 1978 board vote possible. The agreement exacted a price, however, as it ultimately produced an unstructured newsroom integration initiative and less accountability for local editors.

The ASNE newsroom integration proposal that the board approved in April 1978 had been agreed upon, in principle, by ASNE members and newsroom integration advocates at the meeting at Oak Ridge in February. During the discussions leading up to the hiring initiative agreement, Quinn said editors were "hidebound" and about evenly divided between "the ones who felt that [newsroom integration] was none of ASNE's business and the others who felt that the time had come for some specific, positive action." The most insistent advocates argued for a structured hiring program, including concrete quotas for nonwhite hiring. At an impasse, Quinn, Robert Maynard, and Seigenthaler went to the men's room and negotiated a compromise proposal in which, Quinn recalled, "the year 2000 target was . . . a working goal, with the specific pursuit of it left to individual editors." In other words, integration programming would specify the ends, not the means, respecting the editor's prerogative for overseeing newsroom operations, including hiring decisions. Quinn had seen the principle of local autonomy work in the Gannett system, where editors were expected to diversify their newsrooms but the details of implementation were left to them. "We felt that if ASNE could take a position encouraging the pursuit of diversity as part of its obligation to the First Amendment, then we could get a consensus to set a goal in principle and leave the practical aspects . . . to the local editors," he explained.[29]

The discussion that produced the Urinal Manifesto was influenced by another side conversation, this one among the nonwhite male journalists who participated in the Oak Ridge sessions. Fitzpatrick said he and other black integration activists also were concerned about the inflexibility of many of the white editors at the meeting.

> Most of the top brass of ASNE was at that meeting, and what happened in the morning was a lot of talk, but it looked as though there was not going to be any kind of resolution to the situation, so Bob Maynard and Jay Harris and myself—it was just before lunch, we said, "Look, we're doing a lot of talking but we're not going to get anything done on this thing unless we go in there and push it, you know." And so what happened actually, we started working on the formula and so as a result we came—they came up with this solution that by the Year 2000 we would reach parity in the newsrooms. . . . We even felt that that was awful long, twenty-two years, but on the other hand we felt that that was going to be the best thing that would come out of that committee at that time.[30]

As a result, the compromise proposal had the resigned support of the African American journalists who sought to open newsroom doors.

In this way, the ASNE was able to ameliorate the objections of some editors who feared a more directive integration initiative would infringe upon their editorial autonomy. As such, the principles of editorial independence and free press provided a loophole that allowed many editors to escape responsibility for upholding democratic imperatives, specifically those that guaranteed equality of opportunity for all Americans. To integration advocates, a limited integration initiative with a goal but less structure may have seemed a better bargain than no initiative at all, but what remained unreckoned in this calculus was the question of the editors' incentive for diversifying their newsrooms. While those in the Gannett system had not only the ethical imperative but also their annual bonuses to motivate local action, most of their fellow editors were left with nothing more than their scruples to incite good works. For many editors, that simply would not be enough.

A Faltering Start

The euphoria of success faded as integration advocates soon realized how difficult it would be to sell even an unstructured newsroom integration plan to the ASNE membership. Unmistakable signs of resistance appeared at every turn. The census increases in the first two years after the board's 1978 vote failed to raise nonwhite employment even a full percentage point. The response rate for the third newsroom census, conducted in 1979 for release at the 1980 convention, was so low that the survey coordinators were forced to do a second mailing.[31] "Fear of legal reprisals from participation in the annual survey, fear of backlash from sharing experiences, fear of 'raiding' from publicly acknowledging some success all work to defeat good faith efforts," the 1980 Minorities Committee reported.[32] In a pointed scolding of the membership, Tom Winship of the *Boston Globe,* the 1980–81 ASNE president, said, "The Kerner Commission barely pricked our conscience. The effort to increase the number of minority journalists simply never has had broad-based backing among editors and publishers. The majority of the daily newspapers in the nation still do not employ minority journalists and never have." Winship, who was one of the ASNE's outspoken integration advocates of the 1980s, framed the issue in terms of professional responsibility: "Our casual attitude toward minority employment is particularly embarrassing because our mission is semipublic and because it is protected by constitutional guarantees. Yet newspapers, with a nearly all-white face, attempt to portray accurately a mixed society."[33]

Such appeals to emotion and reason failed to produce substantial change in the editors' familiar hiring patterns. After a full five years had passed, nonwhite employment in daily newspaper newsrooms had risen to 5.6 percent, an improvement of just 1.65 percent over the 1978 level, and the slow rate of progress, just one-tenth of 1 percent in 1982–83, caused Minorities Committee chairman John Seigenthaler to worry that "progress in the employment of minorities came to a virtual halt," despite concerted efforts on his watch.[34] During these early years of Goal 2000, the ASNE began plowing substantial resources into the newsroom integration program. In 1983, ASNE President Creed Black reported that "since 1980, we've put more than $75,000 into our minorities effort, with generous grants from the Gannett and Knight foundations, the Dow Jones Newspaper Fund, plus our own resources." The ASNE board also decided that year to hire a full-time minorities affairs director. "ASNE is experiencing a growing discomfiture over our declining rate of success, especially when we believe achievement of the goal is absolutely essential for the health and future of our industry," Black lamented.[35]

Apart from such expressions of distress, what should have been the major bombshell in the early going of the integration initiative was the 1982 report of the Minorities Committee, then chaired by Albert Fitzpatrick. When he joined ASNE in 1978, Fitzpatrick became only the third African American member, after John Sengstacke and Louis Martin of the *Chicago Daily Defender,* and the first to have qualified for membership as an editor in the newsroom of a white-run daily paper. Under Fitzpatrick's leadership, the

Minorities Committee's detailed forty-page report included not only the 1982 newsroom census figures but also a comprehensive survey of editors' attitudes about newsroom integration and a stern warning that Goal 2000 already was in deep trouble.[36]

In announcing that the latest newsroom census showed nonwhites accounted for just 5.5 percent of the journalists in daily newsrooms, the report also asserted that even if higher numbers of nonwhite journalists were available, they likely would have difficulty finding jobs. In boldface type, the report proclaimed, "There is a major and noteworthy disagreement among the editors of the nation's daily newspapers whether there is any professional imperative to hire minorities. This disagreement has not been discussed at meetings of editors—at least not publicly. But it is there and its resolution will ultimately determine the extent to which staffs of large numbers of daily newspapers will be integrated—and, in some cases, if they are to be integrated at all."[37] Attendant to this conclusion, the report contained a section titled "Tensions in Newsroom," which claimed "there continue to be substantial problems with the acceptance of minorities in newspaper staffs," and those problems were caused by "prejudice."[38]

This powerful report was informed by comments gathered from editors, journalists, and educators who attended symposia held at university campuses between December 1981 and March 1982, as well as by excerpted responses to an *ASNE Bulletin* survey of editors' attitudes about hiring nonwhite journalists. While some editors indicated a commitment to the concept of newsroom integration, others used their anonymous survey comments to express attitudes toward the hiring initiative ranging from mild annoyance to disdain. Among these unusually candid remarks were the following:

> "I have made no effort to recruit minority journalists. I do not think I should. I have never persecuted a Negro. Neither has anyone in my family. I feel no guilt. In case of equal (or almost equal) qualifications, I would hire a black over a white. I feel somewhat guilty about that."
>
> "The purpose of a small town newspaper is to inform the readers and to serve the community, not to embark on social engineering."
>
> "Jesus Christ! Are we going to bus journalists????"
>
> "Likely benefits, frankly, largely in looking better on the EEOC report. Practical benefits most unlikely since we circulate amongst an almost entirely white, Protestant population whose intolerance of minorities is legendary."[39]

The survey also asked editors directly whether they believed the year 2000 parity target was a fair and attainable goal, and this data, coupled with the individual responses, substantiated an acute disconnect between the ASNE leadership and the rank-and-file membership on the issue of newsroom integration. Of the 382 editors who completed the survey, just 289 answered that specific question; of them, 40 percent said the goal was fair and attainable while 38 percent said it was neither and 22 percent were uncertain.[40] About 20 percent of respondents said adding nonwhites to their newsrooms would reduce the quality of their newspapers. The report's authors took care to reproduce white editors' comments verbatim, offering a backhanded response to those who claimed nonwhite journalists had inferior writing skills. "It's difficult to get minority candidates . . . who's [*sic*] qualified," said a Midwestern editor, while a Texan responded, "Yes, it is fair although I am scepticle [*sic*] as to if it is attainable."[41]

While the Minorities Committee report clearly was calculated to highlight an injustice and stir editors' consciences, the response from the ASNE membership was decidedly anticlimactic. Two decades later Fitzpatrick recalled,

> There was virtually no response. . . . We published that report and distributed it all throughout . . . the whole convention, and we gave the report—we didn't read line for line . . . and the response was just a quiet—I don't even remember now getting an applause. You know, sometimes you give reports they will give applause to them. . . . But it was just quiet. And also, it was interesting at that time in 1982, . . . when it was time for the Minorities Committee to report, a lot of the editors got up and walked out of the room.[42]

While some ASNE members objected to Goal 2000 on philosophical grounds, a very real obstacle to newsroom integration was the deep personal discomfort many editors experienced as they negotiated the racial divide in journalism.[43] Smyser said his own understanding of racial dynamics evolved, sometimes awkwardly, during a series of conferences at half a dozen universities during 1980 and 1981. At these gatherings, nonwhite journalists and white daily newspaper editors from the area were invited to spend a few days together discussing their concerns about newsroom integration. Smyser said these conferences demonstrated how little understanding many white editors had of the nonwhite journalists who were seeking entry into the profession.[44] In fact, for some white editors, these conferences were the first opportunity for prolonged interaction with nonwhite journalists. "I thought those were enlightening conferences. I know they were enlightening to me," Smyser said. "They were enlightening because, to be very honest with you, I realized I had no conception of the talent and the intelligence and the journalistic excellence of these minority journalists, who I must say in my own mind I tended to have low expectations about. And I think most of the [white] editors who we rounded up, many of whom were from smaller papers in the state, had the same experience, and just sitting down with them [nonwhite journalists] for a couple of days, I think was enlightening most of all to us white editors."[45]

This social unfamiliarity sometimes manifested as what Smyser called "gaffes," racially charged comments that betrayed the white editors' self-consciousness about skin color. "I shudder when I think back to some of the things that I said that were the wrong things to say because I was not sensitive to some of the minority perceptions," Smyser said.[46] In this vein he offered an anecdote that is worth quoting at length, because of its assessment of interracial relations in the ASNE and in journalism at the time of the hiring initiative's founding.

> I always had Jay Harris and [his wife] Christine Harris at my side, and they would frequently come up and said, "Dick," in a polite way, "that was not a good thing to say." I remember at Northwestern I was at a session there and I guess I was the committee chairman, and I came into this big conference room and I walked around and I recognized some people and I got their names wrong. I called them the wrong name and so forth, so when it was my turn to speak, I thought I would say something that would—and I said, "You know, I just had this experience here in this room with mistaking so-and-so for so-and-so and so-and-so for so-and-so. Maybe I do think they all look alike." At the moment I thought it was funny, but it was greeted with a loud thud. The minority people did not think it was funny. I learned from that then that you don't make jokes. You be very careful as far as humor is concerned.[47]

Nancy Hicks Maynard, who attended many of the early Minorities Committee sessions at university campuses and delivered the keynote speech at an ASNE conference at Pennsylvania State University in 1980, said that if the nonwhite journalists who were working to open newsroom doors recognized such slights, they did not dwell on them. "We didn't parse the language then closely," she said. "I don't remember too many conversations of, 'Can you imagine that so-and-so said that?' That wasn't the issue, what they said." Rather, she said, nonwhites' concern was one of "'just give us the goddamn jobs and we'll be fine. We can clean it up then.'"[48]

A Different Imperative

Not everyone was surprised that the hiring initiative had gotten off to such a wobbly start, though the degree of resistance may have been unexpected. Some, like Smyser, had anticipated that the inertia and indifference of the newspaper editors would be an ongoing challenge. While supporters of Goal 2000 insisted that newsroom integration was a moral and ethical imperative and hoped editors would see the rightness of this position, they also suspected that, without coercion, many would not join them on the high road. To appeal to the stragglers' practical concerns, the integration advocates devised another inducement, namely the argument that newsroom integration was tied to the economic future of the daily newspaper industry.

This line of reasoning generally held that unless daily newspapers hired nonwhite journalists who would create content of interest to and sensitive toward nonwhite readers, the industry would lose access to an underdeveloped and potentially profitable market. To those who bought into the idea that newsroom integration was a moral and ethical necessity, the business imperative argument looked like a reasonable, practical incentive, even if it smacked of cynicism and shortchanged the moral argument conveyed by advocates for social justice. Although newsroom integration proponents generally did not see the trade-off in a negative light, an inescapable conclusion is that the business imperative argument, which continued to be refined and recirculated within the ASNE into the twenty-first century, was a principle, if unacknowledged, source of ambivalence toward the integration initiative and one of the key weaknesses that undermined the effort's good intentions.

The business imperative, which Smyser characterized as "enlightened self-interest,"[49] was such a central component of the newsroom integration initiative from its founding that it was mentioned near the top of the Minorities Committee's 1978 recommendation that the board launch the newsroom parity initiative: "This is simply the right thing to do. It is also in the newspaper industry's economic self-interest."[50] Through repetition, the business imperative became a chief justification for the initiative—almost a slogan—when ASNE leaders attempted to sell the concept to members. When the Minorities Committee recommended that editors develop a five-year plan for recruiting nonwhite journalists, the business imperative and the moral rationale were side-by-side in the suggested preamble for such a plan: "We believe it is in the economic interest and fits the moral commitment of our newspaper to monitor the employment of minority journalists."[51] Even newsroom integration proponent Tom Winship, in a 1981 "appeal with all my heart to the conscience of the leadership of the print media to confront our failure in minority hiring,"[52] said the crisis was not only one of morality but also of blindness to reader demographics. "The time has come to cease being shy about mentioning profits in connection with minority hiring," he said.[53]

Nonwhite advocates for newsroom integration also advanced this argument as part of their case for the hiring and promotion of nonwhite journalists. Albert Fitzpatrick said the argument was formulated in this way: "Goodwill is a fine thing, the right thing to do is a fine thing, but it makes good business sense to diversify your operations, because the question is, who are going to be your readers and your constituents and customers ten years from now, with the changing demographics in this country?"[54] Jay Harris, another of the hiring initiative's chief tacticians, said the argument appeared necessary in the context of the time. "There was a sense that I felt, and others, that . . . the moral or social justice argument, if you will, was losing its efficacy, and it was losing it in the society as a whole as well as in . . . this industry discussion," he said. "And at the same time, the newspaper industry was becoming more focused on profitability. . . . More and more newspapers were coming under the control of large corporations, and so the greater concern of people was circulation growth, [market] penetration, et cetera. And so a new and, I would say, a complementary line of argument developed, which said [newsroom integration] is good business, too."[55]

While the business imperative rationale was present from the beginning of the hiring initiative, it became a more frequent tool of persuasion in the mid-1980s when a new group of activists within the organization began to sound the alarm, routinely and with greater urgency, about the improbability of attaining the year 2000 goal. Their message forecast certain economic doom for the newspaper industry, unless editors embraced the concept of racially diverse newsrooms. "What is at stake here is, ultimately, our relevance to our readers," David Lawrence of the *Detroit Free Press* wrote in 1986. "Unless we can make real progress, and at a faster rate than heretofore, the price we pay will be fewer readers and customers."[56] In her address at the 1988 convention, President Katherine Fanning predicted that one-quarter of the U.S. population in 2000 would be nonwhite. "Enlightened hiring and promotion is not only the right thing to do," Fanning said, "it creates a dynamic newspaper with a diversified content that will more likely attract the alienated reader. That is good business."[57] In 1989, when nonwhites accounted for just 7.54 percent of newsroom employees, Bill Ketter of the *Quincy (Mass.) Patriot Ledger*, chair of the Minorities Committee, cited U.S. Commerce Department estimates that nonwhites' spending power would reach $650 billion by the end of the century. "We need to do more faster or face further declines in circulation, market penetration, advertising revenues and profits," he said. "Minorities are fast transforming the face of America, and if we do not mirror that change, the economic and social consequences could well be disastrous."[58] In an article for the *ASNE Bulletin,* Ketter conceded that the business imperative was a hard sell in the newspaper industry. At a Michigan Press Association meeting, about half the audience left before the start of the session on business reasons for hiring and promoting nonwhites, he reported.[59]

Although the business imperative became an article of faith for newsroom integration advocates during the 1980s, it failed to mobilize the ASNE rank and file. For most editors at newspapers that had circulations under 100,000 and were not located in metropolitan areas, the grim predictions of financial ruin for daily newspapers with unintegrated newsrooms did not match their experiences in their own communities, even on the eve of a recession that would dampen advertising sales from 1990–92.[60] At the end of the 1980s, 54 percent of daily newspapers, representing 18 percent of daily circulation, still employed no nonwhites in their newsrooms, and the profitability of their newspapers had more to do with the health of the local economy than the racial diversity of the news staff.[61]

The argument that nonwhite readership was somehow more volatile or elusive also could be disproved. In 1979, when 70.2 percent of U.S. adults read a daily newspaper, 71.9 percent of white people were readers, 55.7 percent of Spanish-speakers, and 58.7 percent of nonwhites. By 1985, the adult readership had dropped to 64.2 percent of the population, and 65.5 percent of whites were newspaper readers, 49.6 of Spanish-speakers, and 57.7 percent of nonwhites. The trend of declining readership across the board continued through 1990, when 63.4 percent of adults read a daily paper, including 63.7 percent of white adults, 43.7 percent of Spanish-speakers, and 55 percent of nonwhites.[62] During the 1980s, newspaper readership in every category eroded, with the decline in white readers outstripping that of nonwhites. No clear correlation was evident between a newsroom's racial diversity and the newspaper's readership and revenue levels. In this context, *Bulletin* articles with such titles as "Newspapers' Survival Depends on Serving a Changing Constituency, and Minority Journalists Are Essential to That Effort" simply did not ring true to many editors.[63]

In short, the newsroom integration advocates overplayed their hand, and editors who had not been persuaded of the journalistic exigency of newsroom integration saw through the maneuver. Looking back, however, Eugene

Patterson insisted that the business imperative was not inconsistent with the moral objectives of newsroom integration, that the discussion of profitability was merely an extension of the credo that mandates ethical conduct in every aspect of newspaper operations. Patterson explained his vision of the business imperative as "simply an understanding that unless you try to live up to the title deeds of this country, you're going to pay an economic price, and you're not going to prosper. And if you do the right thing, you will."[64] That conceptualization, a karmic view of newspaper profitability, is a long way from other editors' concrete predictions of lower circulation and advertising sales for newspapers that did not hire nonwhite journalists.

Had editors ever been convinced that racial injustice in the industry posed a financial threat to newspapers, their enthusiasm—or at least that of the publishers who monitored profitability—likely would have been greater, and to this extent the business imperative argument was a logical move. At the same time, the glaring contradiction between the newsroom integration advocates' dire and hyperbolic predictions and newspapers' continued profitability was an irreconcilable credibility problem for the initiative. Many editors apparently felt so confident that ignoring the hiring initiative would have no repercussions for their newspapers' standing in their communities, in terms of both economic viability and reputation, that they devoted little or no energy to recruiting nonwhite journalists and routinely walked out on newsroom integration discussions at ASNE conventions. Jay Harris recalled, "One of the jokes used to be that if you wanted to clear a convention session at ASNE, to clear the hall, one of the best ways to do it would be to say that the next session will be on diversity. And, you know, large numbers of people would leave."[65]

The ASNE hiring advocates missed an opportunity in failing from the beginning to link newsroom integration concretely to the core values of journalism. While ASNE leaders spoke of moral imperatives and the need for social justice, there was comparatively little talk, as the 1980s wore on, of journalism's ethical obligation to serve the entire community and to accurately reflect social reality.[66] The relationship between a diverse newsroom and sound journalism was not incorporated into the ASNE's Statement of Principles, which enumerates the organization's values, ethical precepts, and commitment to a free press. Moreover, the hiring advocates' embrace and exaggeration of the business imperative equivocated on the moral necessity of newsroom integration. In a just world, no other rationale for the hiring initiative would have been necessary. When leaders of the initiative insisted that integrating newsrooms also was a business imperative and introduced an alternative justification for Goal 2000, they said, in effect, that Goal 2000 was not premised on an ethical absolute after all. In this way, proponents unwittingly undercut their most substantial arguments for newsroom integration and validated the white professional norm within the ASNE and its members' newsrooms.

Counting Heads: The Quantification of Social Justice

When the ASNE board approved the "minority hiring" initiative in 1978, it did not simply endorse the idea of newsroom integration but it created and institutionalized a goal for nonwhite inclusion, chiefly the year 2000 parity target. The centerpiece of the effort was the annual newsroom census, which was to be a permanent mechanism for motivating and tracking compliance. In this way, Eugene Patterson recalled, the early newsroom integration advocates sought to ensure that the initiative was more than an empty promise. The objective of the newsroom census, Patterson said, was "not to just do it the first year to determine the status and go on from there, but to make it an annual survey, . . . so that every year we have to maintain in American newspapers a consciousness of the fact that the numbers are going to be counted at the end of the year and reported to our Society's convention, and if we don't make progress, we feel bad about it."[67]

As he and Richard Smyser envisioned it, the census and the Goal 2000 parity target were to function in tandem, augmented by programs to facilitate nonwhite hiring. "Dick and I decided that we should set goals that would be made permanent and to kindle, for the first time, a really permanent and sustained effort to hire and train and promote minority journalists," Patterson said.[68] Smyser recalled that the numerical goal was controversial within the ASNE and required a certain amount of finesse on the part of the newsroom integration leaders. "There was always a resentment of this idea of a quota," Smyser said, "and we tried to phrase our committee reports in ways that avoided the term 'quota,' but in fact that's what we were seeking. We were seeking a certain percentage of minority journalists, so call it what you will."[69] Raising editors' sensitivities about quotas was the anti-affirmative action backlash that had manifested in the U.S. Supreme Court's *Bakke* decision in 1978, which questioned the constitutionality of racial quotas in university admissions.[70] In addition, African American journalists had brought a number of lawsuits over discrimination in newsroom hiring, pay, and promotions, including high-profile litigation against the Associated Press, *Washington Post, New York Times,* and *New York Daily News.* Some of the cases had noted the percentage of nonwhite employees as a specific grievance.[71]

But Patterson, Smyser, and their allies were undeterred by the strong current of opposition within the ASNE membership to the concept of a census, and insisted on its value in achieving their greater objective of newsroom inclusion. In practice, however, the census was no corrective mechanism. At the most obvious level, the annual ASNE census was useful for quantifying the lingering problem of racial exclusion and the degree to which nonwhites had gained access to newsrooms generally. What the census could not do was offer qualitative evidence of whether the nonwhites who had been hired were being allowed to participate meaningfully in newsroom decision-making and whether their job satisfaction was comparable to that of white journalists. Albert Fitzpatrick recalled that marginalization of nonwhites within newsrooms and bogus promotions were a longstanding problem. "We used to joke about it years ago and say, 'Well, they could go find somebody and they'd sit him at the front desk there. They'd call him vice president in charge of the door.'"[72] In its focus only on outward appearances, the census provided a superficial and not entirely representative measure of the newspaper industry's response to segregated newsrooms. In addition, the obsession that some hiring advocates developed during the 1980s with numbers that crept upward only in tiny increments tended to reduce nonwhite journalists to a commodity and to emphasize statistics rather than the human and democratic issues at stake.

Each year from 1978 forward, the ASNE made a public report of the number of white and nonwhite journalists employed in daily newspaper newsrooms and, beginning in the mid-1980s, routinely classified nonwhite journalists according to four racial categories: African American, Hispanic, Asian American, and Native American.[73] This process reveals much about the ASNE's conceptualization of race and exposes a key flaw in the Goal 2000 initiative. While the census' democratic intent, according to Patterson and Smyser's vision, was as a tool for motivating recalcitrant editors and tracking progress, in practice it functioned as a means of measuring racial difference against a white norm. The census reported the number of white as well as nonwhite newsroom employees, but the census did not account for white employees as members of a racial category in the same way as nonwhites, whose numbers were the real purpose of the count. Because the percentage of nonwhite journalists was emphasized in the goal and in the ASNE's annual publicity about the census, the white employee total became incidental to the census. After all, the ASNE would have had no motivation for a census if not for the historical absence of nonwhites in newsrooms. As a result, the census functioned as a mechanism of objectification that affirmed whiteness as the professional norm and nonwhiteness as its opposite.

The discussions of race by the numbers that accompanied each year's census further objectified nonwhite journalists and often exacerbated the us-them dynamic between nonwhite journalists and white editors. This could happen even when an editor's conscious objective was to advance the cause of inclusion. Take, for instance, this seemingly progressive statement by William Ketter, the passionate and committed hiring advocate who chaired the Minorities Committee in 1989. In a pitch for viewing newsroom integration through the prism of human resource development, Ketter wrote, "To fully use this expanding *human capital* in the newsroom, *we* must not only hire more minority journalists, *we* must promote more of *them* into management positions. Absent the opportunity to get ahead and share power, some minorities end up leaving newspapers and younger ones shy away from entering *our* business"[74] [emphasis added]. In this statement, nonwhite journalists are reduced to a commodity, "human capital," and whiteness is clearly inscribed as the "we" in control of the situation as opposed to the nonwhite "them" who are subject to these personnel decisions. Moreover, the reference to nonwhites who "shy away from entering our business" reasserts white editors as insiders and grants them a certain ownership as opposed to nonwhites who are described as tentative outsiders. Similarly, a racial dichotomy emerged during a board of directors discussion in 1981, when the minutes paraphrase ASNE President Mike O'Neill referring to the tensions between "staffs and minorities" in integrated newsrooms, as if the nonwhites who had been hired were something other than members of the staff.[75]

Throughout the 1980s, the annual census and diversity advocates' preoccupation with the numbers, which were reported in press releases, *Bulletin* articles, and Minorities Committee reports to the convention, generally distilled the nonwhite newsroom experience to a tabulation. In this environment, in which nonwhites often were discussed as no more than items to be accumulated and counted, discussions of recruitment took uncomfortable twists. For example, the difficulty that some editors claimed to have in diversifying their newsrooms led to the portrayal of nonwhite journalists as elusive quarry. This was evident in the predatory title of a *Bulletin* article on the importance of the junior high and high school journalism experience in a teenager's career choice—"Best Way to Find Minority Journalists Is to Get Them While They're Young"[76]—as well as in a story urging editors to be flexible in hiring black journalists. Editors were advised to "be prepared to hire when one turns up," because, according to Paul Hanensch of the *Courier-Journal and Louisville Times*, "Sidney Poitier is not going to come walking through the door."[77]

The J-School Connection

From the early years of the ASNE, when the self-educated Casper Yost, the first ASNE president, and his contemporaries decided that journalists needed not just a college diploma but instruction in a specific curriculum, the ASNE felt a duty to intervene in and police higher education in journalism. The ASNE has maintained its reach into academia through representation on the Accrediting Council on Education in Journalism and Mass Communication, which typically has been chaired by an editor.[78] Throughout the twentieth century, the ASNE assumed wide latitude in dictating to journalism deans and department chairs, through the accreditation system, what they should teach and who should teach it. Because the First Amendment proscribes the licensing of journalists, accreditation was one of the few ways the ASNE could confer a measure of professional legitimacy on some journalists but not others, without running afoul of the Constitution. As described in the introductory chapter of this book, the exclusionary function of the accrediting mechanism contributed to a sense of elitism in the profession as well as to the journalistic exceptionalism that allowed the naturalization of double standards favoring whiteness and masculinity and excluding those who did not represent the professional norm. The white editors' stake in the accreditation system would become one of the internal contradictions that worked against the credibility and efficacy of Goal 2000.

When the newsroom integration initiative was founded in 1978, ACEJMC accreditation was entrenched as an industry tool for regulating entry into the profession, and the ASNE remained one of its fiercest champions. Specifically, however, none of the accredited journalism programs at institutions of higher education was located at a historically black college or university or at a school with a significant nonwhite enrollment. Because journalistic qualifications and graduation from an accredited program had become so closely linked in the ASNE's culture, the failure of journalism programs at historically black institutions to merit accreditation was prima facie evidence, within the ASNE's logic of journalistic professionalism, of the deficient qualifications of nonwhites rather than of racially exclusionary standards that favored white journalism students. Because many editors saw nonwhite journalists as lacking in professional qualifications, the ASNE pointed its finger at the quality of the journalism education they received.

Soon after it adopted the integration initiative in 1978, the ASNE began pushing journalism programs at historically black institutions to meet accreditation standards. In many cases, such schools had no formal journalism program, and in those that did, the faculty frequently had no professional experience in daily newspapering, owing to the industry's legacy of segregation. During a 1981 Minorities Committee meeting with nonwhite educators in Tallahassee, William Kearney of the historically black Hampton Institute was quoted as saying, "Until the 1960s, journalism was a no-future occupation for blacks. How can we have well-trained black journalism faculty when there simply weren't any blacks with substantial newspaper experience until recently?"[79] Interestingly, in citing a dearth of appropriate faculty, Kearney discounted journalists who had worked for the black press. Compounding the problem, nonwhite faculty who had an interest in journalism but had not found opportunities in the newsrooms of white-run papers or who had worked in the nonwhite press were unlikely to encourage students to seek careers in daily journalism. In such an environment, it comes as no surprise that, prior to the implementation of Goal 2000, many editors of the daily papers publishing closest to historically black institutions had never met the journalism faculty at those schools.[80]

The ASNE concentrated its energies on historically black colleges and universities because approximately half of all nonwhite journalism majors were enrolled there,[81] a stunning demonstration of the segregated nature of journalism education. To correct perceived shortcomings of nonwhite job candidates and quickly elevate their skills so daily newspapers would hire them, the ASNE not only encouraged schools that educated large numbers of nonwhites to seek accreditation but also offered remedial training and crash courses for nonwhites who were available to work but did not meet the standards for hiring. The ASNE pursued the education quality and training issue through a series of programs, beginning with one in 1980 that offered newspaper internships for nonwhite faculty.[82] By 1988, the ASNE diversity director could report that the organization was "channeling" more than $500,000 in grant money and other funding into minority programs, scholarships, and job fairs, much of it targeted at students and faculty at historically black institutions.[83] At the end of the decade, the ASNE was offering "flying short courses" taught by traveling editors who stopped at historically black institutions to offer journalism workshops and also was helping these colleges and universities get computer equipment for their journalism programs.[84]

Although no historically black institution offered an accredited journalism program when the ASNE adopted the newsroom integration initiative in 1978, that changed fairly quickly, with the accreditation of journalism programs at Florida A&M University in 1982 and Howard University in 1986. To make progress in newsroom integration and overcome the perception that nonwhites were less qualified to be journalists, however, the ASNE had to encourage more historically black institutions to seek accreditation. Unfortunately, the accreditation structure was tailored to programs at larger state and elite colleges and universities where resources were more plentiful, making it difficult for all but the most prominent historically black institutions to have a shot at being accredited.

To smooth the way, the ASNE board in 1990 approved a resolution endorsing a six-year exemption from the rule specifying the proportions of liberal arts and journalism coursework—an incongruous move, given the ASNE's somewhat strident insistence that liberal arts standards be maintained. In 1987, for example, the ASNE's Education for Journalism Committee had voted to recommend that the ASNE consider withdrawing from the Accrediting Council for Education in Journalism and Mass Communication "if the council in any accreditation action fails to enforce the liberal arts standard fully and firmly."[85] To roll back the liberal arts standards for historically black institutions after making those standards the central plank of an argument for higher quality in journalism education merely heightened the perceived disparity between the quality of institutions that served primarily whites and those with majority nonwhite enrollments. Rather than help integrate newsrooms, the exemption from the standard may have deepened the stigma attached to journalism education at historically black institutions. A more constructive move would have been to waive enforcement of the rule for all institutions for six years. Similarly, the use of such stop-gaps as the flying short courses appeared to contradict the ASNE's insistence that journalism skills be learned within an established and regulated framework.

At the same time that the ASNE was skirmishing with the accreditors over the liberal arts issue, it also was pushing the adoption of Standard 12 to require accredited institutions to recruit a racially diverse student body and faculty and ensure that women were adequately represented as well.[86] In this way the ASNE attempted to shift some of the onus for integrating the newspaper industry onto the predominantly white educational institutions. While this was an appropriate move, it left the basic racial framework of the journalism education establishment intact. Nowhere is this clearer than in the ASNE's competing emphases on accreditation and hiring nonwhite journalism graduates, recurring themes in the *Editors' Exchange*. This monthly ASNE newsletter, published from 1978 to 1998 to circulate practical information among editors of daily newspapers, became a primary vehicle for the hiring effort through a page called "Minorities Memo." This feature, which appeared most months from January 1984 to July 1995, offered information about recruiting nonwhite journalists, including lists of nonwhite journalism graduates and contact information for placement officers at their colleges and universities.

Beginning in August 1984 with publication of a roster of sixty-nine nonwhite journalism graduates, the "Minorities Memo" urged editors at the conclusion of every semester to hire journalists from this list. After four of these rosters had run during the 1984–85 academic year, however, the *Editors' Exchange* juxtaposed the roster of graduates with a different list. Under the heading "Will You Be Recruiting J-School Grads This Year?" the August 1985 "Minorities Memo" itemized the eighty-six colleges and universities with accredited journalism programs, clearly implying that recruiting should target only those students who graduated from accredited programs.[87] This honor roll of journalism programs stood in contrast to and undermined the lists of nonwhite graduates, many of whom did not receive degrees from accredited programs. This was not an isolated occurrence. In January 1987, an updated list of accredited journalism programs appeared, awkwardly followed the next month by a roster of nonwhite graduates available for hire—and again, the contrast was clear.[88] While graduates of such schools as Alabama State, Prairie View A&M, North Carolina Central, Southwest Texas, Alcorn State, Grambling State, Hampton, and Lincoln College were noted as available for work in the January list, the accreditation list in February suggested that they were not qualified to work in daily newsrooms after all.

Lest students, faculty, and alumni of unaccredited journalism schools miss the subtext in these lists, the *Editors' Exchange* added a petty insult. In an item about a change in its distribution policy, the *Editors' Exchange* announced, "A new mailing list will enable every daily newspaper and *accredited* journalism school in the United States to receive one copy of the newsletter free of charge"[89] [emphasis added]. Apparently, students at the unaccredited schools would have to purchase a subscription to see themselves slighted.

Marginalizing Gender

While the ASNE did not ignore the disadvantage of women after it launched the newsroom integration initiative in 1978, the issue of gender equality clearly took a backseat to racial considerations as the organization's leadership focused its attention on hiring nonwhite journalists. The most obvious manifestation of this marginalization of gender was in its omission from the hiring initiative's annual census. Not until 1998 would gender be quantified alongside race. As a result, the structure of the hiring initiative pitted white women, who also were underrepresented in newsrooms, against nonwhites of both genders, forcing them to compete for the ASNE's attention and resources. Tensions between race and gender undermined whatever common interest in social justice all women may have shared and forestalled the opportunity for all women to present a unified front in matters relating to gender discrimination in newsroom employment.

At the same time, some of those who participated in the founding of the hiring initiative saw race and gender as separate issues bearing different degrees of urgency. Nancy Hicks Maynard remembered that while no women of any race were represented adequately on newspaper staffs or in editorships in the late 1970s, white women had greater access to newsrooms than nonwhites of both genders, who were still trying to get through the newsroom door. "Experiencing it both as a woman and as a black person, they were different things that we were working against," Hicks Maynard said.[90] This comment is revealing for what it tells us about the intersection of race and gender within the newsroom diversity movement, where the two identities became mutually exclusive for nonwhite journalists. While Hicks Maynard recognized herself as having at least two identities, she deferred in her activism to race, and it, not gender, defined the goal of her important work. Rather than advocating for all journalists whose opportunities had been curtailed based on inequities of identity, Hicks Maynard and her allies were forced—by the opposition of race and gender—to choose and to privilege one signifier over the other. As a result, a progressive movement to enact democratic principles in newspaper newsrooms functioned, de facto, as a mechanism of exclusion.

The same logic, though in a different context, may have influenced the perspective of white women as well. Linda Grist Cunningham of the *Rockford (Ill.) Register Star,* a white member of the ASNE board from 1985 to 1991 and a committed supporter of the ASNE's newsroom integration effort, recalled that the goals of the initiative were narrowly focused on race because leaders believed racial inequality represented the more pressing need. "I don't totally disagree with that," Cunningham said. "I certainly was among those who pushed for more involvement of women and bringing women in and things like that, but as a white woman, I know that I didn't have it as hard as a black woman coming in in the same position. I looked like the editor's daughter, and because I was the same color, if you will, as the editor's daughter, he was more comfortable with me, so it made it easier for me as a white woman than if I'd been a black woman."[91] Cunningham's thesis is congruent with the numbers. Using ASNE membership as a gauge of race and gender in newsroom management, a third as many nonwhites of both genders as women of all races belonged to the organization in 1980, and despite their exclusion from Goal 2000, women would end the decade with higher numbers on the ASNE membership roll than nonwhites.[92]

Because women as a category fell outside the scope of the hiring initiative while nonwhite women were counted in one of four racial classifications, a reference to "women" within the newsroom diversity conversation was, by default, a reference to white women. White women, meanwhile, were left in a sort of identity limbo within the ASNE. While they accounted for just 4 percent of ASNE membership in 1980,[93] white women were excluded from both the census and the vast majority of programmatic initiatives associated with inclusiveness. At the same time, many men in ASNE seemed not to know how to deal with women within the professional milieu of the organization or the newsroom. This point was underscored during a 1980 directors' meeting when board member Judith Brown complained that the women members of ASNE were required to wear the same convention badges as editors' wives, which designated them as female guests rather than full-fledged members of the organization.[94] Among the ASNE leaders during the 1970s and 1980s who took an interest in women's issues or recognized the disparity in opportunity for women was John Seigenthaler Sr. During the 1983 convention program, Seigenthaler, then the Minorities Committee chair, said the talent pool for women was adequate but that lingering gender discrimination thwarted opportunities for women. "The difficulty is attitudinal and it has to do with this male-bastion idea," Seigenthaler said. "Just look around this room. I wish it were not a reflection of what's been happening. But I fear it is."[95] Such gestures as the stereotypical assignment of convention badges and the relative exclusion of women from the ASNE offer a glimpse into the institutional attitude toward women, white and nonwhite. When the ASNE did add women to the census in 1998, a full twenty years after the founding of the hiring initiative, it did so merely to count them, as gender would remain outside the scope of the reformulated hiring targets, which determined the allocation of diversity resources.

While the ASNE's lack of interest in formal, programmatic responses to the disparity in opportunity left white women at a disadvantage in terms of access to the organization's resources, this neglect also created a space for them to agitate for reform. The most prominent effort to disrupt the ASNE's masculine professional norm was led by Dorothy Misener Jurney, who had retired in 1975 as an assistant managing editor at the *Philadelphia Inquirer.* In Jurney's career, the reality of women's subordination within newsroom culture was emphasized at the end of World War II, when she lost the city editor post at the *Washington News,* which she had held during a male editor's military service, and was again exiled to the women's pages.[96] Over the years, Jurney would be reminded that gender had thwarted her efforts to make a career in newsroom leadership, as men received opportunities for which she was equally qualified. Jurney, who had won numerous awards during her career and had been the first woman elected to the board of the Associated Press Managing Editors, had substantial professional credibility when she began openly advocating for women in journalism. In 1979, as a parallel to the launch of the ASNE's annual newsroom racial census, Jurney began to issue annual reports on the number of women in newsroom management. In her first report, Jurney found that 212 women held directing editorships on daily and Sunday papers, which represented 6.5 percent of newsroom management, a 1.3 percent gain from 1978. During this period women won several Title VII lawsuits against newspapers and the Associated Press, an indication that gender discrimination was under scrutiny. At the end of the 1980s, the annual survey Jurney had begun indicated that women held 16.2 percent of directing editorships and that their share was increasing about 1 percent a year.[97]

Operating without the resources that would have been available inside the ASNE diversity infrastructure, Jurney used the annual newsroom directory published by the trade journal *Editor & Publisher* as her source of data. Her methodology, which consisted simply of counting the number of women listed in directing editorships at each U.S. daily newspaper, totaling them up, and noting the difference between the number of male and female editors, was primitive; however, as a strategy of political intervention, the project demonstrated considerable wile and sophistication. By focusing on the number of *directing editors,* the term used in the ASNE constitution to denote eligibility for membership in the organization, Jurney's reports suggested the need for women to have a greater role in both newsroom management and in the ASNE.[98]

From 1979 to 1986, Jurney submitted her reports to the ASNE to be published in the *Bulletin,* where they documented the exclusion of women from editorships and from the annual newsroom employment census.[99] As an ASNE member from 1973 until her retirement from active newspaper work two years later, Jurney had developed a keen appreciation for the value of access to the ASNE's professional sanctum. When she joined ASNE, she had been one of just seven women in the 749-member organization.[100] In a 1990 interview, she recalled that through participation in ASNE, "I learned that all of these men that I had been working for and thought were so smart got many of their ideas by going to conventions of the ASNE. And women did not have this opportunity."[101]

While Jurney supported female journalists in general, she would focus her postretirement activism on increasing the number of women promoted to newsroom leadership as well as the number in the management "pipeline," namely those in assistant editorships and other supervisory newsroom jobs. Jurney's decision to focus on women's representation in newsroom management likely was dictated, at least in part, by her lack of access to resources other than the *Editor & Publisher* newsroom directory, which listed the various editors for each daily newspaper. As a result, her reports contained little information about any difficulty women might have had finding initial employment in journalism or working at lower levels of the newsroom hierarchy. Moreover, by framing the women's issue as one strictly of access to management, the reports appeared to underscore the point made by Hicks Maynard and Cunningham that white women did not encounter the same obstacles in obtaining entry-level newsroom jobs. In addition, as an oppositional maneuver, the annual reports on women in management further sedimented the division between gender and race, and also reaffirmed the definition of women's concerns as white women's concerns.

The key development of the 1980s that appeared to demonstrate a greater measure of progress for women was Katherine Fanning's assumption of the ASNE presidency in 1987. In contrast to Jurney, Fanning, editor of the *Christian Science Monitor,* was no hardscrabble journalist who had worked her way up through the newsroom desks. Rather, Fanning's entry into the newspaper business came tangentially in 1950 with her marriage to Marshall Field IV, owner of the *Chicago Daily News*; in 1966 she married Larry Fanning, the paper's editor. They then purchased the *Anchorage Daily News,* which Katherine Fanning took over after her husband's death in 1971. When she became ASNE president, she had been editor of the *Christian Science Monitor* since 1983.[102] While Fanning's leadership of the ASNE had significant symbolic value, it also tested male editors' commitment to equal opportunity. In his biographical profile of Fanning for the *Bulletin,* newsroom integration advocate Tom Winship wrote, "The American Society of Newspaper Editors and Katherine W. Fanning took a tortuous route growing up. It took some 60 years of maturing before the all-male ASNE hierarchy could bring itself to elect a woman as its president."[103] Apparently, the maturation process still had a way to go, as Winship could not resist the temptation to open the article with a crack that stereotyped Fanning as a poor driver.

A New Generation of Advocates

One of the most significant developments of the 1980s was the succession of leadership within the newsroom integration initiative from such early stewards as Gene Patterson, Richard Smyser, and Albert Fitzpatrick to the next wave of advocates, a zealous prodiversity contingent that dominated the ASNE board by the end of the decade. The most fervent of these Goal 2000 proponents was Loren Ghiglione. The owner of Worcester County Newspapers, a small newspaper group in Massachusetts, Ghiglione began a two-year term as chairman of the Minorities Committee in 1984. Ghiglione traced his advocacy for social justice to the civil rights movement and his work as a teacher at Rust College, a historically black institution in Mississippi, during Freedom Summer in 1964.[104] Other hiring advocates may have matched Ghiglione's passion for social justice, but none was as evangelical or uncompromising in commitment to the cause.

Although the stridency of Ghiglione's message clearly did not resonate with some ASNE members, and it certainly did not prompt the newsroom integration numbers to rise at a greater pace than they had before, Ghiglione's leadership of the Minorities Committee and his term as ASNE president in 1989–90 significantly shifted the ASNE paradigm on newsroom integration. As Ghiglione saw it, if the ASNE was going to sponsor the hiring initiative, then members needed to be accountable for the results. "ASNE's efforts won't succeed if editors don't push now for more minorities throughout their papers," Ghiglione told his peers. "Leadership, as always, begins at home."[105] By pressing the theme that editors—both ASNE leaders and rank-and-file members—were individually responsible for the outcome of the newsroom integration effort, Ghiglione reenvisioned the initiative as a central component of the ASNE mission rather than a single project among many that the organization directed at any time.

Ghiglione opened his tenure as Minorities Committee chair in spring 1984 by exhorting fellow editors to join him on the high road and announcing a plan of action that would be carried out by the committee he had assembled, which he noted was "the largest in ASNE history" with thirty-five members. In his opening salvo, Ghiglione wrote in the *Bulletin,* "At the present rate, ASNE's minority employment goal for the year 2000 will not be achieved until the year 2055. That's almost three generations late."[106] Ghiglione proposed an array of conferences and initiatives to encourage papers to hire and promote nonwhites, to allow nonwhite junior high and high school students to see journalism as a career option, and to collaborate with historically black colleges and universities. Along the way the committee started regional job fairs, which gave nonwhite job applicants a time and place to meet with prospective employers and refuted the claim that qualified journalists were not available for hire. The committee also reached out for the first time to the professional organizations for black, Hispanic, Asian American, and Native American journalists, which were offered adjunct memberships on the Minorities Committee.[107] The National Association of Black Journalists, founded in 1975, was followed in the 1980s by associations representing the interest of journalists in the other three racial categories.

For editors who had viewed newsroom integration as something they could casually ignore, Ghiglione's ascension to ASNE leadership changed the experience of ASNE membership. Such editors had no place to hide as Minorities Committee members began calling on their peers at other newspapers to urge participation in the hiring initiative.[108] In February 1985, material assembled by Ghiglione's committee consumed thirty-two pages of the *Bulletin,* and the cover story by Ghiglione was anything but subtle. "If schools and other government agencies desegregated as slowly as America's newsrooms, many of us would label them dawdling defenders of the status quo," he wrote.[109]

But Ghiglione strayed even further from the customary Goal 2000 cheerleading narrative. He referenced anecdotal evidence of "bias" in newsrooms, quoted *Boston Globe* editor Tom Winship, former ASNE president, as saying the newspaper industry had a "downright racist attitude toward employment of minorities," and noted that Ellis Cose of the Maynards' Institute for Journalism Education had declared the working environment in newsrooms as "something approaching a crisis," with the number of nonwhites leaving newspapers eroding the hiring gains that were being made.[110] ASNE members were not used to such direct and unyielding criticism from one of their own, and the quantity of the material on race confronting them in the *Bulletin* and on the convention programs was overwhelming and off-putting to some.[111] Any thought that Ghiglione and his committee would retreat was disabused during the 1985 board meeting. The minutes note, dryly and cryptically, that following Ghiglione's Minorities Committee report, "there ensued a discussion of just how hard ASNE should push in behalf of achieving the 'Year 2000' goal. Those who wanted to be 'thoughtfully shrill' seemed to carry the day."[112]

Initially, the results of the hiring campaign were disheartening for Ghiglione, as the 1985 newsroom census number came in at 5.7 percent, unchanged from the previous year and the first time that the numbers showed absolutely no growth since the newsroom integration initiative began in 1978.[113] Undaunted, the Minorities Committee pressed even harder, promoting a new scholarship program for nonwhite journalism majors and hitting the road to evangelize recalcitrant editors into integrating their newsrooms.[114] In an article for the *ASNE Bulletin*, Rolfe Neill of the *Charlotte Observer*, who headed up the outreach project, offered a frank assessment of his fellow editors' performance on nonwhite hiring—one that reached a bit too far to demonstrate empathy with African American journalists.

> Promises. Promises. Promises. I'm beginning to feel I know what it's like to be black.
>
> America's editorial pages talk of a racial equality that editors don't practice within their own shops. It's a remedy more easily prescribed than taken.
>
> The truth about achieving racial balance in newsrooms is that commitment isn't enough. There must be more. There must be an *inconveniencing* commitment. America is 20 percent nonwhite. Our newsrooms are only 5 percent blended. And 60 percent of U.S. newsrooms are 100 percent white.[115]

In addition to such proselytizing, the Minorities Committee sponsored sixteen regional minorities conferences during the 1985–86 ASNE year, forty campus visits by minority professionals in residence, and fourteen newsroom internships for nonwhite faculty members. When it reported its census results in April 1986, the Minorities Committee was able to show a .58 percent increase, the largest jump in five years.[116] A year later, even though the committee continued its aggressive program of advocacy and education, the increase was smaller, as the nonwhite census rose from 6.3 percent to just 6.56 percent.[117]

At the fall board meeting in 1988, Ghiglione, who was on the ASNE leadership ladder to assume the presidency in April 1989, announced development of an extensive and ambitious plan to increase nonwhite employment in newsrooms, including mentorship of faculty and students at historically black colleges and universities and collaboration with professional organizations for nonwhite journalists.[118] At the same time, the ASNE was receiving clear indications that once nonwhites landed jobs in journalism, they often found newsrooms inhospitable places to work. For example, during a 1989 convention session titled "Minorities: Ascending the Newsroom Ladder," panelists discussed the white backlash that sometimes occurred in newsrooms and the white resentment of nonwhites who were promoted. "It can be even worse than usual for a black person when everyone knows there is a push on for diversity," said Karen Howze of *USA Today,* who noted that white coworkers often assumed a promotion for an African American employee resulted from affirmative action, not merit.[119] In other cases, nonwhites reported being subject to different standards, the result of lingering concern over their qualifications. Mervin Aubespin of the *Louisville Courier-Journal,* the Minorities Committee chair in 1989, recounted the story of a black journalism-school graduate who had completed two internships yet received just one offer in response to the fifty resumes she mailed out. The offer was for a "special" one-year internship, rather than a permanent job. Aubespin said the young woman asked, "'Why should I have to go through a minority program? My white classmates don't and seem to have less problems finding a job.'"[120]

While the ASNE supported newsroom integration as a matter of policy, the census results and the anecdotal reports from newsrooms suggested Goal 2000 was a source of tension between those who embraced the cause and those who still resisted it. By the end of the decade, the friction between the most passionate newsroom integration advocates and the editors who had not bought into the initiative came to a head. The difference now was that newsroom integration advocates had a foothold on the board of directors and in committee chairmanships, and had reinvigorated the cause of social justice, even portraying the hiring laggards as pariahs within the organization.

During an "ASNE Gripe Session" at the 1989 convention, Goal 2000 advocates vented about editors who had not done their part to integrate newsrooms. George Blake of the *Cincinnati Enquirer,* a longtime member of the Minorities Committee, said he resented the anonymous nature of the annual newsroom census results and suggested it was time to out the newspapers that were not hiring nonwhites. He said, "The number that bothers me is not the 7.54 percent of the workforce that is minorities, but the 54 percent of the newspapers in the country that do not have a single minority on their news staffs. I do not know what the Society should do about that. But as I stick with this minority recruiting issue and maintain my personal commitment to it, I get madder and madder every year and wonder when it is time to name names."[121] Interestingly, Mireille Grangenois, the ASNE minority affairs director and an African American, sought to dissuade the hiring advocates from ending anonymity for survey respondents. "I would caution editors on the idea of 'exposing' newspapers," she said. "The editors of these noncomplying newspapers are not some breed apart—they are your colleagues and golf partners."[122] David Lawrence of the *Detroit Free Press* was unpersuaded.

"For us to let 54 percent of the daily newspapers in this country off the hook, even inadvertently, would be a terrible mistake," he said.[123] And so, with the 1990 census, editors were given the option of identifying their papers with their nonwhite employment totals, but just 54 percent of respondents agreed to go public. Aubespin, the Minorities Committee chair, sharply scolded the anonymous respondents. "There's some doubt about the determination of the industry, as a whole, to do more than patch together something that looks like a real commitment to diversity," he wrote in the *Bulletin*. "Only half of us are willing to sign our names to what we're doing."[124]

This was a crucial moment in the history of newsroom integration because the hiring initiative had produced a good guys-bad guys construct among the white ASNE members, which suggested, contrary to Grangenois's argument, that enthusiastic supporters of the effort did indeed view the laggards as "a breed apart." Moreover, the ASNE leadership defied the wishes of a sizeable portion of the membership by proceeding with the plan to name names. In 1992, the option of voluntary disclosure would disappear and the percentages of nonwhite employees in each newsroom would be published in the *Bulletin*.

This accountability push was the culmination of the changes brought by the Ghiglione era of the newsroom integration effort. While the hiring initiative still encountered tacit resistance from editors, the organizational culture in which ASNE leaders worked in the late 1980s was substantially different than when Goal 2000 was launched a decade earlier. Even if whiteness still represented the status quo within the ASNE and a significant number of members—half or more, if the percentage of newsrooms with no nonwhite professional employees was an indication—had reservations about the newsroom integration initiative, they acquiesced to the leadership to some degree because support for racial diversity had become a social and professional expectation. The hiring initiative had finally gained legitimacy, if not universal support, within the ASNE. The power that now accrued to the initiative's leaders did not obviate the entrenchment of the white professional norm within the organization, however, and cynics and fence-sitters found subtle ways to protect their stake in the racial status quo. For the true believers, newsroom integration was a moral absolute and a central value of journalism; for others, a commitment to racial inclusiveness might be fine, if it did not interfere with the business of newspapering.

The 1956 convention panel titled “The Press Looks at the Problem of Integration” ignited controversy when racist remarks by Harry Ayers of the *Anniston (Ala.) Star* were reported in the Washington papers. Members of the panel were, from left, Herbert Brucker of the *Hartford Courant,* Lenoir Chambers of the *Norfolk Virginian-Pilot,* Erwin Canham of the *Christian Science Monitor,* Ayers, and John Mahaffey of the *Texarkana Gazette and News.*

During the mid-1950s, when the ASNE was led by Southern editors who opposed the U.S. Supreme Court's school desegregation ruling in *Brown v. Board of Education*, the monthly *ASNE Bulletin* sometimes carried cartoons that asserted Confederate identity. The caricature of George Healy (top right) of the *New Orleans Times-Picayune*, the 1958–59 ASNE president, offers a clear statement of his position on desegregation. The other two cartoons, both published in 1957, refer to the ongoing G.A.R.-C.S.A. tennis tournament played during ASNE conventions.

Virginius Dabney of the *Richmond Times-Dispatch* was the 1957–58 ASNE president.

Among the internationally prominent ASNE convention speakers was Cuban leader Fidel Castro, pictured here with ASNE President George Healy in 1959.

Civil rights leaders, seen here at the 1964 convention, were the first African Americans to address the ASNE. Their panel was rescheduled and shortened because ASNE members elected to attend a presidential press conference that posed a time conflict. The last-minute rescheduling prevented the Reverend Martin Luther King Jr. from being able to participate. Pictured here are, from left, Whitney Young, National Urban League; Roy Wilkins, NAACP; James Farmer, CORE; John Lewis, Student Nonviolent Coordinating Committee; and ASNE members Dick Peters of the *New York World-Telegram* and John Colburn of the *Wichita Eagle and Beacon*.

Following his term as the 1969–70 ASNE president, Norman Isaacs of the *Louisville Courier-Journal* would lead the organization's first effort to encourage daily newspaper editors to hire nonwhite journalists.

C. A. "Pete" McKnight of the *Charlotte Observer,* the 1971–72 ASNE president, visited with Vice President Spiro Agnew, an outspoken critic of the press, who spoke to the ASNE in 1972. The same convention would feature the ASNE's first program on newsroom integration.

Jay Harris, associate director of the Gannett Urban Journalism Center at Northwestern University, presented results of the first Goal 2000 newsroom census to the 1978 ASNE convention.

Eugene Patterson of the *St. Petersburg Times,* the ASNE's 1977–78 president, addressed the 1978 convention. During the convention, the ASNE board voted to launch the Goal 2000 parity hiring initiative.

Robert Maynard of the *Washington Post* was widely regarded as the leader of the newsroom diversity movement. In addition to advocacy, he and his wife, Nancy Hicks, led a series of journalism training programs to prepare nonwhites for newsroom employment.

John Quinn of Gannett Newspapers was an early supporter of the Goal 2000 initiative.

Richard Smyser of the *Oak Ridger* in Oak Ridge, Tennessee, was the Minorities Committee chair in 1978, when the ASNE board adopted the Goal 2000 initiative.

Carl Morris, the ASNE's first Minority Affairs director, discusses job hunting with college students attending a 1984 minority journalism conference at the University of Washington. The conferences, along with job fairs and scholarship programs, were designed to increase the number of nonwhites entering the journalism job market.

Katherine Fanning of the *Christian Science Monitor,* the ASNE's first woman president, was succeeded in 1988 by newsroom integration advocate John Seigenthaler Sr. of *USA Today.*

Loren Ghiglione of the *Southbridge (Mass.) News,* who became ASNE president in 1990, was one of the organization's most uncompromising advocates for Goal 2000.

William Hilliard of the *Oregonian* in Portland was the ASNE's first African American president. Hilliard served in 1993–94.

Edward Seaton of the *Manhattan Mercury* in Kansas was ASNE president in 1998, when the organization recalibrated the hiring initiative and set a new goal for 2025.

Tim McGuire, of the *Minneapolis Star-Tribune,* became ASNE president at the 2001 convention, where African American journalists protested low retention of nonwhite journalists and a racist comedy sketch touched off a nationwide controversy.

4

The Gay Nineties

Reimagining and Renegotiating a Multicultural Newsroom

What began as a fairly routine report at the 1990 convention of the American Society of Newspaper Editors ended with the iconoclastic revelation that a gay man was on the organization's membership roll. Leroy Aarons had been out in the newsroom of the *Oakland Tribune,* where he was senior vice president for news, but until he took the podium that April day in Washington, D.C., he had remained inside the closet that constrained gay members of the ASNE.[1] Aarons was not, of course, the only gay editor among the 983 members of the ASNE; he was simply the only one who had ever come out within the organization.[2] At the end of his report on an ASNE-sponsored survey of the newsroom experiences of 205 gay and lesbian journalists, Aarons uttered a single sentence that by one account "sent shockwaves through the news industry."[3] Although the survey results showed that bias against gays and lesbians was a fact of life in many daily newspaper newsrooms, Aarons found cause for optimism in the ASNE's willingness to sponsor his research. As he concluded his summary of the survey, Aarons said, "And I, as an editor, and a gay man, am proud of ASNE."[4]

Aarons's acknowledgment was considered so extraordinary that it warranted mention in the *New York Times*'s coverage of the ASNE convention, and *Time* magazine columnist Ellis Cose soon quoted Aarons as "an acknowledged gay" in a piece about the survey results and the prevalence of newsroom homophobia.[5] While Aarons was an established activist for newsroom integration issues, having been involved for years with Robert Maynard and Nancy Hicks Maynard's efforts to increase daily newspaper job opportunities for nonwhite journalists, his coming-out before the ASNE now allowed him to work openly to counter the intolerance that circumscribed opportunity for gay journalists and kept many of them closeted within their profession. The most obvious result of Aarons's self-emancipation was his founding later that year of the National Lesbian and Gay Journalists Association, which would have nearly 500 members when it held its first convention in 1992 and 1,200 by the time of Aarons's death in 2004.[6] Aarons's announcement also freed him to agitate for reforms within the ASNE. He would be instrumental in passage of ASNE resolutions in 1990 and 1995 to urge daily newspapers and wire services to add sexuality to their nondiscrimination policies and, in 2000, would direct a tenth-anniversary follow-up survey to gauge newsroom progress following his historic disclosure to the ASNE convention.[7]

Aarons's disclosure from the ASNE convention podium was a signal event for gay and lesbian journalists and editors, exposing the irony in a movement for greater professional inclusion that had left them out in the cold; however, it also marked the beginning of a new era in the ASNE's hiring initiative, expanding the conversation about social justice in newsrooms beyond the narrow parameters of race and, occasionally, gender. In effect, Aarons's speech to the ASNE asked editors to imagine a multi-identity newsroom hiring initiative rather than the one-dimensional effort studied each year by the Goal 2000 newsroom census, which quantified employment based solely on race.

With his remarks, Aarons inaugurated the era of diversity, ushering the ASNE hiring initiative out of its infancy, a period in which social justice was defined simply as the "integration" of racial "minorities" into newsrooms. In its place, he introduced a new idealism in which identity politics were more variegated and complex but the possibilities grander and more optimistic, namely the fulfillment of a truly democratic vision in which all journalists could recognize themselves within the professional norm. Even the nomenclature and organizational structure would evolve to reflect this reorientation until, in 1996, the ASNE would rename its Minorities Committee as the Diversity Committee.[8] But such change remained superficial as the ASNE's diversity efforts during the 1990s would remain fixated on the four traditional categories of race.

Taken to its logical conclusion, Aarons's call for greater inclusion of nonheterosexual journalists, a category that transgressed race, gender, sexual orientation, and other identities, might have opened opportunities for broad collaboration among various identity interest groups pursuing the mutual objective of social justice. Aarons's long tenure with the Maynards' training institute for nonwhite journalists should have signaled that his advocacy for gay rights was one cause among many to which he had committed, not a play for resources earmarked for some other constituency. But when Aarons took the ASNE podium in April 1990, he stepped into a crosscurrent of cultural and political forces that would transform the newsroom diversity movement into a turf war.

A source of tension within the ASNE's diversity movement of the 1990s would be the post-civil rights movement emphasis on multiculturalism that had been growing throughout the 1980s, largely through public school initiatives to celebrate difference. Although multiculturalism was defined and implemented differently throughout American culture, its main contribution was to erase the insistence on assimilation of nonwhites, often referred to as a "melting pot" approach, in exchange for a "salad bowl" vision of diversity.[9] In addition to focusing on race and ethnicity, multiculturalism also brought identities based on sexual orientation, religion, and physical disability into the diversity conversation. While multiculturalism attracted a range of criticism, a relevant strain argued that multiculturalism celebrated difference while leaving intact a white, male norm. As Angela Davis observed, "Multiculturalism can become a polite and euphemistic way of affirming persisting, unequal power relationships by representing them as equal differences."[10]

Aarons's coming-out and his founding of the NLGJA complicated the ASNE's conceptualization of diversity in significant ways. For one thing, gay identity was closely identified during the 1980s and 1990s with HIV/AIDS, diseases that many Americans associated with illicit and taboo sexual behavior. In the minds of some Americans, homophobia was a logical response to AIDS. Although gay Americans were targets of discrimination, they were not widely viewed as a cohort deserving of civil rights protection. It is important to note that public attitudes, specifically those of many white Americans, toward the rights claims of all identity-based groups took on an unabashedly critical tone during the 1990s, a rejection of the demand for political correctness that had governed discussion of race, gender, and other differences in recent decades. During the 1990s, the most prominent manifestation of this impatience with the complaints of marginalized groups was the anti-affirmative action backlash. Although it had festered since the 1960s, opposition to affirmative action would find its voice in high-profile denouncements of "racial preferences," most notably in Dinesh D'Souza's wildly successful *The End of Racism,* which was published in 1995, and Stephan and Abigail Thernstrom's *America in Black and White: One Nation, Indivisible,* which followed two years later.[11]

At the same time that remedies for historical racism were under attack, news events during the 1990s would offer repeated reminders of a continuing sense of injustice in some quarters of the African American community. In 1992, fifty-three people died during a six-day riot in Los Angeles, after four police officers were acquitted of beating black motorist Rodney King. Then, in 1995, the American public was sharply divided along racial lines by O. J. Simpson's acquittal on murder charges, which was cheered by many African Americans and scorned by many whites.[12] Such reality checks for American race relations, along with the competing calls for an end to affirmative action and a commitment to multicultural diversity, demonstrated the complexity and contentiousness of identity politics during the 1990s.

Within the ASNE, discourse about the hiring initiative registered the contradictory impulses of American society throughout the 1990s, when the push for multiculturalism and the anti-affirmative action backlash continually chafed against the race-exclusive model of Goal 2000. The ASNE leadership redoubled its commitment to Goal 2000, however, and proponents, both inside and outside the ASNE, either ignored or were blind to the corrosive impact of identity politics, which foreclosed any kind of consensus on newsroom diversity. Consistently, many of Goal 2000's advocates acknowledged only with scorn the white journalists and editors who questioned affirmative action and declined to compromise with other marginalized journalists, most notably gays and lesbians, who now wanted to be incorporated into the newsroom hiring initiative. In this climate, Aarons's coming-out, which made sexual orientation visible and offered a more elastic notion of multiculturalism, fragmented the newsroom diversity movement rather than expanding it.

The Closet in the ASNE

Aarons's effort to bring gay identity into the conversation about newsroom employment would encounter resistance from advocates of the race-focused newsroom diversity model, but it also would be hindered by the ASNE's general ambivalence toward homosexuality. This was not the first time that the closet within the ASNE had been challenged, and the organization's previous response is telling. Two years before Aarons made his historic disclosure to the 1990 ASNE convention, Lee Stinnett, the ASNE's executive director since 1983, had come out to the organization's board of directors. Stinnett had been elected president of the Arlington (Virginia) Gay and Lesbian Alliance and anticipated that the media might contact him to speak for the organization. For several years, Stinnett had been on the board and executive committee of the Whitman-Walker Clinic, which provided health services to the gay community in Washington, D.C., but his activism had remained under the radar. Now that he was in a higher profile position with the AGLA, Stinnett recalled, "I felt that ASNE ought to know. In fact, I wanted to know whether I was going to be fired if I did that."[13]

When Stinnett made his self-disclosure to John Seigenthaler Sr. of *USA Today,* the longtime newsroom-integration advocate who was ASNE president in 1988, Seigenthaler responded with unconditional support. The ASNE board's executive committee also supported Stinnett, but Seigenthaler felt obligated to protect Stinnett in the event sentiments changed as new directors rotated onto the board in the future. For that reason, Seigenthaler asked the full board to pass a resolution endorsing Stinnett and praising him for his fine performance as ASNE executive director—but, according to Seigenthaler, the resolution did not mention that Stinnett was gay. Indeed, the resolution is not recorded in the ASNE board minutes, which suggests that it was passed in executive session. Seigenthaler recalled, "Every member of the board knew what we were doing, and it was a unanimous endorsement of Lee, for his excellence in his performance of his duties as executive director of ASNE. But what we also were saying to each other is that he's coming out of the closet."[14]

Significantly, the board did not make the reason for the resolution of support part of the institutional record or publicize it to the membership. Nor did the board document discussion of the matter, which was initiated by Seigenthaler outside formal meetings.[15] In other words, despite its affirmation of support, the board effectively rejected Stinnett's attempt to come out and kept him closeted within the organization, even though he was publicly gay outside it. This is all the more curious when considered alongside publicity that Stinnett willingly embraced a year and a half after he came out to the ASNE board, when the conservative columnist Cal Thomas called the ASNE in response to a press release announcing its sponsorship of Aarons's survey of gay and lesbian journalists. Stinnett took Thomas's call and, before referring the columnist on to the chair of the committee directing the study, told Thomas that he himself was an "openly gay person."[16] Through the syndication of Thomas's column, Stinnett was out nationwide, but he was only partially out in the ASNE. Not until Stinnett retired would Seigenthaler and other former officers publicly acknowledge Stinnett's sexual orientation. During a retirement tribute to Stinnett at the 1999 convention, Seigenthaler would recount Stinnett's disclosure to the board, and he and another former president, who also made remarks during that program, would mention Stinnett's longtime partner by name.[17]

So constraining was the closet within the ASNE in 1990 that Aarons, though he was openly gay at the *Oakland Tribune,* wavered in his decision to come out at the ASNE convention that year. According to Stinnett, Aarons did not make the final decision to identify himself as a gay man to ASNE until he was standing at the convention podium that day in 1990. Stinnett recalled, "He talked to me about this immediately afterwards, and he said, 'You know, I didn't know what I was going to do until I did it. I debated it, whether I would say I was gay or not, and I got finished and I just heard my voice say [it].'"[18] Aarons's coming out to the ASNE in 1990 provided the incentive for many gay and lesbian journalists to follow suit in the newsrooms where they worked, but it did not inspire other editors to self-identify as gay or lesbian within the ASNE. In the wake of the founding of NLGJA, Stinnett, as ASNE executive director, agreed to plan a reception for gay editors in the ASNE president's suite during the 1994 ASNE convention. "However," Stinnett told Aarons, "I cannot count on anyone showing up."[19] Indeed, announcements were made that year and for some other conventions during the 1990s but, Stinnett recalled, "Almost nobody showed up. One time one person did and he was frightened to death."[20]

Nor did gay members of the ASNE, many of whom were out in their newsrooms and belonged to NLGJA, become more comfortable disclosing their sexual orientation within the ASNE in the years that followed Aarons's announcement. Pamela Strother, who succeeded Aarons as executive director of NLGJA, said that when she resigned her position in 2006, she could count on three fingers the number of gay and lesbian ASNE members who were out.[21] One of them, Pamela Fine, former editor of the *Indianapolis Star,* said in 2008 that gay concerns continued to be downplayed in ASNE nearly two decades after Aarons's announcement. "I'm a gay person. I'm a former leader of newsrooms and I look around and I start to see a few gay editors in place, but ASNE does not even include . . . attention on that issue," she said.[22]

This trend in the ASNE's neglect of sexual orientation as an identity deserving of formal recognition is significant, beginning with the ASNE board's apparent discomfort with Stinnett's coming-out in 1988. Although the ASNE board included newsroom-integration diehards, it missed an opportunity to advance the cause of broader diversity. Had the board publicized its resolution of support for Stinnett's disclosure, it might have modified the perception by gay and lesbian editors that the closet was a condition of membership in the organization. When Leroy Aarons took the convention podium in April 1990, the ASNE would have been fully on record as supporting gay and lesbian journalists and editors, and his disclosure might not have caused him such personal angst or "sent shockwaves through the news industry."

The early 1990s was a time of reimagining and renegotiating the terms of engagement for the ASNE's demographic parity objective, but despite Aarons's activism and the injection of a multicultural vision into the ASNE's diversity discussions, race remained the organization's primary focus throughout the decade. An indisputable factor in the ASNE's continued embrace of the outdated integration model of newsroom diversity was the sizeable political clout of the professional organizations for African American, Hispanic, Asian American, and Native American journalists. The considerable individual influence of the four associations grew exponentially when they formed the coalition UNITY Journalists of Color, which became an unyielding advocate for Goal 2000's race-based newsroom-integration model. After thousands of nonwhite journalists attended UNITY's first convention in 1994, proponents of a more inclusive model of social justice in newsroom hiring simply could not compete. Throughout the 1990s, the parallel professional organization for gay and lesbian journalists would be relegated to the margins of the diversity movement.

The Politics of Competing Goals

At the same convention at which Aarons gave his speech, the ASNE learned that the percentage of nonwhite newsroom employees had risen to 7.86 percent, but it was no cause for celebration. "My guesstimate is that the percentage of minorities in the general population increased .5 percentage points last year," wrote ASNE President Loren Ghiglione. "So a .3-percentage point increase in the newsroom population really represents a decrease."[23] To those tracking the numbers, it was becoming painfully apparent that the ASNE's unceasing rhetoric about Goal 2000 was merely a display of idealism. Even though nonwhite journalists accounted for 20 percent of newsroom hires and one-third of interns, attaining the end-of-the-century target was not just improbable but impossible.[24] As such, the 1990s quickly took shape as the decade of dissonance, in which the disparity between the ASNE's stated intention and the annual newsroom census results could no longer be explained away. Not only had most daily newspaper editors failed to hire enough nonwhite journalists to match the nonwhite populations in their own communities, but, at the beginning of the decade, more than half of daily newspapers' newsroom staffs remained entirely white.[25]

In many newsrooms that did hire nonwhite journalists, the atmosphere was distinctly inhospitable, and nonwhite journalists quickly moved on, many of them leaving the profession altogether.[26] "There was widespread assumption within newsrooms that people of color were hired only because of affirmative action and only because they were people of color," said Walterene Swanston, former executive director of UNITY, the coalition of the four nonwhite journalist organizations. "The second assumption was that they weren't qualified. And the perspective of those people of color was that 'I'm looking at the leadership in these newsrooms and there is nobody that looks like me. I'm not getting the opportunities to do the kind of reporting or editing or photography that I want to do. There is no way for me to develop my career here, so why would I stay here?'"[27]

Even as progressive editors labored in the diversity trenches, the U.S. nonwhite population was growing at a pace unforeseen by the hiring initiative's architects. Indeed, the original Goal 2000 projections had been crafted in 1978, when nonwhites accounted for 17 percent of the U.S. population, and had assumed the nonwhite percentage would be perhaps 20 percent in 2000. By 1990, that figure already was 19.7 percent.[28] Given the slow rate of progress in hiring during the 1980s, this population trend, fueled by increased immigration, would continue to widen the gap between the nonwhite numbers in the ASNE's annual survey and the percentage of nonwhites in the United States.

The disconnect between the ASNE's rhetoric and mathematical reality would exacerbate tensions between ASNE and the four professional organizations for nonwhite journalists, which were raising their profile and gaining strength, both individually and through the UNITY coalition. Although the ASNE had no actual control over whether Goal 2000 would be achieved in newspaper newsrooms, the organization would be blamed in increasingly strident terms for the parity initiative's failure. For example, in 1991 John Greenman of the *Akron Beacon Journal* wrote, "A number of editors explain the lack of progress as a lack of will. I reject that view. The newsrooms of this country will not become integrated by wishing that more white men do the right thing. What's needed is better organizing, more agitation, and perhaps a few well-placed lawsuits."[29] Greenman also noted that few editors who attended the ASNE's annual convention were participating in meetings of the Minorities Committee, which had become dominated by representatives of nonwhite journalist organizations and other outside diversity advocates.

Despite the dimming prospects for success at what increasingly seemed like an impossible and thankless task, ASNE leaders continued to hold up the hiring initiative as a key objective of the organization. During this period, the rhetoric focused on the business imperative for diversity more often than its social justice implications. In 1991, ASNE President David Lawrence urged editors not to use a slumping economy as an excuse for scaling back newsroom diversification efforts but to see hiring nonwhites as an investment. "For newspapers to be necessary to multicultural Americans, we simply *must* have people of diverse backgrounds in key positions, deciding what stories will run, where they will run and how they will be displayed. We need diverse people deciding who will be hired and promoted," Lawrence wrote. To delay action on newsroom diversification, he said, "is to operate with one arm tied behind our back at a time when competition for the reader's attention is fiercer than ever."[30] Yet as the newspaper industry struggled to recover from recession and a growing number of newsrooms felt pressure from corporate ownership to cut overhead, editors who had never bought into the need for nonwhite hiring found an excuse to remain disengaged.

Linda Grist Cunningham, who was named executive editor of the *Rockford (Ill.) Register Star* in 1991, was one of the exceptions. A white editor, she heavily recruited nonwhite journalists during the 1990s and, under her leadership, the *Register Star* became one of the few midmarket papers whose newsroom was integrated in proportion to the nonwhite demographic in its community.[31] Yet Cunningham also watched as other editors ignored the call for diversity. For one thing, she said, recruiting nonwhite staff members took effort and it was easy to detect an "early '90s kind of ennui that began to develop where everybody was just tired of working at this and wanted to turn attention elsewhere. I mean, there was some snarling that went on, like, 'This is wrong. We shouldn't have to do this.'" During this period, attendance at diversity workshops during the annual ASNE conventions was low, she said. "Now as numbers began to grow among women and racial minorities [within the organization], some of the, those who were resisting, some of the—well, how do I put this gently? I can't—some of the white editors who were beginning in the late '80s and early '90s to resist the hard work that was involved were then shamed into doing another sort of push again, because the numbers of women and racial minorities had increased and we were more visible. We said things, we pushed the point."[32] Yet the passion of those committed to the cause failed to resonate sufficiently with the membership at large, and peer pressure did little but engender resentment among skeptical editors, particularly those whose circulation areas had a small nonwhite population. For many of them, newsroom integration seemed irrelevant.

As the annual census numbers continued their sluggish rise, conflict intensified between nonwhite journalists who felt betrayed by the false promise of Goal 2000 and the predominantly white editors of ASNE, many of whom remained ambivalent about newsroom integration. This tension shaped the conversation after the broader concept of multiculturalism emerged in the early 1990s. As long as the business of the original, race-specific hiring initiative remained unfinished, many nonwhite journalists would see proposals for an expanded definition of diversity—one that included nonheterosexuals, white women, and persons with disabilities, who now were protected by the Americans with Disabilities Act—as coming at their expense. As a result, the multicultural 1990s would also be a time of reentrenchment.

An Uneven Commitment

Despite growing evidence that Goal 2000 was a pipe dream, the decade opened with ASNE leaders adamant, at least in public, that the hiring initiative's race-focused goal was still within reach. Leading the cause was a new wave of diversity advocates, many of whom had joined ASNE after adoption of the hiring initiative in 1978. In addition to David Lawrence of the *Miami Herald,* the 1991–92 ASNE president, other white editors who campaigned tirelessly for nonwhite hiring included Gregory Favre of the *Sacramento Bee,* who would be president in 1994–95. For some time, the ASNE leadership ladder, the series of offices that directors ascend before becoming president, had been dominated by champions of Goal 2000. Although some presidents were more outspoken diversity proponents than others during the 1990s, it is no coincidence that Lawrence and Favre, among the most passionate Goal 2000 advocates of the decade, were elevated to the presidency. Nor is it a coincidence that the ASNE's first African American president, William Hilliard of the *Oregonian* in Portland, also led the organization during this period.

Like other nonwhite editors of his generation, Hilliard started in the newspaper business during the 1950s, when all but a few newsroom staffs were all-white. The *Oregonian* even denied Hilliard a paper route when he was eleven years old because of his race.[33] Despite being told in college that the daily newspaper business was no place for a black man, Hilliard said he immediately sought a newsroom job at his hometown paper when he graduated. "They took my application and said there were no openings. I left," he recalled. "Two weeks later, someone told me there was a copy boy position open at the *Oregonian.* So I went up to apply for it. They said, 'Well, you'll have to make out an application, and we don't normally use college graduates as copy kids, but we'll give you an application.' I said, 'Well, I already filled out one here several weeks ago.' They couldn't find it, which means that they probably had thrown it away, hadn't paid any attention to it. And that's how difficult it was. This was in 1952."[34]

But the *Oregonian* eventually gave Hilliard his chance, and he became the first African American hired by a daily newspaper on the West Coast.[35] Thirty-four years later, Hilliard was named the *Oregonian*'s editor in chief, and seven years after that, Hilliard became the first black president of the ASNE.

In the ASNE of the 1990s, the leadership's passion for the hiring initiative kept it at the top of the organization's agenda. In addition, the leaders' preoccupation with the annual newsroom census, whose results were announced at the annual convention each spring, had produced an institutional culture dictating that all editors, regardless of the size of their papers, hire nonwhite journalists; those who failed to do their part to increase the annual survey numbers, many of them editors of smaller papers, were scorned by the initiative's most vocal supporters, most of whom were editors from high-circulation metropolitan papers that enjoyed a corporate commitment to diversity and the resources for recruitment and training that entailed. Increasingly, some of the small-town editors pushed back. A month before the 1992 ASNE meeting, Brian Cooper of the *Telegraph Herald* in Dubuque, Iowa, anticipated the convention segment devoted to release of the annual Goal 2000 numbers. "Then comes the ASNE Guilt Trip," Cooper wrote in the *ASNE Bulletin*. "Editors are chided for slow progress in minority employment. And then we're invited to scan the list of newspapers answering the survey . . . to see which papers aren't holding up their end."[36] During the 1990s, the disparities in commitment to diversity and results at small and large papers would jostle the ASNE's long-standing fault line between small dailies and the newspaper industry's Goliaths, which historically had functioned as a class divide within the ASNE.[37]

In April 1990, the same month Aarons made his historic speech, the *ASNE Bulletin* carried twenty-four pages on newsroom integration and cited survey data showing a resistance to hiring nonwhites among editors at papers with circulations less than 50,000, which were the traditional training ground for larger papers. While all newspapers with circulations above 100,000 employed nonwhites, the performance in smaller circulation categories, accounting for the majority of U.S. daily newspapers, was decidedly lower. Just 21 percent of daily newspapers with circulations below 10,000 had broken the race barrier in their newsrooms.[38] Without a steady stream of nonwhite journalists in the hiring "pipeline," the frequent industry term, integration at the top of the profession would be slowed. But many editors at smaller papers declined to accept responsibility for the problem, the *Bulletin* reported.

> They don't buy the idea that after three centuries of reserving virtually all newspaper jobs for whites, U.S. newspapers should be moving positively to encourage minorities to practice journalism.
>
> They don't even respond to the economic argument that all-white work forces are at a competitive disadvantage in trying to attract increasingly diverse readers and advertisers.[39]

The *Bulletin*'s strident, even accusatory, posture reflected a deep frustration among ASNE leaders and newsroom-integration advocates with the failure of the organization's staggering investment of resources to reverse the pattern of industry discrimination. Lee Stinnett said that during his tenure as ASNE executive director from 1983 to 1998, the organization devoted more resources year in and year out to Goal 2000 than any other project but the annual convention.[40]

In 1993, following a poor showing in the 1992 census, which pegged the nonwhite portion of the newsroom work force at 9.39 percent, ASNE President Seymour Topping of the *New York Times* announced that the focus of diversity programming would expand to include newspaper content. This was a subject that had been on the periphery of the Goal 2000 project from the beginning, when founders such as Gene Patterson and John Quinn had understood that comprehensive news coverage could not be achieved with an all-white news staff. This concern also had been reflected in rhetoric about the business imperative of newsroom integration; however, little attention had been paid to how the perceptions of readers and journalists about bias in newspaper content affected readership or the working environment in newsrooms. "Newspapers cannot hope to sustain [market] penetration unless they reach out more effectively to the broadest possible cross section of their communities," Topping wrote. "The largest untapped pool of potential readers may be among blacks, Hispanics and Asians, particularly as their education and income levels continue to rise."[41]

As part of a new Blueprint for 2000 project, which Topping described as a "newsroom multicultural initiative," the ASNE launched a nationwide content survey program, to be headed up by Gregory Favre of the *Sacramento Bee.* Newspapers would be encouraged to quantify the representations of nonwhites and their communities that appeared in their pages and to gauge whether these portrayals were positive or negative. Results could be reported confidentially. The ASNE's new focus, Topping said, was a move away from a strictly race-based, hiring-focused approach to diversity and toward an appreciation for the value of difference as an element of news coverage. "A multicultural approach that makes allowance for distinctions of race, ethnic origins and gender, rather than insistence on uncompromising assimilation into the white male work force, is at the core of the program," he wrote. Favre, whose committee produced "Covering the Community," a fifty-eight-page publication on how to conduct a diversity audit of a newspaper, said the point was to determine whether newspapers were reflecting their communities. "And I'm not just talking about counting numbers, because that's not necessarily the way you do it," Favre said. "But to see the richness of your coverage, take a look at your index, your Rolodexes, and see who you're calling [for interviews]. Do you go back to the same people all the time because they give good sound bites and most of those people are white, middle-aged men? There's nothing wrong with white, middle-aged men, . . . but they shouldn't be the whole mix."[42]

Although the ASNE's push for newspapers to audit coverage expanded the conversation about diversity to include newspaper content rather than just newsroom employment, the auditing process, which quantified representations of and references to nonwhites, reenacted the process of racialization entailed in the newsroom census. Just as the annual Goal 2000 count of nonwhite newsroom employees asked editors to measure news coverage against a distinct norm, the audits counted representations that were not white, not straight, and not male. As a result, the center of power in news coverage—the white, male, and straight norm—remained intact and undercut the corrective benefit of the audits. In this vein, Christopher Campbell has concluded that news stories produced by integrated news staffs "reflect the dominant newsroom values, which dictate similar coverage of events by minority and nonminority newspeople."[43]

Attendant to the multiculturalism goal, Topping said, were efforts to address the challenge of nonwhite retention in newsrooms. While recruitment of new hires was fairly strong, "the alarming drift of young minorities away from newspaper jobs has continued, presumably because of disillusionment with what they encounter in newsrooms."[44] Nonwhite attrition would create a continual and circular set of tensions in newsrooms during the 1990s. In the view of some white editors, the quick departure of many highly recruited, hard-to-come-by nonwhite hires, whether to jobs at other papers or in other professions, reinforced the perception that newsroom integration was difficult to achieve. This appeared to validate many editors' lack of commitment to nonwhite hiring. This self-sustaining process of failure was a subject of "Race: The Conversation You're Not Hearing in Your Newsroom," a roundtable session at the 1996 convention. Max Jennings of the *Dayton Daily News* said nonwhite turnover was an obstacle to achieving newsroom diversity. "It is not easy to find people, and when we do find them, the retention problems are tremendous," Jennings said. "Many of us have been trying to do that for a long, long time, and this is something we haven't addressed as an industry. It is not easy for us to find the right people, and then it is not easy for us to retain them."[45] Andrea Ford, a staff writer at the *Los Angeles Times,* said many nonwhite journalists did not stay in the profession because they saw no future in newsrooms. "One thing that is not openly stated is that a whole lot of people are frustrated and are getting the hell out," Ford said. "They are leaving the business—not just individual papers. People have stopped plantation-hopping. When they bump up against that glass ceiling, which is very, very real, and realize what is at stake, what you have to give up to be in these places, they ask, 'Why am I here? What am I doing?'"[46]

Backlash on All Fronts

By the 1990s, the newsroom-integration effort had produced an uncomfortable working environment for white as well as nonwhite journalists. While the ASNE record contains infrequent direct references to the resistance of white journalists and midlevel editors to newsroom integration, white backlash was a continual subtext in ASNE diversity discourse. Sometimes the problem was implied through calls for training midlevel editors to lead multiracial staffs more effectively, as in the publication of an "ASNE Multicultural Management Guide," which cited problems of cultural sensitivity and even racism in newspaper newsrooms.[47] Other times, backlash was implied by the ASNE's defensiveness on the subject of quotas, even though the critics often went unidentified and their complaints were vaguely outlined.[48] More often, nonwhite journalists mentioned the racial hostility they encountered in newsrooms in anecdotes describing the skepticism of white coworkers and supervisors. For example, Delma Francis, night city editor of the *Richmond Times-Dispatch,* told a session at the 1991 convention, "I do think we are held to a different standard. If you are a minority and a woman, heaven help you. If you happen to be a woman as well as a minority, you do not have to work twice as hard, you have to work three times as hard."[49]

One of the few bold, public statements of philosophical opposition to the newsroom hiring initiative by a white editor was offered in 1991 by Philip Terzian of the *Providence Journal,* who was alarmed by the hiring initiative's emphases on race and numbers. "I wish the American Society of Newspaper Editors had better things on its mind than the imposition of racial quotas in newsrooms," Terzian wrote in the *Bulletin,* arguing that percentages have nothing to do with the quality of journalism. "These are not matters of substance; these are painful obsessions. For if there is any axiom in race relations worth following, it is that progress must be measured by the extent to which race does not matter, does not pervade, does not influence decisions, or the way people think, or businesses operate."[50] Terzian noted that journalism had indeed been predominantly white and male. "Happily, those days are over, and not likely to return. This is not to say, however, that the balance has shifted radically, or is destined to do so, or must do so at all." Rather Terzian worried that recruiting people who were not called to the news business by an affinity for the work would diminish the quality of the news product. "In short, this is not a business that lends itself to recruitment by quotas or will necessarily appeal to all kinds of people," Terzian wrote. "And anyone who must be drafted into service is not likely to adorn the vocation as a whole."[51]

In most cases, however, standards of political correctness obviated frank discussion of white backlash in newsrooms that had integrated their work forces. Or, the backlash was framed as concern for the integrity of the profession, much as it had been in the 1970s, when editors worried openly about the professional qualifications of nonwhite journalists. Occasionally, a direct indictment of newsroom diversity did filter into the ASNE's formal discussion of Goal 2000, but it was usually offered as evidence of the continued need for a hiring initiative and greater sensitivity by newsroom managers. In 1996, for example, the *American Editor* (*ASNE Bulletin,* renamed in 1995) reported on the results of a newsroom diversity study conducted by the Associated Press Managing Editors, which found dissatisfaction among both white and nonwhite journalists. The study quoted an anonymous white journalist as saying, "Our paper has bent over backwards to hire blacks and women for high-profile jobs at the expense of equally or more qualified white males. . . . We don't look for the best people anymore but the best blacks or women. That, to me, destroys credibility as much as not seeking diversity."[52]

The APME survey followed a bombshell that had rocked journalism's professional community in 1995, when the *New Republic* published a 13,000-word investigative piece by journalist Ruth Shalit on staff dysfunction produced by the newsroom-integration program at the *Washington Post.*[53] The newspaper's management responded angrily—publisher Donald Graham condemned the article as "big lie propaganda" among other things[54]—and the piece, which was found to contain factual inaccuracies, was partially discredited. Even so, Shalit's article, which one observer described as a "depth charge,"[55] quoted the bitter complaints of named and unnamed white staff members about what they perceived as affirmative action hires and promotions in the newsroom.

The article also quoted nonwhite journalists who were aggrieved by the white backlash in the newsroom. Although Shalit may have botched some of her facts, the article was broadly perceived as having accurately reported "racial strife" within the newsroom of a major U.S. newspaper that held itself up as a leader in newsroom integration. The article followed publication in 1993 of *Volunteer Slavery: My Authentic Negro Experience,* the memoir of Jill Nelson, an African American journalist who reported racial hostility at the *Post.*[56] In an internal report following publication of the *New Republic* piece, *Post* ombudsman Geneva Overholser wrote, "Much of the power of the article derives from its airing of sentiments that are deeply felt but usually narrowly circulated."[57] Said *Post* columnist Richard Cohen of Shalit's reporting, "It's not a question of whether she got this or that wrong. What she didn't get wrong was the phenomenon."[58]

Although the *New Republic* article was notable for documenting white discontentment with newsroom affirmative action, it also affirmed complaints of nonwhites who had been hired into newsrooms whose editors were aggressive supporters of a diversified workforce, only to find a chilly reception from white coworkers suspicious of nonwhites' qualifications. Betty Winston Baye, an assistant editor at the *Louisville Courier-Journal,* said black journalists had no margin for error.

> Because I'm black, I rarely have the luxury of just being able to do my job.
>
> Instead, in order to survive, I must devote energy to watching my back, being fully aware that I am resented by some of my white colleagues. From their perspective, all newsroom jobs are "white" jobs; therefore, if I am hired or promoted, I've taken what "rightfully" belongs to them.
>
> Being a black journalist in a mostly white newsroom means always having to pass another test and knowing that no matter what your credentials or how hard you work, your talents are always suspect. [59]

Many nonwhite journalists sensed a double standard from their earliest experiences in the newsroom. Cindy Rose Stiff, placement director at Florida A&M University, said this had become a recurring theme in her contacts with African Americans in their first job.

> In my teaching I have found blacks often believe they have to be better just to be equal. Beginning minority reporters are especially vulnerable.
>
> For example, what happens in your newsroom when a young reporter makes a grammatical error? I recently received a note from an award-winning veteran white reporter who used "hear" twice when she should have used "here." Just a mistake.

> Is that what your editors would think if black reporters make the same mistake?[60]

Some nonwhite journalists also complained that once they were hired into newsrooms, opportunities for promotion to positions of influence were closed to them. Gilbert Bailon of the *Dallas Morning News* wrote, "Minority journalists are often bypassed for key assignments and responsibilities that they need to prove their qualification, and which lead to promotions and better assignments. The talent pipeline for such plum positions is clogged with white men."[61]

Such sentiments had crystallized and received prominent play in 1993, following release of "Muted Voices: Frustration and Fear in the Newsroom," a twenty-four-page report based on a survey conducted by the National Association of Black Journalists. In a damning comparison, the NABJ found that most newsroom managers, the majority of them white, believed the industry had made progress toward newsroom integration while a majority of their black employees believed it had not. Among the most striking findings of the NABJ survey were the following two statistics:

- 67 percent of black journalists believed their employers were not committed to newsroom integration while 94 percent of managers said the news organization did indeed have a serious commitment to hiring, retaining, and promoting nonwhites.
- 92 percent of employers said blacks and others were subject to the same standards for promotion while just 28 percent of NABJ respondents agreed.[62]

"African American journalists and the bosses of the newsroom are operating in different worlds," the report stated. "The gulf in communications between reporters and managers is so great that journalists are afraid to speak up about race issues and are hitting a glass ceiling of opportunity that leads to frustration."[63]

ASNE President William Hilliard responded to the NABJ report by asking editors and journalists alike to recommit to the hiring initiative, but Hilliard now framed the concept in terms of multiculturalism, which in theory included everyone and excluded no one. "Our industry must make up for mistakes of the past," Hilliard wrote. " . . . We can do so without alienating any one person because of color, race, gender, religion or sexual orientation, and without quotas. We have the creativity."[64] Interestingly, Hilliard deemphasized the newsroom census at the same time that he emphasized the need for broad inclusion, beyond the race-based Goal 2000 objectives. "How we count the numbers doesn't matter a lot," Hilliard wrote. "What really matters is creating newsrooms that reflect America's diversity and that recognize the strengths, talents and viewpoints of people in all their variety. Managers should make a major change in attitude and step outside the comfort zone of demanding that everyone be just like themselves. There is strength in unfamiliar packaging: in women and men, in people of different colors and sexual orientations."[65] This multicultural turn in ASNE discourse would not placate white editors and journalists whose impatience with the ASNE's hiring-by-the-numbers approach was growing and would further alienate the disaffected African American journalists whose frustration registered in the just-released "Muted Voices."

The NABJ report was a sobering blow for ASNE's leaders, who found themselves caught between the promise entailed by Goal 2000 and the virtual certainty—understood by many but rarely articulated—that demographic parity would not be achieved by the century's end. Moreover, in a key finding of the NABJ survey, ASNE leaders had learned that cultural difference and fear had produced a toxic newsroom climate in which tokenism, double standards, and disparities in perception were commonplace. Stunningly, just 51 percent of black journalists who responded to the NABJ survey planned to remain in journalism more than five years.[66] For those ASNE members who had worked hardest to advance the cause of newsroom integration, the report was an especially bitter pill. In reality, few in the newsroom were happy with the newsroom hiring initiative—certainly not the nonwhite journalists who were its purported beneficiaries or the white, male journalists who believed the gains in diversified hiring, which were supposed to make for a better newspaper, were coming at their expense.[67]

Despite the sting of the NABJ survey results and increasing reports of a white backlash festering in newsrooms, the Goal 2000 project passed two significant milestones in 1993. For the first time, more than half of daily newspaper newsrooms employed at least one nonwhite journalist or editor, and nonwhites now accounted for more than 10 percent of the professional work force in daily newspaper newsrooms. To anyone who was paying attention, however, many nonwhite journalists were sending the ASNE a clear warning that the multicultural shift and the new emphasis on programs not designed to accelerate the racial integration of newsrooms and create opportunities for nonwhite promotion were being viewed with suspicion. Laurence O'Donnell, former *Wall Street Journal* managing editor, cautioned that recruiting of nonwhites was still a necessity.

> Over the past few years, industry efforts on minorities have shifted away from recruitment to the problems of managing multicultural newsrooms and, ultimately, measuring multicultural content. ASNE has participated in this reallocation of resources. The shift is good if it really helps with the training, advancement and retention of minorities already on staff. The shift is also good if it succeeds in prodding newspapers to take a broader, more inclusive approach to covering the news.
>
> But the shift is a mistake if it comes at the expense of minority recruitment, assuming that problem has been met. It hasn't. The fight to attract the best minority students into our newsrooms is as difficult today as it was 25 years ago, when we as an industry first got serious about hiring minorities. Recruiting the best is still a struggle.[68]

As the ASNE expanded the conversation about diversity to include not only gender and sexual orientation but also religious differences and disabilities, many nonwhite journalists would view the ASNE's embrace of multiculturalism as a breach of faith. Although the census and most programs supporting Goal 2000 focused on race, many nonwhite journalists believed they were being asked to share newsroom power and diversity resources with other marginalized groups when they themselves still felt unempowered and marginalized.

Most outspoken on the subject were African American journalists and diversity advocates. The National Association of Black Journalists, founded in 1975 as the flagship organization for nonwhite newsroom professionals, had been joined during the 1980s by the National Association of Hispanic Journalists, the Native American Journalists Association, and the Asian American Journalists Association. Now, Leroy Aarons's National Association of Lesbian and Gay Journalists had emerged, eager for a role in the diversity movement. In this new order, the political complexity of multiculturalism was coming into focus.

Navigating the Fissures in Diversity

As William Hilliard completed his term as ASNE president in 1994, the organization could point to his leadership as evidence the ASNE was diversifying itself as well as its members' newsrooms. While elevating a black editor to its presidency earned the ASNE a certain amount of credibility with the increasingly politicized and polarized diversity community, the significance of his leadership extended beyond symbolism. Even before he became president of ASNE, Hilliard had championed the cause of multiculturalism and had demonstrated in his leadership of the *Oregonian* that his vision of diversity was not limited to the concerns of African Americans. In 1991, Hilliard had directed his sports department to stop referring in print to sports mascots that conveyed stereotypes of Native Americans, such as the Redskins, Braves, and Savages. Though the decision had been unpopular, Hilliard insisted it was the right thing to do. "People got all upset. Readers were upset," he recalled. "And *Sports Illustrated* and different newspapers around the country called trying to figure out what we were trying to do."[69]

In his president's address to the 1994 ASNE convention, Hilliard made an important rhetorical move by identifying diversity as a journalistic value rather than simply a politically correct cause to embrace, and defined diversity as transcending race and incorporating sexual orientation, disability, gender, and age. "In my view a newspaper that does not look like a cross-section of the community it serves will not and cannot serve that community as it wants and deserves to be served," Hilliard said. "No newspaper can claim immunity from a role in helping to build and maintain the cultural collaborations that comprise rich and successful societies. A successful society's greatest virtues, the wellsprings of its greatness, are tolerance, respect and unyielding commitment to common values. And such are the values of great newspapers."[70] By placing the commitment to diversity on the same plane with such journalistic values as freedom of information, and by drawing a more porous boundary around the profession of journalism, Hilliard attempted to redefine the terms of the employment debate within the ASNE and its members' newsrooms. Even so, the principle of diversity would remain outside the ASNE's official framework of journalistic values for another decade.

In his final communications as ASNE president, Hilliard also had a message for the editors who still resisted the idea of the inclusive newsroom, as well as for the white journalists who were swept up in the backlash that played out as resentment of nonwhite hiring. Noting he had received letters from four members who criticized the ASNE's annual effort to quantify nonwhite journalists in daily newspaper newsrooms, Hilliard wrote, "Some of them say the survey invades the privacy of their employees, while others see the survey as a disguise for what amounts to a quota system based on racial and/or gender representation."[71] He reminded editors of America's shifting demographic and warned that a newspaper industry that ignored multiculturalism would be irrelevant when nonwhites became a majority during the twenty-first century. "To those few who are threatened by that prospect, let me remind them that this is not a case of winners and losers," he said. "No one has to be disenfranchised when we accommodate and nourish cultural diversity. . . . The Oregonian did not fire a white male reporter to make room for me, and I was not promoted at the expense of more competent and deserving colleagues. Nobody lost because I succeeded." Hilliard added that newsrooms did not have to lower their professional standards to diversify their staffs. "I have tried to make sure that when any prospect applies for work at the Oregonian, that person's only cause for anxiety should be, am I good enough—not am I man enough, or white enough, or young enough? Not can I cut it as a black reporter or as a lesbian reporter or as a disabled reporter—just can I cut it as a reporter? That is all that counts."[72] Sixteen years after the adoption of Goal 2000, however, this was a line of argument that still had not found consensus within the ASNE rank and file.

Diversity Fatigue

As the rhetoric of ASNE leaders took a multicultural turn, ASNE discourse began to reflect a growing sense of what frequently was referred to as diversity fatigue. By one definition, diversity fatigue was rooted in frustration over lackluster results despite what many editors believed had been their extraordinary efforts to integrate newsrooms. At the same time, a second definition emerged in the ASNE discourse surrounding newsroom employment in the 1990s. Despite many ASNE members' passion for Goal 2000 and the organization's commitment of resources to that end, editors who were not intent upon diversifying their newsroom workforce found the reiteration of the diversity message in ASNE publications and on the annual convention program tiresome and redundant. Whatever caused the diversity fatigue of the 1990s, editors tended not to vocalize their sentiments, at least not publicly, as doing so would have entailed a direct challenge to the ASNE's orthodoxy on diversity. Instead, diversity-weary editors voted with their feet.

Throughout the 1990s, newsroom diversity advocates expressed dismay at the comparatively low turnout for convention sessions dedicated to nonwhite hiring. Attending his first convention in 1994, Gilbert Bailon of the *Dallas Morning News* was troubled by the obvious lack of interest in diversity programming. "Based on some lobby chatter and relatively low attendance at 'The Multicultural Newsroom' workshop, I concluded that some members have grown weary of what they perceive as multicultural homilies or boot camps on political correctness," Bailon wrote. "That's disconcerting when one considers the dearth of minority members at the convention."[73] A year later, Kenneth Bunting of the *Seattle Post-Intelligencer* suggested that flagging interest in diversity programming was a response, in part, to white backlash against affirmative action. Bunting chided "the cynics among us who are tired of all the emphasis on diversity, and . . . the fainthearted who might be tempted to give up the battle in the face of growing political pressures." He urged editors not to give in to the "concerns of white males who nowadays are feeling cheated, victimized and oh so righteous in their indignation over what they perceive as reverse discrimination."[74]

The discussion of diversity fatigue in the 1990s was really just the latest riff on the long-standing complaint about low attendance and mass departures at race-related convention sessions. Recall, for example, at the 1964 convention, the first time African Americans had appeared on an ASNE panel, that many editors snubbed the nation's leading black civil rights advocates to observe a presidential press conference. The ASNE leadership rescheduled the panel and shortened its time allotment, making it impossible for the Reverend Martin Luther King Jr. to attend. Many editors took a pass on the abbreviated panel, whose presenters were forced to condense their remarks on short notice.[75] At the time, there were no newsroom-integration activists in the wings to complain.

In the 1970s and 1980s, however, supporters of nonwhite hiring began to remark on the cause-and-effect relationship between the introduction of race as a convention topic and the number of editors moving toward the exits.[76] During the mid-1990s, when this phenomenon became linked in ASNE discourse with the concept of diversity fatigue, criticism about white editors' attendance reached a heightened pitch. A case in point was the 1995 convention, which included a heavy dose of diversity programming. In addition to "Voices of UNITY" testimonials from nonwhite journalists who had attended the first UNITY convention the previous summer, the program included sessions explicitly about race.

On the first morning of the convention, following Gregory Favre's presidential address, editors had the opportunity to attend two such sessions. The first, a plenary, featured public intellectual Cornel West, author of the 1994 nonfiction best seller *Race Matters*. Wanda Lloyd of *USA Today* introduced West, who is black, to the convention and had a clear view of the audience. "I walked onto the stage with him and you could just see the bodies get up and fleeing [*sic*] out of the room," she recalled. "Well, Cornel West is a pretty darn big deal in this country and in the area that he speaks, diversity. That was very embarrassing to me and it was embarrassing to ASNE, and that has happened in several of those sessions."[77]

Observers reported a similar audience response in a second race-focused session later that morning. *Chicago Tribune* columnist Clarence Page, who moderated a session called "Race in America Near the End of the Anglo Century," handled the mass departures with poise. Page, who is black, told audience members who remained, "One of my fellow panelists happened to notice that after Gregory Favre spoke, half of the white men in the audience got up and left. And I said, 'That is OK.' I looked out and said, 'Everybody here is a friend of mine.' No wonder. I am glad to see so many familiar faces."[78] Kenneth Bunting of the *Seattle Post-Intelligencer* was less magnanimous in published remarks after the convention. Bunting worried about the impression the departures had made on the nonwhite journalism interns working on the convention newspaper. "Some of the young, aspiring journalists who worked on the Reporter noticed, as the program continued later in the week, that the trend appeared to continue whenever one of the poignant reflections on UNITY was about to be delivered," Bunting wrote. "More troubling to me were murmurs, whines and complaints of those who thought there was too much emphasis on diversity. There was not. There needs to be more. Our industry will suffer if we lack the vision and common sense to finish what we started."[79]

In fairness to ASNE members, it should be noted that the annual conventions, a mix of tightly scheduled plenary and concurrent sessions, are a backdrop for professional networking. Editors routinely leave the meeting rooms to visit with their peers and many spend much of the convention engaged in conversation in the hallway. Moreover, there traditionally has been a great deal of movement in the meeting rooms in the short space of time between one session's end and another's beginning as people go out and others come in. Given the structure of the program, it seems an odd decision to have scheduled the "Voices of UNITY" testimonials between sessions, when many conventioneers would not be in their seats. Once a session is under way, popularity of the topic can be determined a few minutes after it starts simply by observing the number of full and empty seats. Wanda Lloyd believed, however, that what happened at the Cornel West and Clarence Page sessions at the 1995 convention was part of a pattern. "One of the things we have observed in ASNE is that every year when we have a diversity program at the convention, it's very traditional that a lot of people leave the room," she said. "Now, are they leaving the room because they're opposed to diversity? Are they leaving the room because they've heard it all before? Are they leaving the room because we're not putting on a program that engages them and they just don't want to do it? Or are they leaving the room because they just have to go check their e-mail and call the office? I don't know. All I know is that people leave the room on diversity programs it appears more than they leave the room on other programs, as a general theme."[80]

The issue of attendance at race-focused programs would come to the fore again in 1998, when some ASNE members observed a similar response by white editors to a session featuring African American history scholar John Hope Franklin, whom President Bill Clinton had chosen in 1997 to lead his national initiative on race. Again, a prominent African American appeared on the program and, again, the audience evaporated. "Many in the ballroom hit the exits when John Hope Franklin took the stage to discuss U.S. race relations with Dorothy Gilliam of the Washington Post," wrote Gilbert Bailon of the *Dallas Morning News.* "The sparse crowd was not lost on Franklin, who commented on the many empty chairs after his public conversation."[81] For diversity advocates within ASNE, the audience response to Franklin's presence on the program was shocking, but for Rick Rodriguez of the *Sacramento Bee,* who chaired the Diversity Committee in 1998, Franklin's rebuff was a personal affront. "I actually wrote a letter to John Hope Franklin apologizing," he recalled. "I was the one that got him to come to speak at the convention, because what happened is we're right in the middle of the Clinton diversity initiative. We had had a pretty good panel leading into John Hope Franklin. He was the speaker before lunch, and this very distinguished man came up to talk about the Clinton diversity initiative, the talks that were going on in communities throughout the country. Editors just got up and walked out, turned their backs on him as he was speaking. It was embarrassing to me."[82]

UNITY and Fragmentation

In contrast to the ASNE board's ambivalence about the Maynards' National Conference on Minorities and the News in 1978, the leadership offered an unequivocal endorsement of the first UNITY gathering, held in Atlanta in 1994. The emergence of UNITY, a coalition of the four national organizations representing black, Hispanic, Asian American, and Native American journalists working in all media, not just newspapers, was undoubtedly the most important development in the newsroom diversity movement of the early 1990s. Spurred in part by nonwhite journalists' growing impatience with the pace of industry self-reform initiatives, the most prominent of which was the ASNE's Goal 2000, the first UNITY convention attracted more than six thousand people, which the coalition claimed as the largest attendance ever at a meeting of U.S. media professionals.[83] The 1994 convention would be followed by others in 1999 and 2004, and scheduled on a four-year cycle thereafter.

Formation of the UNITY coalition was an important display of political clout for the constituencies targeted by the newsroom-integration movement. While the National Association of Black Journalists, National Association of Hispanic Journalists, Asian American Journalists Association, and Native American Journalists Association each retained their autonomy and would continue to hold meetings each year, the collaboration and solidarity represented by UNITY transformed a fragmented movement into a unified center of power. Among those attending the first UNITY convention was Wanda Lloyd of *USA Today,* who had edited the NABJ's 1993 "Muted Voices" report and would serve on the ASNE board of directors from 1997 to 2003. Lloyd recalled that many white editors who attended UNITY were surprised by the size of the nonwhite journalists' turnout and their lingering sense of injustice. "I think it was kind of an eye-opening experience for a lot of people to see the numbers of people and the numbers of people who in some of the workshops were . . . quite angry sometimes at the lack of progress or at the way certain people were being treated, or the lack of progress in just individual assignments," Lloyd said. " . . . There was a lot of anger at UNITY that first time when there were workshops on . . . how to get ahead in your career."[84]

The UNITY experience also shifted the diversity dynamic because white editors who attended were in the minority. Lloyd said a number of newspapers, especially those affiliated with chains committed to diversity, sent several representatives, many of them white, to the convention. As a result, Lloyd said, "there were a lot of people at that first UNITY who had never been in the presence of large numbers of people of color."[85]

Significantly, the formation of the UNITY coalition also entailed a closing of ranks in opposition to the concept of multiculturalism in newsroom employment. Mirroring the ASNE's newsroom-integration initiative—which had defined "minority" journalists as those having black, Hispanic, Asian, or Native American ancestry—the composition of the UNITY coalition and its collective influence further cemented that restrictive template into the newsroom diversity concept in the 1990s. The result was an affirmation of the exclusively race-focused remedy embraced by the ASNE since 1978 and a rejection of the ASNE's more recent multicultural turn. This is apparent in UNITY's marginalization of gay and lesbian journalists within the diversity movement. In 1994, the coalition formally and resoundingly rejected a request by the National Lesbian and Gay Journalists Association for a seat at the UNITY table. Leroy Aarons, the NLGJA founder, would recall in 1999 that "UNITY at the time (was) dead-set against 'diluting' the effort for racial equality by absorbing the gay-lesbian equality claim as well, especially when the large majority of gays in the industry are white."[86] In 1995, the NLGJA forged an informal alliance with UNITY, but its role at UNITY conventions generally was limited to sponsoring sessions that focused on the concerns of nonwhite journalists who also were gay or lesbian.[87] A 1998 decision by the coalition to change its name to UNITY Journalists of Color sent an unequivocal message that the organization's collaborative mission was to remain exclusively racial. UNITY would maintain its arm's-length relationship with the NLGJA until 2011, when that organization finally would be allowed to join the coalition.

Despite the ironic exclusion of the NLGJA from UNITY's social justice mission, the first convention in 1994 demonstrated that the race-based professional journalism organizations had achieved critical mass and come of age. Gregory Favre, who succeeded Hilliard as ASNE president, said the UNITY convention's ability to command the attention and attendance of thousands of nonwhite journalists showed how far the newsroom-integration movement had come in thirty years. "When the Kerner report came out [in 1968], you could probably have maybe held it in a telephone booth," Favre said following the 2004 convention. "Today there are thousands of people, journalists, working journalists, who show up and participate in UNITY. So that is progress."[88]

The formation of UNITY and the enormous success of its first convention lit a fuse that would burn for the next four years. In 1998 the ASNE would reconsider the newsroom hiring initiative implemented by ASNE leaders twenty years earlier, recalibrate its hiring goal, and attempt to bring other disaffected journalists under the diversity umbrella. As will be described in chapter 5, the political explosion touched off by these efforts in 1998—the culmination of years of tension over newsroom integration—would alter the dynamics of the newsroom diversity movement. UNITY's leaders would be front and center in those negotiations, wielding the influence represented by the 1994 UNITY convention and effectively vetoing some ASNE proposals.

As the 1998 showdown loomed, diversity advocates within ASNE found themselves managing a variety of constituencies, all of them dissatisfied. Internally, the ASNE diversity program met with apathy from white editors who lacked the resources and inclination to accelerate hiring of nonwhites even as the conversation about diversity was expanding into a vision of multiculturalism. From outside the organization, the ASNE came in for frequent criticism from a now-unified racial constituency at the same time the impracticality of attaining Goal 2000 and the unfairness of its limited focus on race were becoming hard to ignore. As a result, the hallmarks of the hiring initiative in the 1990s would be the tension created by the push for multiculturalism and the divergent backlashes by white and nonwhite journalists. At the end of the decade, competing self-interests would make it difficult to identify anything like unity across the broader newsroom diversity community.

Heading toward the Diversity Waterloo

When Sandra Mims Rowe assumed the ASNE presidency in 1997, exactly ten years had passed since Katherine Fanning became the first woman to lead the organization. In the previous decade, the ASNE had begun elevating more white women and nonwhites of both genders to its leadership ladder; however, the simple fact that Rowe's presidency was notable for her gender was a reminder that she was just the second woman to lead the ASNE. In part, this was a reflection of daily newspapers' failure to promote women at the same rate as white men. ASNE members had to be top editors, so the demographics of ASNE membership and leadership reflected promotion patterns in newsrooms. While this began to change in the 1990s, as the ASNE elected a disproportionate number of women and nonwhite men to its board of directors, Rowe's presidency was for white women the first payoff from that organizational strategy. Over the next ten years, half of the ASNE presidents would represent the organization's multicultural agenda: a white man with a physical disability, a white woman, a black woman, and two Hispanic men.[89]

In 1997, at the beginning of Rowe's term in office, women constituted 17.3 percent of the ASNE's active membership. Ten years earlier, at the beginning of Fanning's term as president, 7.6 percent of active ASNE members were women. Although the ASNE had deliberately sought to increase the number of women members and had succeeded, partly by expanding the membership criteria in the 1970s,[90] women's representation in newsrooms did not increase from one decade to the next. In reporting results of a survey profiling the newsroom workforce, Paul Voakes of Indiana University told a 1997 convention session that gains by women, largely the result of recruitment efforts by chains and individual newspapers, had stagnated. "The rapid rise in women's representation in the newsroom in the 1980s seems to have ground to a halt in the '90s. The percentage of women was 35 percent in 1988 and 37 percent in our survey last fall, which doesn't even beat the margin of error." Voakes suggested that many women did not stay in newsrooms long enough to be promoted. "The number of women decreases as age increases: About half the journalists in newspapers who are under 30 years old are women, but less than a quarter of the journalists over 50 are women," he said.[91]

The data on women in Voakes's study filled a gap in the ASNE information stream on newsroom diversity. Because the annual census quantified journalists according to four categories of race, women were relevant to the newsroom hiring initiative only if they were nonwhite. In addition, exclusion of gender from the annual headcount meant that the ASNE had to rely on outside sources for information, like Voakes, about this particular newsroom cohort. Despite Dorothy Jurney's efforts during the 1980s to emphasize newsroom promotions for women and track the number of women in supervisory positions, the ASNE had not incorporated her agenda into its diversity programming.

Gender also was subordinated to race in the priorities exhibited in ASNE publications and convention sessions. During the 1990s, women as a category—and white women in particular—virtually disappeared from the ASNE's worries about newsroom staffing. While this may have indicated that editors no longer perceived gender inequality as an urgent problem in need of a solution, it more likely was a sign that gender, as a discrete category of identity, had been lost in the shuffle of multiculturalism. Certainly, Rowe's treatment upon assuming the presidency was much more dignified than Fanning's. Whereas the *Bulletin* had featured Fanning in a patronizing and sexist article that stereotyped her as a bad driver, Rowe was introduced to readers of the *American Editor* as a competent, well-respected newsroom leader who time and again had demonstrated her commitment to journalism.[92] Even so, the fact that it had taken ASNE so long to elevate another woman to its presidency is a commentary on the priorities of both the ASNE and the newspaper industry as a whole. Despite the ASNE's relative inattention to women in the previous two decades, gender would emerge as a stated priority of the ASNE in 1998, when women would be added as a category to be counted in the annual newsroom census.

Indeed, Rowe's presidency formed a bridge as the ASNE and its many diversity constituencies moved to an as-yet-undefined point beyond Goal 2000, negotiations that will be analyzed in chapter 5. The failure of the newspaper industry to achieve the national racial parity target had been inevitable for more than a decade, but it was formally acknowledged for the first time at the 1997 convention, at the end of which Rowe assumed the presidency. In his speech on the morning of the convention's first day, outgoing President Robert Giles of the *Detroit News* announced that the 1997 newsroom census had pegged the nonwhite portion of the daily newspaper work force at just

11.35 percent. While he noted that this represented an increase of 259 percent since 1978, he conceded that the end-of-the-century parity goal would not be met. "It represents a hard-won achievement, but one that will leave us well short of our goal in the year 2000," Giles said.[93] A similar message appeared in the annual activity summary of the Diversity Committee, filing its first report after changing its name from the Minorities Committee: "We can see now that the ambitious goal ASNE set for itself nearly 20 years ago—to have the percentage of minorities in the nation's newsrooms reach parity with the national minority population by the year 2000—will not occur, not by a long shot."[94]

The Diversity Committee, chaired by Narda Zacchino of the *Los Angeles Times,* offered three reasons for the ASNE's failure to meet the goal. Its report noted that nonwhites comprised 27 percent of the continually expanding U.S. population, far outstripping the 1997 newsroom census' 11.35 percent. Second, some newspapers still did not have a single nonwhite newsroom employee. And finally, the committee speculated that white backlash had dampened enthusiasm for nonwhite hiring. As it happened, several states were reexamining affirmative action policies and California voters had approved Proposition 209 in 1996, which banned affirmative action in state hiring and education. "In the last year," the committee said, "affirmative action programs have come under attack across the nation, and it may be just a coincidence that for the first time, the total number of minorities has remained unchanged in the ASNE's annual survey."[95] Though the percentage of nonwhites in the 1997 report was up from 11.02 percent a year earlier, the number of nonwhite newsroom employees remained steady at 6,100.

While both Giles and the Diversity Committee emphasized that newsroom diversity would continue to be a centerpiece of ASNE programming, Giles told the 1997 convention that as far as Goal 2000 was concerned, the game was over. He also anticipated the criticism that ASNE would receive for failing to reach its target.

> ASNE's leadership and influence go well beyond the numbers, with our commitment of resources and energy to job fairs and a broad range of other programs that serve the cause of broadening diversity and that show the way for the rest of the news industry.
>
> But at the end of the day, we will be judged, as a Society and as an industry, by the numbers, by the opportunities. Our critics acknowledge our effort and leadership, but they believe the pace of change has been glacial. As one critic observed recently: "If the newspaper industry had been as committed to technology as it is to diversity, we'd still be using manual typewriters."[96]

Although it had been apparent for many years that the census numbers would not match the parity goal, the rhetoric of ASNE leaders had always insisted that the target was still within reach—if editors just worked harder to diversify their newsrooms. While many editors did do their part, many more did not. Along the way, the myth that Goal 2000 was attainable had fueled public perceptions of the newsroom hiring initiative and, within the organization, had served as the justification for the continual exhortation for editors to diversify their newsrooms. Wanda Lloyd, the ASNE director who had edited the NABJ's "Muted Voices" report, said even though the disparity between the census numbers and the parity target had been obvious, Giles's acknowledgment of the futility of Goal 2000 was a profound moment in the newsroom hiring initiative's history. "It was an admission of defeat . . . ," Lloyd said. "Well, you know, we're all pretty smart people, so we can count. We knew we weren't going to get there. But . . . for ASNE, it was a bold statement for Bob to stand before the body and say it's not going to happen."[97]

While a truth, even an obvious one, can still have the power to shock, Giles's assessment followed the findings, published a year earlier, of the Joan Shorenstein Center for Press, Politics and Public Policy at Harvard University. In a study funded by the Ford Foundation, researchers noted that underrepresentation of nonwhites in the elite stratum of society, where the press resided, was partly to blame for the failure of the newspaper industry to integrate its newsrooms. Consequently, researchers found that professional qualifications for newsroom jobs, specifically the college or postgraduate degree, were an impediment to the proportional hiring of nonwhite journalists.[98] In addition, they noted, the claim that nonwhite journalists would contribute to more complete reporting of the news had not been reconciled with journalism's tradition of objectivity, in which truth is supposedly nonnegotiable. And finally, the report cited as obstacles to newsroom diversity wide skepticism about affirmative action, a shortage of nonwhite students in college journalism programs, and the failure of readers and advertisers to pressure those who make hiring decisions.[99]

While the Shorenstein report addressed both the print and broadcast press and did not single out the ASNE in offering its critique, the ASNE, as the spearhead of the newsroom-integration effort, was clearly on researchers' minds as they explained the press's failure to hire and promote nonwhites in sufficient number. "There has been little direct confrontation with many of the existing obstacles to such progress," researchers concluded, noting that "many of the advocates for increased racial and ethnic diversity in the American press have acted as if the soundness of the idea of increased racial and ethnic diversity were a sufficient condition for its widespread acceptance and adoption."[100] Indeed, in 1978, ASNE board members, so convinced of the moral rectitude of their mission, had expected the newspaper industry to achieve the newsroom parity goal well before the year 2000. That the initiative might not succeed was then unthinkable.

Now, twenty years later, the failure of good intention would place another group of ASNE directors directly in the line of fire but would offer them a chance for redemption. The ASNE would have the opportunity to set a realistic and achievable goal, given the patterns of newsroom hiring and population growth, or reaffirm the existing model and the industry's status quo. In the end, old habits would prove hard to resist.

5

Diversity in Crisis

ASNE's Time of Reckoning, 1998–2002

Of the white editors who championed newsroom integration in the hiring initiative's first decade, none could match Loren Ghiglione, a small-town editor from Southbridge, Massachusetts, for intensity of passion and devotion to the cause. Having spent Freedom Summer 1964 teaching in Mississippi, Ghiglione brought a commitment to civil rights when he joined the ASNE. Accordingly, Ghiglione threw himself into the Goal 2000 project as chair of the Minorities Committee from 1984 to 1986 and architect of many of the job fair and outreach efforts during the 1980s. In ASNE discussions about nonwhite hiring, Ghiglione's was often the most insistent voice in the room.[1] As ASNE president in 1988–89, Ghiglione took his evangelism on the road, visiting some fifty newspapers across the country, to go eyeball to eyeball with editors who were not hiring nonwhite journalists in sufficient number—or at all—and to encourage those who were making an effort. Among the already converted who received a visit from Ghiglione was Edward Seaton at the *Manhattan Mercury* in Kansas.[2] Though neither man knew it at the time, that conversation about newsroom integration would be followed by many others a decade later.

As Seaton prepared to become the 1998–99 ASNE president, the most pressing matter the ASNE confronted was the future of Goal 2000. After Robert Giles, the 1996–97 president, declared the end-of-the-century parity target out of reach, Seaton began strategizing to prepare the membership for the difficult task ahead. Given their long professional acquaintance, it is hardly surprising that Seaton chose Ghiglione, by then the journalism director at Emory University, to open the next phase of the ASNE's diversity conversation. Looming over Seaton's term as president, even though it was a year away, were the questions of whether the hiring goal and annual newsroom headcount should be continued at all and, if so, whether a goal other than national parity should be crafted. In addition, the ASNE during Seaton's term would have to decide who, exactly, should be covered by any post-2000 hiring initiative and census. Answering that question would require examination and even redefinition of the concept of newsroom diversity and a discussion of whether the ASNE's exclusive focus on race was realistic and equitable. Following the multicultural thrust of the 1990s, some in the ASNE recognized that white women, nonheterosexuals, and disabled persons, who were now protected by the 1990 Americans with Disabilities Act, had been stranded on the periphery of the ASNE's newsroom diversity project and were not fully franchised members of the journalistic community. With Ghiglione as his front man, Seaton forged ahead.[3]

Nearly a year before Seaton assumed the presidency, Ghiglione, writing in the *American Editor,* noted that in the 1997 newsroom census, nonwhites accounted for a little more than 11 percent of the workforce in daily newspaper newsrooms, compared to 25 percent of the national population. While such comparisons had been made annually, the actual distance between goal and reality, as well as the magnitude of the failure, was now sharply evident as Ghiglione requested input from editors and members of the broader diversity community on whether the hiring initiative should have a future.[4] A few months later, Ghiglione reported on the flood of early responses, the complexity of which hinted at just how difficult the conversation would become. Some respondents wanted to do away with the numerical target for newsroom diversity, while some said abandoning it would signal defeat. Others said the focus should be on parity with the college-educated population rather than the total national population, and still others said the percentage in the goal should be tied to diversity in the local community.[5] Thus it was clear at the outset that many people with strong opinions were personally and professionally invested in the outcome—and that consensus would be elusive.

At the same time, another practical reality was coming into focus: the ASNE no longer owned the newsroom diversity issue, even though the organization was the official steward of the industry's hiring initiative. Political power within the diversity community had shifted in important ways over the previous two decades. The parties to the initial newsroom integration conversations of the 1970s had been a small contingent of progressive, white ASNE leaders, many of them Southerners on a mission for redemption, and a handful of African

American journalists who developed much of the strategy but, as ASNE outsiders, had no official standing in the negotiations. In short, when the Goal 2000 hiring initiative was formulated in 1978, the ASNE board, under Eugene Patterson's leadership, called the shots. Twenty years later, however, the discussion was dominated by an array of identity-based professional groups, the UNITY coalition, and outside diversity experts. ASNE, despite being widely assumed to have ultimate responsibility for the outcome of Goal 2000, now was just one of the factions seated around the table.

That nonwhites and other marginalized groups no longer were entirely subordinate to ASNE and white voices no longer controlled the conversation were clear signs of racial progress. At the same time, however, the ASNE's diminished stake in the diversity conversation—obvious for years as nonmembers routinely outnumbered editors in meetings of the ASNE Minorities Committee and later the Diversity Committee[6]—meant that any policy decision on the future of the hiring initiative would be shaped by pressure from outside constituencies as much as—or more than—by the ASNE's institutional will. In 1998, at the conclusion of Seaton and Ghiglione's inquiry, the ASNE board would acquiesce to a consensus reached not among the editors doing the hiring in their newsrooms but by a few ASNE representatives and the most vigorous advocates in the broader diversity community. As such, the logic undergirding the reformulated newsroom hiring initiative would be political rather than practical, with a goal of appeasement rather than development of an achievable, post-2000 program. Because the contours of a new diversity project would be dictated from without, many ASNE members would not embrace it anymore enthusiastically than their predecessors had in the 1970s and 1980s, when the hiring initiative was driven from the top by a succession of progressive ASNE leaders rather than imbricated into the organizational culture.

As it happened, Ghiglione, more than any other ASNE leader, was responsible for raising the profile of the nonwhite journalist organizations within the ASNE and giving them direct input into ASNE diversity programming. As Minorities Committee chair in 1986, Ghiglione established a category for adjunct members of the committee, which created an avenue for direct participation by representatives of the nonwhite journalist organizations.[7] Then, during his presidency in 1989, Ghiglione invited those organizations to make reports to the ASNE board of directors.[8] A decade later, however, Ghiglione's doctrine of direct participation, and the inclusive effort toward social justice it envisioned, produced an altogether different result. Before Ghiglione could compile the recommendations he would present to the

ASNE board at the convention in April 1998, chaos created by the fragmentation of power within the diversity movement would expose the structural weaknesses that had doomed the Goal 2000 program from the beginning. As a result, the year leading up to the ASNE board's October 1998 vote on the future of the initiative would cap the organization's most contentious episode in at least sixty years.[9]

In addition, the ground had shifted beneath the ASNE as American attitudes toward race and diversity had made an important transition. In the coming 2000 U.S. census, Americans for the first time would be given the option to designate a multiracial identity, the logical consequence of decades of intermarriage.[10] In short, America had become what Michael Lind described as "transracial,"[11] and the ASNE's four-race rubric for quantifying newsroom integration was officially irrelevant and anachronistic. For those clinging to the traditional affirmative action philosophy, the challenge of measuring diversity, which also encompassed sexual orientation, religion, disability, and other identities, was now far more complicated than it had been when Goal 2000's architects sought a straightforward solution to the legacy of Jim Crow. As the turn of the century loomed, America's expanding diversity could no longer be shoehorned into the annual newsroom employment survey.

Taking Sides and Battling for Turf

To gather input into the decision about the future of the ASNE's newsroom employment project, the Diversity Committee, under chair Rick Rodriguez of the *Sacramento Bee,* organized a two-day Diversity Dialogue. Held January 30 and 31, 1998, at the Pacific Coast Center of the Freedom Forum, a nonprofit journalism organization that had sponsored and funded diversity projects, the Diversity Dialogue was attended by seventy-eight ASNE members and representatives of organizations with an interest in the diversity goal. The participants were, in the words of UNITY President Paul DeMain, "the most powerful and influential champions of diversity in the newspaper business."[12] The workshop, which Rodriguez would recall as a "semi-brutal meeting," was dominated by heated discussion about the future of the diversity initiative.[13] "Yes, it was, at times, a very contentious meeting," Rodriguez wrote in his 1998 committee report. "At times, the tone was tough, accusatory and critical."[14]

The ASNE, as the founder and steward of the newsroom integration program, received the brunt of nonwhite journalists' anger over lingering inequity in newsroom hiring and promotion.[15] Although ASNE leaders had noted frequently in recent years that the organization wielded no control over newspapers' performance in the census, the ASNE had for two decades been synonymous in daily newspaper newsrooms with the nonwhite hiring effort and its influence was assumed. "The industry can't mandate, but we know the power of peer pressure," said Felix Gutierrez of the Freedom Forum, who moderated the Diversity Dialogue.[16] Among leaders of the nonwhite journalist organizations who were critical of the ASNE's stewardship of the diversity effort was Vanessa Williams, president of the National Association of Black Journalists. "ASNE needs to be more visible and show more leadership," Williams said at the meeting. "It seems like people of color are fighting on their own."[17] Walterene Swanston, one of UNITY's early leaders, concurred. "We came out of that meeting with a sense that ASNE had just given up and had not done enough to make it happen, and they weren't serious about it. It was pretty widely believed at that point ASNE had never intended to meet that goal and certainly not done everything it could."[18]

For the ASNE members at the Diversity Dialogue, who were among the organization's diversity champions, the stinging criticism of their individual and institutional efforts came as a surprise.[19] It became clear during the workshop, Rodriguez wrote, that many in the room believed "ASNE has more clout than it does over an individual newspaper or group of newspapers. While that may not be the reality, it remains the perception."[20] Sharon Rosenhause of the *San Francisco Examiner*, who helped organize the Diversity Dialogue, said this expectation was unrealistic. "Nobody could force me as an editor in my newsroom to do what I didn't want to do," she said, noting that the ASNE was nothing more than a nagging conscience. "You weren't going to kick a newspaper out of ASNE because, say, they wouldn't participate in the census or because their numbers were atrocious."[21]

From the discussion in San Francisco came a strong recommendation that the ASNE continue the hiring initiative based on a race-based national parity target, after little support emerged for a goal tied instead to parity with local nonwhite demographics. Among those who questioned the practicality of a national parity target was Edward Seaton, one of the ASNE officers at the meeting. In assessing the reasons the original Goal 2000 had failed, Seaton wrote that it was "asking both too much or too little. In Manhattan, Kan., my town, our minority population is just over 10 percent. To achieve parity with the 26 percent national level seems unrealistic. Attracting and retaining minority recruits, who mostly come from urban centers, to central Kansas—even to a university city like ours—is challenging. Meanwhile, if major newspapers in urban centers set the 26 percent national average as their goal, that's only half or less of the minority population in their communities."[22]

Echoing the 1996 Shorenstein Center report, Seaton also worried that any national parity target would be destined to fail if the goal were defined as parity with the population at large rather than the percentage of the population that held a college degree. "Newspaper newsrooms hire college graduates and the demographic makeup of the society is not of college graduates," Seaton said. "And so to set a goal that says that our newsrooms are going to reflect the society as a whole, when in fact we can only hire college graduates, or basically only hire college graduates, it's just an unrealistic aspiration. It's something that is not going to happen."[23] Although Seaton and some other ASNE leaders considered a national parity target impractical, many in the diversity community, inside and outside of ASNE, believed it the only righteous—and politically feasible—path to take. As a result, the message sent back to the ASNE board from the workshop was that anything less than a reendorsement of the national parity model would be viewed by the diversity community as an abdication of commitment to the cause.

A second, even more heated disagreement emerged at the Diversity Dialogue workshop: whether to expand the ASNE hiring initiative to improve employment numbers for journalists who differed from the professional norm by distinctions other than race. "The question of what the definition of diversity ought to be generated the most discussion," Rick Rodriguez reported.[24] Among those who favored a broadly inclusive definition of diversity—encompassing not just race but gender, sexual orientation, and such distinctions as disability and ideology—was Loren Ghiglione. "I don't see diversity as a zero-sum game. . . . I think we can fight on several fronts at once," he said.[25] Since 1978, the annual newsroom census had counted only those journalists who could be assigned to four categories of nonwhite identity: black, Hispanic, Native American, and Asian American. ASNE programming in support of Goal 2000 also had focused only on the hiring and promotion of journalists in these nonwhite categories. Expanding the definition of diversity was the logical outcome of the ASNE's multicultural turn in the early 1990s, yet resistance from UNITY and its member organizations ultimately would lead the ASNE to reprivilege race in the diversity paradigm.

The suggestion to include women generated some opposition during the Diversity Dialogue as well as in the months that followed. While the omission of white women from the Goal 2000 project had received attention in the early 1980s, when retired editor Dorothy Jurney had begun an annual census of her own by counting female names in the *Editor & Publisher Directory,* Jurney's concern had been limited to the promotion of women into newsroom management. Now, with the parity target back on the drawing board, the question of formally incorporating gender into the initiative and tracking women's total newsroom employment in the annual census became part of the conversation. In addition, the founding of the National Lesbian and Gay Journalists Association had raised the profile of nonheterosexuals within the profession of journalism. Although Ghiglione and others were willing to consider a reformulation of the diversity project that would benefit other marginalized journalists, such as people with disabilities and political conservatives, the disagreement ultimately focused solely on gender and sexual orientation.

Many UNITY representatives and their allies, dismayed by the relative lack of progress toward the racial targets in Goal 2000, believed strongly that a diversity initiative that sought to right too many wrongs would be ineffective in increasing the numbers of nonwhites working in newspaper newsrooms. "We need to stick to the plan we haven't met yet," said James Clark of the *Orlando Sentinel.*[26] Vanessa Williams, the NABJ president, agreed, saying, "Racism is the country's most pressing issue, and we want to remain focused on ethnicity."[27] Such sentiments were shared by Walterene Swanston, the early UNITY executive. "While Unity appreciates and realizes the importance of diversity of all kinds, ASNE should continue to focus on race and ethnicity," she wrote to Ghiglione.[28]

Nonwhites who attended the Diversity Dialogue were by no means monolithic on this issue, however. Among those who believed the definition of diversity should have been expanded was Stephen Montiel, president of the Maynard Institute for Journalism Education, who argued that diversity should not be defined only by race but should encompass the "wholeness of society."[29] Also expressing a dissenting view was Keith Woods of the Poynter Institute, a media research and training center. "What I remember most," Woods said, noting that representatives of the NLGJA were sitting near him at the Diversity Dialogue, "was the assertion by several people . . . who essentially used language that sounded like 'it isn't the right time, it will dilute our efforts,' two notions that at the time—and I said it out loud then—struck me as reminiscent of the suffrage movement and the civil rights movement—'not now' and 'it will dilute our efforts,' the sort of have-some-patience-and-wait-your-turn idea, which I found offensive, and I said so."[30]

Despite his belief that an exclusionary diversity program raised ethical concerns, Woods said he understood the fear in which that position was grounded. Woods recalled that tension permeated the room as participants in the Diversity Dialogue came to terms with the industry's poor performance on the original Goal 2000 census and acknowledged that parity might never be achieved. When the conversation turned to expanding the scope of the revised initiative, some nonwhites assumed it would come at their expense. Woods noted that many members of NABJ, founded in 1975, saw newsroom employment as "one pie differently divided" and believed they had been giving up hires, promotions, and finite diversity resources since the 1980s, when the other three nonwhite journalist organizations came on the scene. "So I think that if you're black, . . . a journalist from NABJ, and you join arms with NAHJ [National Association of Hispanic Journalists], then you recognize that the person who is choosing to hire will now not choose a black person and a Latino, but one or the other and that your chances of being the one chosen now have been cut in half. I think that's a rational fear, but in the end an immoral position."[31] Ultimately, however, Woods's appeal for Diversity Dialogue participants to join him on the multicultural high road failed to carry the day.

Reinventing Diversity

After attending the Diversity Dialogue and collaborating with others interested in the future of the ASNE hiring project, Loren Ghiglione drafted a twenty-six-page report, complete with recommendations for where the ASNE should take the initiative next, and presented it to the ASNE board at its April 1998 meeting. Two of his twelve recommendations, arguably the most politically charged, diverged sharply from the key positions taken by many participants in the Diversity Dialogue two months earlier. In one, Ghiglione suggested that ASNE discontinue a hiring goal based only on national parity. Although he quoted Walterene Swanston of UNITY as saying "a numerical goal is the only way to measure progress or lack of progress,"[32] Ghiglione recommended that the ASNE localize the goal by 2000. "It makes little sense," Ghiglione wrote, "to hold the Los Angeles Times to the same newsroom diversity goal as, say, The Caledonia-Record in virtually all-white St. Johnsbury, Vermont. The Caledonia-Record might be applauded for achieving a newsroom diversity equivalent to the nation's diversity (roughly 26 percent). But should the Los Angeles Times—which describes its community as '53 percent minority' as of 1990—be cheered for attaining a workforce diversity half its community's diversity?"[33] This recommendation contradicted the assertion by several attendees at the Diversity Dialogue that a local parity target, which they saw as holding small-town editors to a lower standard, would weaken the effort.[34]

The second recommendation in Ghiglione's report that seemed certain to draw a strong reaction was to "broaden the definition of diversity and think inclusiveness." While Ghiglione noted that diversity was complex and included class and political ideology as well as race, gender, and sexual orientation, he made his strongest pitch for adding sexual orientation to the ASNE diversity project. In doing so, Ghiglione spoke directly to those at the Diversity Dialogue and in other forums who had insisted that the ASNE maintain an exclusive focus on the four categories of race. "While not denying the primacy of race," Ghiglione wrote, "I would hazard a guess that discrimination based on sexual orientation is just as virulent—and almost as violent—as racism in America." An acknowledgment of hate crimes against gay people, this argument would seem more salient later that year, following the brutal and highly publicized murder of Matthew Shepherd, a gay student at the University of Wyoming. Ghiglione urged nonwhite journalists and their allies to avoid seeing efforts on behalf of other excluded groups as coming at the expense of nonwhites. "The point is not to argue over who qualifies as the greatest victim of discrimination but to recognize the complexity of the fight for inclusiveness and to avoid playing a zero-sum game. Viewing diversity as a zero-sum game presumes that to address discrimination against gays and lesbians is necessarily to diminish the effort to address discrimination against people of color. That's ironic, of course, because people of color, like white people, are gays and lesbians."[35]

During the annual convention in April 1998, the ASNE board met at length to consider Ghiglione's report, input from the Diversity Dialogue, and information gathered by members of the board and Diversity Committee. At the end of its deliberations, the board voted to circulate a draft Statement on Newsroom Diversity, which would tie an expanded definition of diversity to the mission of newspaper journalism and set a new, shorter-range employment target that would define progress over just one decade (see appendix A). "Newsroom diversity is essential to the newspaper's responsibility in a democratic society and success in the marketplace," the draft statement said. "To accurately and sensitively cover the community, newsroom staffs must reflect society as a whole. The newsroom should be a place in which all employees contribute their full potential, regardless of their race, ethnicity, color, age, gender, sexual orientation, physical disability or other defining characteristic."[36]

The draft statement also proposed diversity as a core value of journalism, an important philosophical move for diversity programming. That the ASNE had not clearly and from the beginning of the Goal 2000 effort framed newsroom integration as a journalistic value had reduced its priority, even as ASNE leaders had exhorted members to hire nonwhites.[37] Identifying newsroom integration as an ASNE core value would not have changed the institutional culture, but the failure to do so in 1978 had created a rhetorical disconnect between the ASNE leadership's support for diversity and the organization's policy. As long as diversity lay outside the official sphere of journalistic principle, ASNE leaders left editors an excuse for not hiring nonwhite journalists.

Not only did the language of the draft statement, in its references to broader diversity, depart from the exclusively race-focused vision of 1978 and encompass more journalists, but the proposal itself retreated from national parity. In a bulleted list of objectives, the draft suggested the ASNE "encourage and assist all newspapers to have minority journalists representation, to increase representation of journalists of color to reach 20 percent industrywide by 2010, and to achieve parity with local communities as soon as possible" [*sic*].[38] Although the proposed national target extended just ten years past the end of Goal 2000, that objective would have been easier to achieve than national parity, which soon would entail nonwhite newsroom employment of 30 percent and more. "There was very strong feeling on the board that, if we were to give new energy to the effort, the goal had to be realistic and achievable," Edward Seaton wrote.[39]

Following the board's meeting at the April 1998 convention, the proposed Statement on Newsroom Diversity was circulated widely in hopes of building a consensus before facing final approval at the next board meeting in six months. However, many in the diversity community feared they would lose ground with a lower target of just 20 percent and the shortened time frame of 2010. While the Diversity Dialogue in San Francisco had been testy enough, the tension level there was nothing compared to the response the ASNE received two months later when it released the draft diversity statement. The purpose of the multicultural language, which was not clearly tied to a programmatic objective, was vague enough that the extent of ASNE's support of gay and lesbian journalists was unclear. Would ASNE be sponsoring job fairs and other outreach efforts for gay and lesbian journalists, just as it did for nonwhite journalists?[40] In other words, would nonwhite journalists be competing for diversity resources against those who were not straight, a category generalized by many in the UNITY coalition as representing white journalists? Similarly, the combination of national and local parity goals sent a mixed message and tapped into fears within the diversity community that a local parity goal would hold some editors to a lower standard.

Seaton, whose term as president started after the 1998 convention, characterized the diversity community's response to the draft as a "firestorm," ignited in part by misleading published reports, including a story in the trade magazine *Editor & Publisher,* suggesting that the proposed Statement on Newsroom Diversity represented a final action by the ASNE board.[41] In an article titled "ASNE Pulls Back from Diversity Goal," *Editor & Publisher* reported, "Even as it affirmed a commitment to newsroom ethnic diversity at its 75th annual convention, the American Society of Newspaper Editors announced it is scaling back its goal and deadline for parity." Although the story then characterized the ASNE document as a draft, the damage was done. The story also quoted NABJ President Vanessa Williams criticizing the ASNE's presumed action. "Certainly, we're disappointed but I can't say we're surprised," Williams said of the draft. "The industry has not just lost interest in diversity, but there seems to be outright hostility. . . . They treat it as a problem that has to be dealt with rather than as an opportunity for more readers and better journalism."[42]

Editor & Publisher's misleading report about the draft created deep confusion and exposed the lingering tension between ASNE leaders and representatives of the UNITY coalition. In addition, suspicions about the sincerity of the ASNE's commitment to hiring and promoting nonwhites likely were inflamed by the 1998 convention itself. For one thing, even though Goal 2000's future had dominated ASNE business during the previous year, convention planners did not include a session on the revised diversity goal or the challenge of developing a diversity initiative for the twenty-first century. Such a discussion would have given ASNE leaders an opportunity to review the draft with members and other constituencies and might have averted misunderstanding. More significant, however, was a slight that reverberated through the nonwhite professional community in journalism. At the same annual meeting at which the ASNE board endorsed the 2010 target, many members insulted renowned African American historian John Hope Franklin, who had chaired the Clinton Administration's Initiative on Race, by leaving the room when his contribution to the program was announced. Word of Franklin's inhospitable treatment, which was condemned by such ASNE board members as Rick Rodriguez,[43] circulated within the UNITY coalition. Greg Moore of the *Denver Post* said audience reaction to Franklin may have reflected editors' ignorance of African American history. "I think quite a few people didn't know who . . . John Hope Franklin was, quite frankly. They just thought he was some old black guy," Moore said.[44] Franklin's experience before the ASNE was profound enough that he was still recounting it years later and recalled the incident in his memoir.[45] "They stayed away in droves," Franklin told a Fisk University audience in 2005.[46]

In the months leading up to the October 1998 board meeting, Seaton made presentations at the conventions for three of the four nonwhite journalist organizations and Gilbert Bailon, then the Diversity Committee chair, appeared on an NLGJA convention panel about the draft diversity statement. As they sought to explain the ASNE's vision, criticism of its stewardship of Goal 2000 persisted. "I wonder what a newspaper would do with a manager who had a work goal set—and after 20 years he still hadn't achieved it," Juan Gonzales of the *New York Daily News* said at the National Association of Hispanic Journalists meeting.[47] Joe Boyce of the *Wall Street Journal* dismissed the idea that ASNE had no control over members' hiring decisions. "The fact is that ASNE and the 'newspaper industry' are the same; that is, the top editors who make up ASNE are the same ones making the critical decisions on hiring and promotion that result in the unsatisfactory diversity figures," Boyce said. "What is involved here is a matter of will, not know-how."[48] As Seaton himself noted in a message to ASNE members, the broadcast industry already had achieved 20 percent nonwhite employment, compared to the ASNE's 11.5 percent at that point. Moreover, the newspaper industry was losing ground each year: nonwhite employment on newspaper news staffs had risen just 1.21 percent in five years, at a time when the national nonwhite population was expanding 0.5 percent annually.[49]

Faced with irreconcilable math and unrelenting criticism, the Diversity Committee met in August in Chicago, along with five ASNE board members and representatives of nonwhite journalist organizations, to negotiate a final draft of the Statement on Newsroom Diversity. Input from this meeting figured prominently into the ASNE board's discussions at its midyear meeting October 31 in Miami. Months of criticism clearly had made an impression on the ASNE directors. After lengthy discussion, the board approved a mission statement for newsroom diversity that differed in significant ways from the draft it had endorsed at the April meeting (see appendix B). This time, the statement addressed most of the concerns of the nonwhite journalist organizations.[50] In addition, the Journalism & Women Symposium had lobbied the ASNE board members to encourage them to add women to the annual newsroom census.[51]

In the final version approved by the board in October, a two-paragraph newsroom diversity mission statement was embedded in the middle of a longer document. The diversity mission statement, which adopted the inclusive language from the previous draft, offered a broad definition of diversity but maintained the original initiative's narrow focus on race.

> To cover communities fully, to carry out their role in a democracy, and to succeed in the marketplace, the nation's newsrooms must reflect the racial diversity of American society by 2025 or sooner. At a minimum, all newspapers

> should employ journalists of color and every newspaper should reflect the diversity of its community.
>
> The newsroom must be a place in which all employees contribute their full potential, regardless of race, ethnicity, color, age, gender, sexual orientation, physical ability or other defining characteristic.[52]

Moreover, the board kept both national and local parity goals. In the final version, the board, following the consensus reached by the Diversity Committee, also moved the national parity target fifteen years further down the timeline than the 20-percent-by-2010 target proposed in the April draft. In approving an unattainable 2025 target, the ASNE board gave up on the idea of setting a realistic hiring goal and, in essence, agreed to pursue diversity as an ideal rather than a concrete and achievable condition. In that sense, the new initiative replicated the one it replaced.

Noticeably absent from the new preamble was the inclusive definition of diversity and the conviction that "newsroom staffs must reflect society as a whole," which opened the April draft. While the inclusive list of marginalized identities was now part of the mission statement itself, that language did not appear until the fourth paragraph of the restructured document approved by the board. The statement called for continuation of the annual census to quantify newsroom employees according to the four categories of race and, for the first time, gender. Additional language within the final draft indicated an intention to "expand ASNE efforts to foster newsroom diversity." New to the statement was the goal of establishing three-year benchmarks to assess the progress of the diversity effort.

1998's Aftermath

An uneven commitment across the ASNE membership had dogged the hiring initiative from its inception in 1978, but as time passed, resistance to the objectives of the project rarely invited insinuations of overt racism as they had in the early days. Instead, ASNE diversity advocates had come to accept that a good many editors, particularly those in regions of the country with low nonwhite populations, did not view the diversity initiative as particularly relevant to their newspapers. Many of these editors represented the 42 percent of daily newspapers that still had no nonwhite employees in 1998,[53] as well as another tier of papers that had—and probably always would have—just a few. In many of those smaller markets, editors believed beating the drum for newsroom diversity would not impress readers or advertisers or attract enough nonwhite employees to make a difference in the annual census. Moreover, many remained unpersuaded that the demographic shift altering the urban marketplace would ever reach them.[54] Although his newspaper in Manhattan, Kansas, made a respectable showing in the newsroom census each year, Seaton understood, even if he disagreed with, the mindset of many editors at community newspapers like his own.

As a result, when he took leadership of ASNE's 1998 work on diversity, Seaton had hoped a deliberative and collaborative approach, one that allowed a broader cross-section of members to mix practical considerations with idealism, would result in a more realistic goal and a commitment by more editors than simply the ASNE board and the relatively small group of diversity faithful among the membership.[55] It was a tall order at a time when the newspaper industry was teetering precariously on the edge of a financial decline that would see employment in daily newspaper newsrooms shrink by more than 11 percent over the next decade, at the same time that the paid circulation of the daily and Sunday editions of newspapers would drop by 18 percent nationally.[56]

Economically, the worst was yet to come, but by 1998 editors already felt competitive pressure from the Internet, frustration in seeking a formula for making money off their own online sites, and, in many cases, heat from stockholders who demanded their share of declining newspaper profits. If some editors already saw newsroom diversity as a misplaced priority, they soon would have more company. In 1998, the newspaper industry was about to enter a fight for its life, during which most American newspaper editors would feel they had no choice but to divert their attention from diversity in their newsrooms. Keith Woods of the Poynter Institute said the link between newspaper profitability and the commitment to diversity became clear as newspapers' fortunes declined in the new hiring goal's first decade. "When the economy as a whole took the hit that it did and journalism, especially newspapers, started taking the financial hits that they have, diversity has suffered disproportionately because it was always so tenuous to begin with," Woods said. "And that's not just in funding, that's in practice and in thinking and in activism as well."[57]

In addition, many editors recognized that the backlash against affirmative action, so prominent in the early 1990s, remained entrenched in their newsrooms. Some white journalists continued to perceive nonwhite hires and promotions as coming at their expense, and anecdotes circulated within the industry of newsroom managers telling white journalists that they had not received jobs or promotions because of mandates to increase newsroom diversity. Hiring targets, wrote Vanessa Williams, NABJ's president, were "seen as a burden that must be borne to comply with corporate edicts or to mollify belligerent interest groups." As a result of weak commitment from the top, she argued, the new ASNE diversity target was introduced into a newsroom culture where "many white journalists feel emboldened to openly criticize such efforts without feeling disloyal to their companies or intellectually dishonest with themselves." Even twenty years after the initiation of Goal 2000, many white journalists still believed that nonwhites were less qualified to be working in the profession than they and, Williams lamented, were not keeping these sentiments to themselves. "The mere announcement of a new diversity initiative is enough to send the newsroom into a tailspin," she said.[58]

Charlotte Hall of *Newsday,* a Diversity Committee member during the discussions in 1998, saw the formal emphasis on diversity as a journalistic value, which now was part of the ASNE's diversity mission statement, as an important step toward eliminating ambiguity in editors' commitment to nonwhite hiring and white journalists' resistance to it. "When the goal finally got restated, it was not simply . . . a diversity and staffing goal, but it was a goal that united that concept with the concept of the journalistic imperative," she said. "And the journalistic imperative is really simple to state. It's that you can't do accurate and fair and full journalism unless the communities—all the communities—that make up your larger community, are represented in your paper. And in order to do that, you need a great diversity of voices in your newsroom." Hall, who would become the ASNE's 2008–9 president, said framing newsroom diversity as necessary to sound journalism "became more compelling to people."[59]

But many editors were unmoved. Twenty years after the ASNE first committed itself to newsroom integration, some editors, even those who embraced racial diversity generally, remained unpersuaded that journalism professionals should be engaged in the activism entailed in righting societal wrongs. For editors in this camp, the ASNE's new diversity mission statement, which linked newsroom diversity to "full and accurate news coverage," appeared to contradict their belief in objectivity as an ethical standard. "To advocate diversity as a journalistic 'core value' implies that journalism's mission should be social change as opposed to disinterested news coverage," wrote retired editor Claude Sitton. Sitton, who had gained national prominence while reporting on the civil rights movement for the *New York Times,* continued, "Social change is certainly a legitimate goal for editorial pages but the board would be wrong to urge social change as a goal of reporting, although that may be the result."[60]

For pragmatists in the ASNE, the new goal was another lost cause. Based on 1998 projections, which did not anticipate job losses linked to declining profitability during the following decade, newsrooms would have had to increase nonwhite employment by 1 percent each year—a level not seen in any year since the hiring initiative began in 1978—to reach the goal. In addition, the workforce in daily newspaper newsrooms would have had to increase by 14,850.[61] Reconciling these numbers had not been the priority, Edward Seaton said. "The minority organizations, particularly NABJ but the others as well . . . said a realistic goal . . . isn't going to get the job done, and what we needed was just an aspiration, an aspirational goal. . . . And partly because of the pressure that they brought and what . . . I described as a firestorm that had to be dealt with, we decided to set an aspirational goal." In the years following the recalibration of the hiring target, however, Seaton second-guessed his decision to lead the board in that direction. "If I had this to do over again, I would not have gone this route, I think, but under those circumstances, it was the politically wise thing to do," he said, but added, "There's no question that this goal will never be met."[62]

The editors who launched the hiring initiative in 1978 primarily as a remedy for historical racism against African Americans did not know that immigration would lift the U.S. nonwhite population to near 30 percent by the end of the century and that ASNE's annual census would measure newsroom hiring against a rapidly growing segment of the population that included a high proportion of children and people without college educations. "I think the 1978 goal was not well thought-out and, but once we had that, we had, well, found it virtually impossible to . . . set a realistic goal," Seaton said. Moreover, the membership was alienated by "getting beat over the head all the time in an area that they can't . . . realistically achieve," he said.[63] Even so, the national parity target remained an ASNE article of faith. Richard Oppel of the *Austin American-Statesman,* ASNE's 2000–2001 president, suggested that under the new initiative, good intention mattered, even if results were elusive. "I will retire before our industry achieves the goal," he said. "It will not surprise me if my son and daughter retire before the goal is met. But the effort must go on in every newsroom."[64]

Doomed to Failure

The certainty of the new initiative's failure also dampened the enthusiasm of many of the funders that had underwritten the ASNE's ongoing diversity effort. Seaton, who also had chaired the ASNE Foundation, which assumed responsibility for diversity funding, said outside foundations, news corporations, and other traditional supporters of the diversity initiative did not want to be associated with failure.[65] In the years after the ASNE committed to the new target of national parity by 2025, it was still possible to locate funding for new initiatives, but it quickly became difficult to secure support for the ASNE's ongoing expenses for diversity programming. By 2002, when Diane McFarlin of the *Sarasota Herald-Tribune* became president, the external funding situation had become dire.

While the economic slump following the September 11, 2001, terrorist attacks undoubtedly played a role, diversity clearly had lost its allure. Directors of the ASNE Foundation, which obtained diversity funding from external sources, learned in April 2002, just two years into work toward the new 2025 hiring target, that "diversity funding has run out" and it was now necessary to find new sources of support to cover the foundation's $170,000 annual contribution to the ASNE's diversity programming.[66] "As we appealed to potential funders, we were turned down again and again," McFarlin wrote, noting that organizations that had supported the ASNE's diversity initiative in the past no longer were funding continuing efforts but favored new initiatives. "We were being told, in polite code, that our programs had become too institutionalized and routine," she said. "We certainly weren't well armed to debate the point. Year after year, our annual newsroom census reflected glacial movement toward ASNE's goal of parity with the communities we serve."[67] Despite efforts to reformulate and rejuvenate diversity programming to make it more effective and attractive to funders, the ASNE's diversity effort was bankrupt. Although the foundation board agreed to cover a $113,000 deficit in the diversity budget in 2003–4, directors also turned off the tap by resolving to limit spending from their restricted funds to $50,000 in 2005–6.[68]

In the short term, until it became clear that diversity-as-usual was economically doomed, the UNITY coalition had emerged from the 1998 goal renegotiation process the apparent winner. At no point in the future would any media company or professional association doubt the collective muscle of the nonwhite journalist organizations or dismiss the concerns of nonwhite journalists as peripheral. Significantly, the relationship between the ASNE and the UNITY coalition actually seemed to improve immediately following the contentious goal renegotiations. In the years that followed, the ASNE recommitted to diversity programming through such initiatives as a partnership with the Associated Press Managing Editors for a national Time Out for Newsroom Diversity and Accuracy, which encouraged simultaneous diversity programs at newspapers across the country; a Diversity

Institute to redesign the ASNE's diversity programs; a partnership with the Newspaper Association of America to incorporate the diversity mission into the NAA's Readership Institute; regular job fairs; and a talent bank.[69] Such initiatives were trumpeted in ASNE publications in the same spirit of optimism as similar efforts twenty years earlier.

At the same time, the annual census numbers would affirm that despite the new goal, the 1998 recommitment to diversity had done nothing to boost the momentum in hiring. In the decade after Seaton led the renegotiations, the nonwhite percentage of the workforce in daily newspaper newsrooms crept upward from 11.55 percent in 1999 to just 13.41 percent in 2009, including two years when the percentages actually declined.[70] Despite a census peak of 13.73 percent in 2006, the increase for the ten years after the 1998 goal renegotiation represented a slower rate of progress than in either of the previous two decades of the initiative.[71] In addition, daily newspapers performed poorly on a series of five 3-year benchmarks the board approved in September 1999 in an attempt to nudge the census numbers along incrementally, rather than simply asking editors to achieve the daunting goal of national parity over a twenty-five-year period.[72] By 2003, when the nonwhite employment census stood at 12.53 percent, the number already trailed that benchmark by about 3 percent, with performance on the other measures telling a similar story.[73] By 2009, when the overall target was 21.55 percent nonwhite employment, the census total trailed by more than 8 percent. In addition, the benchmark reporting showed daily newspaper newsrooms collectively were performing worse than they had in 2003 on three of the measures: percentage of nonwhite interns, number of newspapers with no nonwhites on staff, and number of newspapers achieving local parity.[74] As a result, the benchmarks merely offered more detailed proof that the national parity goal was an unworkable objective.

It was folly for diversity activists inside and outside the ASNE to have expected different results from a program that, in its basic format and philosophy, was unchanged from the failed Goal 2000. During the 1998 renegotiations, the ASNE and the UNITY coalition revalidated the outdated race-focused numerical model that had been set in place in 1978 and assumed that identities exist in isolation, as objectifiable traits that can be sorted out for counting, when in fact people are composites of multiple overlapping and intertwining identities. The ASNE census had always oversimplified race as being quantifiable according whiteness and four categories of nonwhiteness, and the 2025 goal perpetuated this error. Ironically, it did so just as a multiracial golfer, Tiger Woods, began his meteoric athletic career and just a decade before U.S. voters would choose a mixed-race politician, Barack Obama, as president. The ASNE census model readopted in 1998 reaffirmed the archaic definition of race as a pure distinction, without allowance for nuance. In addition, by privileging race over other identities, the post-2000 census not only attempted to measure American culture as it did not exist, but also reaffirmed the element of exclusion that had tainted the census project from its inception in 1978. While white women would no longer be omitted from the census after 2000, they very pointedly would not be covered by other diversity programming or the 2025 goal, which were reserved for journalists who could be identified and quantified according to the four categories of race.[75]

While the slight against women certainly weakened the credibility of the post-2000 diversity initiative, the wholesale exclusion of gay and lesbian journalists and its painful irony compromised the entire project. A diversity effort that allows one marginalized cohort to insist on the exclusion of another is simply not sustainable as a movement for social justice. And the need to redress discrimination against gay and lesbian journalists was indisputable. In 2000, Leroy Aarons repeated his landmark 1990 survey of nonheterosexual journalists and found lingering concerns in both working conditions and perceptions of news coverage of gay issues. While 93 percent of respondents said they were openly gay in the workplace, compared to 59 percent who were out in 1990, just 48 percent rated their news organization's coverage of gay life and issues as good or excellent.[76] Moreover, 53 percent reported hearing derogatory comments from newspaper coworkers about gay people in general.[77] Clearly, gay and lesbian journalists had developed the organizational infrastructure to advocate for their inclusion as, just a decade after its founding, the NLGJA had one thousand members and twenty-four local chapters.[78] Yet without full inclusion into the ASNE hiring initiative, nonheterosexual journalists would remain on the margins of the newsroom diversity movement.

The Retention Crisis

The goal of national parity on the four-race model was a symbolic, if not an empty, gesture when the ASNE recommitted to it in 1998, but the reasons the initiative was a lost cause were many and complex. Since 1978, when the hiring initiative began to reverse the legacy of racial segregation within the newspaper industry, a disconnect between the ASNE's pro-diversity rhetoric and its industry's performance had undermined good intention and guaranteed that daily newspaper newsrooms would remain predominantly white and male. The easy explanation was lingering racism, occasionally cited by those who had grown increasingly frustrated with the annual census results—yet pointing that finger oversimplified the problem and ignored many ASNE members' passionate commitment to the cause. Although the census had continually registered the diversity initiative's lost ground against the U.S. nonwhite population, the lackluster census numbers represented more than simply a failure of enough editors to hire enough nonwhite journalists to achieve parity. Instead, the numbers reflected a systemic dysfunction in the ASNE and its industry, one that crystallized and became painfully evident during the organization's 2001 convention, where a confluence of events—an alarming census report, a protest by the National Association of Black Journalists, and racially insensitive convention entertainment—brought into relief the distance between the ASNE's diversity vision and lived reality.

As usual, the ASNE's annual convention coincided with the April announcement of the annual newsroom survey results, though in 2001 the census report met with greater anticipation as it would gauge the newspaper industry's early momentum in the effort to achieve parity by 2025. By the standards of the ASNE newsroom census, the diversity initiative was coming off a good year. In 2000, the census had pegged nonwhite employment at 11.85 percent, up just 0.3 percent from the previous year, but those results had been buoyed by the addition of 1,100 newsroom employees to total newsroom employment, including a gain of three hundred nonwhites. These were the largest such increases since the mid-1990s. In an ASNE press release announcing the 2000 numbers, Diversity Committee chair Wanda Lloyd of Gannett Newspapers had suggested the results might be the beginning of a new phase in the diversity effort: "We've spent the past year developing initiatives to move these numbers up faster in the future. We need the industry to support these initiatives. I'm optimistic about more progress in the near future."[79]

In April 2001, however, the news was bleaker than Lloyd and others had hoped. Although 30 percent of the U.S. population now was identified as nonwhite, nonwhite employment in daily newspaper newsrooms had declined from 11.85 to 11.64 percent. This occurred despite a redoubled focus on diversity programming and daily newspapers having achieved the fourth-highest number of first-time nonwhite hires since the diversity initiative began in 1978 and the highest in ten years.[80] What quickly emerged as the most important number in the census data was not the 11.64 percent nonwhite employment but the difference between first-time hires and departures. Although the hiring numbers were not moving the census anywhere close to parity, nonwhite journalists were in fact coming through newsroom doors. The problem was that they were simply replacing nonwhite journalists who were leaving the industry, and in this particular year they did not fully compensate for attrition. The 2001 data showed a troubling loss of 698 nonwhite journalists against just 600 first-time hires.[81]

Instantly, retention of nonwhite journalists became an ASNE priority; however, the organization's diversity director appeared to struggle with how to frame the problem. In announcing the annual survey results in the *American Editor,* LaBarbara Bowman externalized the cause of nonwhite attrition by positing that newspapers were "victims of talent theft."[82] Although many nonwhite newspaper employees undoubtedly found a ready market for their skills in other industries, internal factors, including the working environment in newsrooms, likely played a more significant role.

This uncomfortable point was driven home during the 2001 convention by nonwhite journalists who appeared on a panel called "Advice on Keeping the Best and Brightest Minorities in Newsrooms."[83] William Sutton, president of the NABJ, and four other nonwhite journalists discussed the availability of mentorship, coworker attitudes toward diversity, opportunities for advancement, and other aspects of professional life that influenced nonwhites' decision to stay in journalism or seek a different career. Sutton emphasized that editors were responsible for the quality of experience that nonwhite employees had in their newsrooms. "I want to challenge ASNE members to work with NABJ and tell us within the next 90 days what specifically you'll do as individuals, because I don't want this to be an ASNE thing," Sutton said. "It has to be individual editors, paper by paper, to make a difference."[84]

In conjunction with this fairly low-key roundtable discussion, NABJ released "Voices of Anger, Cries of Concern," a forceful report addressing issues of retention from the perspective of black journalists who worked in daily newspaper newsrooms. In addition to concern about nonwhite retention, Sutton said the organization was alarmed to see that the African Americans counted in the 2001 census had dropped to 5.23 percent of newsroom employees from 5.31 percent a year earlier. In the preface of the report, Sutton scolded ASNE members for the most recent census results. "Our newspaper industry has entered a crisis state," he wrote. "You can't possibly be comfortable with the latest report that the number of journalists of color has declined for the first time since ASNE started keeping track of the numbers 23 years ago." Sutton disputed the notion that external factors, such as talent theft, were to blame. "Please don't make this a 'them' issue by pointing somewhere else," he wrote. "Either you've done your job and contributed to the solution by bringing in more journalists of color and increasing your total number of journalists of color through retention, or you're part of the problem."[85]

Included in the report were testimonials and anecdotes from several nonwhite journalists describing their experiences in newsroom management and as reporters, copy editors, and interns. At all levels of employment, African Americans reported being treated differently and inequitably. Former editor Dwight Cunningham was among those who cited white managers' reluctance to give blacks challenging story assignments or real responsibility as reasons for high nonwhite turnover. He wrote, "At the NY Daily News, for example, I sat for four months as the ranking African-American editor on the metro desk . . . yet I had no reporters as direct reports, no daily responsibilities. When it came time for me to offer my resignation, I was told by my supervisor, 'Well, I guess there's no need in talking about retaining you here.' I could only smile." In some cases, NABJ members reported being subjected to blatant racism in newsrooms. Dena' McClurkin, a senior at Clark Atlanta University, described the hostile environment in one of the newsrooms in which she had interned. "At first, I had no problem, I went in there and tried to be a team player. But I had an editor who made racist jibes to the other minority reporter, such as 'Chinky Chan,' across the newsroom. I found those statements to be very offensive." LaMont Jones, fashion editor of the *Pittsburgh Post-Gazette,* said the working environment in newsrooms "is beyond bad; it's tragic. And the excuses just don't wash. For example, the industry says blacks want to go to better-paying jobs, such as public relations or law. But the reality is, people who love their work, no matter how low-paying, don't jump ship the way black journalists do."[86]

Such anecdotal reports of greater job dissatisfaction among nonwhites were substantiated by data. A report issued that same month by the Freedom Forum found that since 1994, the annual departure rate for nonwhites working in newsrooms had averaged 7 percent versus 4 percent for their white counterparts.[87] At least for the journalists whose stories were told in the NABJ's new report, little had changed since the organization's 1992 study "Muted Voices: Frustration and Fear in the Newsroom." As it happened, though, the NABJ's "voices of anger" and "cries of concern" would be drowned out by a public relations debacle during that same convention, which would raise questions about the sincerity of the ASNE's institutional commitment to diversity.

The Joke Backfires

Any other year, the disappointing census numbers and the lambasting by NABJ would have generated enough negative publicity for one convention. In 2001, however, both were eclipsed by a public insult to the Asian American community that was exposed by Amy Leang, a Ball State University student who, ironically, was working as a photojournalism intern on the *ASNE Reporter,* the convention newspaper that served as a training ground for young nonwhites aspiring to careers in daily newspaper newsrooms. In a column in the *Reporter,* Leang recounted her experience taking photos of a performance by the comedy ensemble Capitol Steps, whose political satire provided entertainment at the convention's opening reception.

> On stage and in the spotlight was the troupe, Capitol Steps. Dressed in costumes, the performers presented a skit concerning current Chinese and U.S. relations. They were white males impersonating a Chinese official and his translator. The Chinese official sported a black wig and thick glasses and spoke in a disconcerting version of "Chinese."
>
> "Ching ching chong chong," the man shouted as he gestured wildly with his hands.
>
> What was disturbing was not just the fact that this was happening, but that hundreds of editors, my future bosses, were laughing. I felt myself swallowed by all the loud laughter. Each time the "Chinese" voice became more jarring, the editors would laugh even harder. Despite feeling humiliated, I finished the job and turned in my pictures.
>
> The next morning, I woke up crying.[88]

As word circulated nationally of the Capitol Steps performance at the ASNE convention, which included not only the derogatory Chinese skit described by Leang but a blackface impersonation of Diana Ross as well, the ASNE came in for sharp rebuke from the Asian American Journalists Association and the leadership of UNITY, as well as the broader civil rights and professional media communities.[89] "That this could occur at an ASNE convention is almost unbelievable," Dwight Ellis, a human resources officer at the National Association of Broadcasters, told the *Washington Post.*[90]

For his part, ASNE President Tim McGuire of the *Minneapolis Star Tribune* sought to distance himself and the organization from the content of the comedy sketch. "ASNE had nothing to do with the skit," McGuire told the *Post.* To the *San Francisco Chronicle* McGuire insisted that the ASNE had no reason to apologize. "Very few people reacted the way (Leang) did," he said, noting that "of course" he was among those who laughed at the performance. "I don't think we can make an apology because we didn't control anything."[91]

Although the controversy was fueled by external criticism, McGuire also took heat from within ASNE, some of which also became public. "We're encouraging people to get into the (newspaper) business and we let something like this happen under our watch," Carolina Garcia, chair of the ASNE Diversity Committee, told the *San Francisco Chronicle.*[92] Gilbert Bailon, former UNITY president and future ASNE president, said the skit demonstrated that racial humor about Asian Americans was not taboo. "I was sitting next to Rick Rodriguez, ironically, and we both thought, 'Wow, this is really over the top.' Now, nobody stood up and said . . . 'Stop this thing,' nothing that dramatic, but there were some of us, particularly some of the minority editors who thought, 'I really can't believe they went that far.' I mean, political parody is political parody, but as many people in other groups said, you can't imagine them doing a Step 'n Fetchit or . . . some type of really stereotypical drunken guy with a sombrero." With the damage done, Bailon said ASNE should have responded more quickly and directly to condemn the content of the skit.[93]

A month later, McGuire informed his members that he had moderated his position on the controversy. McGuire also sought to explain why the incident reflected badly on the ASNE diversity mission, while insisting upon the free-speech rights of the comedians and their audience. He did not explain, however, why the First Amendment, which protects freedom of speech only from government censorship, ever was a consideration in the ASNE's response to the skit. Moreover, his attempt to find middle ground on the subject of racial humor came across as an equivocation on the ASNE's commitment to diversity. McGuire continued to isolate the affront as an injury to one Asian American college student, downplaying the broad outcry against the ASNE's initial response to the skit.

> Most of us saw the Capitol Steps skit as political satire and parody. We accepted it as such and that construct allowed us to laugh.
>
> It was not until I read Amy Leang's words that I realized that skit could look profoundly different to someone who saw it as making fun of them. I am convinced few of our members saw that skit as mocking Chinese Americans but at least one Chinese-American did and that matters. Our critics would argue that our sensitivity antenna should have been on and they are probably right.
>
> Another learning [*sic*] for me has been the importance of balancing competing values. As this situation developed, I was very intent on protecting the

> First Amendment right to speak out in satire and parody. Those values are important, but we can't ever lose our focus on the feelings and perceptions of those people who have historically been subjected to demonization, ridicule and stereotyping.[94]

In his mea culpa, McGuire acknowledged a disconnect between the ASNE leaders who make policy and the rank-and-file members who were expected to implement it, a recurring theme in ASNE discourse about diversity. Reflecting on the incident in 2004, McGuire said those who objected to the Capitol Steps skit were not the only constituency whose views he had to consider. "There are still many people in ASNE for whom this is a very divisive kind of issue," McGuire said. "They think that [the skit] shouldn't have bothered people, it shouldn't have become an issue. There are some people who hold that very dearly, and I respect those people."[95]

In a commentary in the *American Editor,* Terry Greenberg, editor of the *Elkhart (Ind.) Truth,* chastised fellow conventioneers for insensitivity to the discriminatory content of the Capitol Steps skit and for having "sent an embarrassing message about our commitment to diversifying America's newsrooms." Even so, Greenberg acknowledged he found the Capitol Steps performance to be humorous. "The jokes were funny," he wrote, "but I remember telling my wife that I wondered if some people would be offended by the stereotypes and, in another bit, one of the women doing Diana Ross in what appeared to be black face."[96] William Woo, a former ASNE board member teaching at Stanford University, did not see the humor. In describing his reaction to descriptions of the Capitol Steps skit, Woo wrote in the *American Editor,* "The more I read about it, the angrier I became. And nobody walked out?" Even so, Woo refuted claims that the ASNE's initial response reflected institutional ambivalence about diversity. "Offensive as the skit was," he wrote, "that it occurred at the ASNE convention says nothing about the organization's deep commitment to bringing more minority journalists into our newsrooms. I've been there and struggled with the problem and I know the folks who struggle with it now. That's a non-issue."[97]

For many observers of the newsroom diversity movement, however, the fact that ASNE members had not exhibited reflexive outrage from the moment the skit was performed was further evidence of a tentative and shallow commitment to diversity. "It just sort of reinforced the sort of negative feelings that the folks that were down on the ASNE had about their sensibilities and questioned their intention," said Walterene Swanston, UNITY's former director. " . . . First of all, you probably should have known more about what the act was going to be before you drop those folks on. But secondly, if they were offensive, then you should have left. That was the buzz."[98] Members of NABJ remembered clearly what had happened at their 1993 convention, when rapper Bushwick Bill made misogynistic comments during a panel discussion. "I was standing outside with the executive, outside the meeting room door," Swanston recalled, "and people just stormed out of that meeting and started surrounding the president of NABJ, telling her what was going on. And she went in and made the guy apologize right then and there. The fact is . . . that people just streamed out because they were so offended. And it was men and women just walked out."[99] Against the standard set by NABJ President Sidmel Estes-Sumpter in 1993, the ASNE's handling of the Capitol Steps incident came up short.

"The Adult Table"

After the 2001 newsroom census showed that more nonwhite journalists were leaving daily newspaper newsrooms than taking jobs in them, ASNE leaders sponsored a diversity summit with presidents of UNITY and the associations for black, Hispanic, Asian American, and Native American journalists.[100] ASNE representatives had hoped the nonwhite journalist organizations would endorse a survey to gauge why nonwhite journalists were leaving the newspaper business, but the strong, negative reaction to the survey proposal merely underscored how disconnected the current generation of ASNE leaders were from nonwhite journalists and how astonishingly little they knew of the history of the newspaper diversity effort. Writing in the *American Editor,* McGuire said representatives of the UNITY coalition forced the ASNE to adopt a new strategy. "We were not prepared for their anger," he wrote. "The Unity partners made it absolutely clear to us they opposed any further interviewing of diverse staffers. They ardently believed minority newsroom employees had been researched enough and that answers to the retention problem should be obvious to us. We later learned that those leaders were prepared to walk out of the meeting if we insisted on going ahead with our research plans."[101]

Instead, the ASNE contracted researcher Larry McGill, director of the Freedom Forum's Media Studies Center, to compile and synthesize a wealth of existing—and largely ignored—data on nonwhite journalists. The result was a meta-analysis that examined thirteen studies of nonwhite journalists in the context of ASNE newsroom census data on hiring and retention. Although about 21 percent of new full-time newsroom hires were nonwhite, McGill found that journalists from this demographic had left newsrooms at twice the rate of their white counterparts.[102] Moreover, "nearly three of every five new hires in the newspaper industry over the next 25 years (58.5%) would have to be journalists of color to achieve racial parity by 2025."[103] In other words, a revolving newsroom door for nonwhites was contributing mightily to the newspaper industry's inability to make substantial progress in nonwhite hiring and would present an obstacle to achieving the parity goal that had been recalibrated in 1998.

McGill's report offered a series of recommendations, none of which departed from advice the ASNE had received previously and repeatedly from nonwhite journalists. Specifically, McGill suggested that "efforts to retain journalists of color should focus on improving the newsroom as a work place and the management skills that influence the work environment."[104] In addition, McGill cited better pay, better hours, and more opportunities for creativity as ways to improve nonwhite retention. Although the analysis merely reworked existing data, McGuire trumpeted McGill's recommendations as new information that provided the key to resolving the newsroom diversity problem. "One of the most amazing of McGill's findings was that 4,800 minority journalists have been interviewed in the last 15 years or so," McGuire wrote. "The Unity partners were correct in their assertion about interview fatigue." With no hint of irony, McGuire concluded, "The findings of the study, while depressing and challenging, should give us confidence we know what the retention issues are. Now is the time for action."[105]

That year the ASNE board voted to invite representatives of the UNITY coalition and the professional associations for black, Hispanic, Asian American, and Native American journalists "to attend the portion of the ASNE board meetings devoted to committee reports for the purpose of strengthening the interaction between ASNE and the largest minority journalist organizations as they work together to enhance the diversity of American newsrooms."[106] The board also committed to holding a diversity summit during each spring convention. Through these gestures, McGuire attempted to repair ASNE's fractured relationship with the nonwhite journalist organizations. "They were angry about everything," McGuire later said of the UNITY coalition members who attended the summit following the 2001 convention. "I mean, they came prepared to tell us to stick that survey idea where the sun never shines. They were upset about the numbers, but it was my judgment, and it was largely my judgment, that they were angry about not being included, about not having a role. They were angry about powerlessness." McGuire said the offer to do the meta-analysis, to analyze existing data, was an "olive branch," as was the invitation to nonwhite journalist organizations to send representatives to ASNE board meetings.[107]

Even so, McGuire's framing of the compromise, in a column in the *American Editor,* sent a contradictory message. In reporting the board decision to the membership, McGuire quoted UNITY President Jackie Green as saying, "We've always felt like we'd been invited to Christmas dinner but we've never been allowed to sit at the adult table," an analogy suggesting that ASNE had treated members of UNITY and the nonwhite journalist organizations like children. McGuire then missed the opportunity to dispel this impression by using language that might have neutralized the hierarchical relationship between ASNE and the groups now invited to the board meetings. Instead, McGuire affirmed that power differential when he wrote in response, "ASNE has now welcomed all the diverse organizations to the adult table, and we think good things will come from that."[108] In addition, McGuire defaulted to the pre-1998, race-only definition of diversity when he indicated that ASNE had conferred "adult" status to "all the diverse organizations." Notably absent from the list was the NLGJA, which held an ex officio seat on the board of the Radio and Television News Directors Association, ASNE's counterpart in broadcasting.[109]

While the ASNE would continue to champion diversity for the next five years or so, until the economic disintegration of the newspaper industry forced a new set of priorities, the organization would never recover the momentum—and credibility—lost in the period from 1998 to 2001. What became apparent during the years bookended by the goal renegotiations and the disastrous Capitol Steps convention was that diversity advocates within ASNE would not be able to suture the rhetorical disconnect between the organization's stated support for the parity goal and the ambivalence, and even disengagement, of many ASNE members. Moreover, by acceding to pressure to continue the national parity goal even as they acknowledged it was unattainable, ASNE diversity advocates signaled they would no longer even try for consistency. By revalidating the race-only newsroom census, the ASNE excluded other marginalized groups from diversity programming—even if identities other than race were now mentioned in the diversity mission statement—and undermined its own moral authority in the newsroom diversity discussion. In the political calculation to readopt the unachievable national parity target, the ASNE declared that words, even empty promises, counted more than deeds.

AFTERWORD

Closing a Chapter of Newspaper History

When he returned from the 2005 ASNE convention, Greg Moore, editor of the *Denver Post,* hung an oil painting of an editor's rolltop desk in his home.[1] Moore, a longtime newsroom diversity advocate and program chair of the 2005 convention, had attempted every day of the annual meeting to elicit silent auction bids for the artwork, which Denver artist Darrell Anderson had donated to ASNE's diversity fund-raising effort. By the convention's end, Moore, who had hoped to sell the painting for $3,000, had received not a single bid, even though the convention had been attended by representatives of the largest daily newspapers and most well-heeled news corporations and media foundations in the United States, any of whom easily might have purchased the painting for an office or board room. At the end of the convention, Moore bought the painting himself. It is not hard to imagine a different outcome, say, a decade earlier, when support for newsroom diversity was still fashionable and representatives of those same media entities might have taken turns bidding up the price of the painting in a public display of support for ASNE's newsroom hiring initiative.

By 2005, however, the ASNE's diversity project had lost its ability to stir passion and mobilize resources. For one thing, the decline of newspaper profitability—the confluence of shrinking circulation and plummeting ad revenue—had become the newspaper industry's overriding focus. Since 2000, four million readers had given up their daily and Sunday newspapers; by 2008, six million more would follow suit. Although print newspapers saw an uptick in advertising revenue in 2005, by 2009 ad expenditures would be half what they had been at their all-time peak in 2000, and online advertising was failing, utterly, to compensate.[2] Even so, the economic crisis in the newspaper industry was by no means the sole or even primary reason the diversity initiative was receding in priority. Instead, the loss of readers and revenue merely accelerated the erosion of the ASNE's diversity programming, which had been inevitable since the original hiring initiative's founding in 1978. Ultimately, the economic crisis in the newspaper industry would provide the ASNE with cover when, in 2009, it eliminated the diversity director's position, a move that sent an unmistakable message to the newspaper industry and broader public about the future of the ASNE's commitment to the issue.[3] Although the ASNE pledged to continue its newsroom census and diversity programming, elimination of the one full-time position dedicated exclusively to diversity since 1983 closed a chapter in American newspaper history.[4]

The ASNE diversity initiative had failed to regain momentum after ASNE leaders declared Goal 2000 a failure and reset the demographic parity target for 2025. The contentious renegotiation of the diversity definition and recalibration of the parity target in 1998 had exacerbated diversity fatigue among the ASNE rank and file. By recommitting to the Goal 2000 structure, based on an outdated four-race model and the unattainable goal of national demographic parity, the ASNE had recommitted to failure and asked its members to embrace a lost cause. Efforts by diversity advocates inside and outside ASNE to reenergize editors, through exhortation to increase their annual census numbers and recrimination when they did not, had generated resentment, particularly among editors at newspapers in communities with low nonwhite populations. In fact, the term "diversity fatigue" may have understated the attitude toward the hiring initiative of editors at those smaller newspapers. "They're damn tired of it," Edward Seaton, ASNE's 1998–99 president, said in 2004.[5]

In short, Moore's unsold painting represented a cold reality manifested in both anecdotal experiences like his at the 2005 ASNE convention and in newspaper industry data. One of the most compelling reports on the status of the newsroom diversity effort, published that same year by the John L. and James L. Knight Foundation, showed that nonwhite employment in the newsrooms of 82 percent of U.S. daily newspapers had already peaked. Despite the concerted effort since 1978 to achieve racial parity between the newsroom workforce and the U.S. population, 37 percent of daily newspaper newsrooms still employed no nonwhite journalists and just 13 percent were at parity with their local community. The study's authors, Bill Dedman and Stephen Doig, also noted that the high rate of layoffs and seniority buyouts affecting older white employees at daily newspapers had skewed the percentages of nonwhite journalists counted in the ASNE's annual newsroom census. "If the newsroom shrinks, and whites leave, the nonwhite percentage can increase without a single nonwhite journalist being hired," Dedman and Doig wrote in 2005. They noted that "newsrooms have lost more than 2,200 jobs since 2001, a 4 percent decline, while the number of journalists of color has increased by 700, or nearly 11 percent. Without the industry contraction, presumably the records on nonwhite hiring would look worse at many newspapers. Even with the contraction, most newspapers are below their peak nonwhite employment, as a share of the staff."[6]

Dedman and Doig's finding, that newsroom diversity at 82 percent of daily newspapers had already reached its highest levels by 2005, confirmed that the hiring effort's moment had passed. The worsening economic crisis in newspapering would erase any optimism about salvaging jobs for nonwhites as layoffs continued to sweep through newsrooms in the years that followed. By the end of the decade, newspaper payroll cuts, in combination with attrition, also would reduce the representation of nonwhite journalists in newsrooms. In its stunning 2010 census report, the ASNE announced that nonwhite employment in newsrooms, which had hit 7,400 in 2007, had dropped to 5,500, a decline of almost 18 percent for the decade, a period when white and nonwhite newsroom employment together declined more than 25 percent. From 2009 to 2010, the number of newsroom jobs held by nonwhites fell 12.6 percent while the overall job total dropped 11 percent.[7]

Goal 2000's failure has been attributed to a variety of factors, few of them accurate. For one, members of nonwhite journalist organizations complained through the years that the ASNE had not committed adequate resources to the newsroom integration project. In fact, throughout the twenty years of its existence, Goal 2000 consumed more of the ASNE's organizational resources than any other effort except the annual convention, according to Lee Stinnett, ASNE's executive director from 1983 to 1999. At the leadership level of the ASNE, Goal 2000 became a more intense organizational focus than even the core issue of freedom of information, Stinnett said.[8]

For their part, ASNE leaders frequently have blamed changing American demographics, namely the unforeseen increase in the nonwhite population, for the failure of the parity project. The newspaper industry was being asked to hit a "moving target," they complained.[9] In fact, this rationale disregards the ASNE's own census numbers. When the ASNE's directors adopted Goal 2000 in 1978, they estimated the U.S. nonwhite population would be 20 percent by the end of the century. That nonwhites accounted for nearly 30 percent of the U.S. population in 2000 had no bearing on the success or failure of the original hiring initiative because that same year the percentage of nonwhite newsroom employees stood at just 11.85 percent. The daily newspaper industry would not have achieved the goal even if the goal had been static. Interestingly, one of the few demographic rationales that helped explain the discrepancy between the parity goal and the annual census numbers did not gain traction in the 1998 renegotiations. Edward Seaton argued that a parity target should have been fashioned around the nonwhite college-educated workforce rather than the nonwhite population as a whole, which would have eliminated children and unqualified adults from the parity calculation.

Critiques of resource allocations and demographic models attempt to identify concrete, quantifiable explanations for the failure of the ASNE's newsroom hiring initiative, but such efforts generally miss the point because they fail to take into account flaws in the conceptualization and design of Goal 2000 and its successor, the 2025 initiative. Specifically, the four-race, census-based model had been doomed to failure since its initial adoption in 1978 and, by the end of the century, had completed a trajectory that was inevitable, with or without the economic crisis in the newspaper industry. This historical analysis, which has traced the ASNE's journey from tolerating inequality—even extreme racism and sexism—in the 1950s to championing equal opportunity in journalism in later decades, has shown that the ASNE failed to deliver on its newsroom integration promise, specifically parity with the U.S. nonwhite population, for four reasons: The ASNE membership and the newspaper industry did not sufficiently embrace the social justice mission of Goal 2000; the initiative was corrupted by its privileging of some marginalized identities over others; the initiative's stewards badly underestimated the intransigence of an institutionalized professional norm that idealized editors and journalists as white, straight men; and the ASNE lacked institutional memory of its own history in the diversity trenches and, therefore, repeated its mistakes.

The Elusive Consensus

When the ASNE board, led by Southerner Eugene Patterson, launched the newsroom integration initiative in 1978, it did so with a deep sense of history and of the need to right a grievous societal wrong. Patterson had been at the *Atlanta Constitution* in the 1960s when the newspaper hired its first black reporter. He and many of the ASNE directors on his board knew the newspaper industry had its own long history of Jim Crow, with white journalists working for white-owned newspapers while their nonwhite counterparts worked for presses that were operated by and served people of their own races. The racial barrier that preserved most daily newspapers as whites-only workplaces was even more consequential than racial discrimination in many other contexts because newspapers served a democratic purpose. And for Patterson and the core group of progressive editors who joined his crusade, it was obvious that newspapers could not report on others' failures to fulfill the promise of the civil rights movement when newspapers were holding themselves to a lower standard. "That has been pretty much the touchstone of the effort," Patterson said. "It's not enough to demand ethical and responsive action at city hall or the state capital. It's required that we look within our own newsrooms and have the same goals."[10]

While it is impossible to know whether Goal 2000 would have been adopted if it had been put to a vote of the 391 members who cast ballots in the ASNE's 1978 election rather than simply the 1978 board's twenty-six officers and directors,[11] it is clear that many ASNE members could accept, at least in principle, that integrating newsrooms was the right thing to do and some could even agree that an affirmative action program such as Goal 2000 was a necessary solution. At the same time, it is also clear that other editors believed the social activism entailed in such an effort undermined the journalistic ideal of objectivity, while some failed even to acknowledge the daily newspaper industry's role in perpetuating social inequality. This lack of philosophical consensus on the hiring initiative was never resolved, even as subsequent generations of editors rotated into and out of the ASNE. As a result, Goal 2000 was always championed by a small group of ASNE leaders and diversity advocates inside and outside the organization, while many disinterested ASNE members sat on the sidelines. Tim McGuire, the 2001–2 ASNE president, defined these two camps as editors who embraced diversity as a "holy mantra" and those who did not. "That holy mantra is absolutely felt at the top levels of the organization. I'm not sure it's felt as a holy mantra all the way through," he said. The result was an uneven commitment to diversity in the newsrooms supervised by ASNE members, where the hiring decisions counted in the annual census were made. "Nobody opposes diversity, most people will acknowledge its importance, but it is not a holy mantra for the entire membership," McGuire said in 2004.[12]

Despite Patterson's conceptualization of Goal 2000 as ethically necessary, the ASNE leadership failed from the outset to connect newsroom diversity to journalistic values, which might have made the social justice dimension of the effort more compelling to the broader membership. Not until 1998, with adoption of the mission statement for the 2025 parity target, did the organization concretely and formally link the hiring initiative to the press' reciprocal obligation under the First Amendment to serve the public. Moreover, ASNE leaders sent a mixed message throughout the years by justifying the hiring initiative as an economic necessity. Attempting to appeal to editors less committed to diversity, ASNE leaders, from 1978 forward, framed diversity as a business imperative, as vital to the financial health of their newspapers, often neglecting to mention a loftier ethical or democratic imperative. Even in the 1998 diversity mission statement, the concepts are muddied: "To cover communities fully, to carry out their role in a democracy, and to succeed in the marketplace, the nation's newsrooms must reflect the racial diversity of American society." In fact, editors in most U.S. newspaper markets saw little relationship between newsroom diversity and their profitability. And they were right. Newspapers that aggressively diversified their newsrooms were neither advantaged nor insulated in the marketplace. A more persuasive rationale for Goal 2000, one that might have made diversity a "holy mantra" for more ASNE members, would have emphasized from the beginning that newsroom integration was a democratic principle on the order of the ASNE's longstanding—and broadly supported—commitment to freedom of information.

While a lack of philosophical consensus on newsroom integration weakened the ASNE's diversity effort, it also kept the broader newspaper industry from fully supporting the concept. White resentment of targeted nonwhite hiring created an inhospitable environment in some integrated newsrooms and contributed to the difficulty of retaining nonwhite journalists. An indication that white hostility toward newsroom diversity initiatives was pervasive in the newspaper industry at the turn of the twenty-first century is found in William McGowan's *Coloring the News: How Crusading for Diversity Has Corrupted American Journalism,* published in 2001. The book quotes several journalists who described antiwhite bias in their newsrooms and said they feared retribution for publicly criticizing the diversity policies of their employers. While McGowan presents his argument as textual analysis and investigative research, he at times rants and the book may fairly be called an anti-affirmative action polemic. McGowan's ideological agenda also is apparent because the work was published by Encounter Books, an imprint of the ideological right, and sponsored by foundations noted for funding conservative projects.[13] While newsroom diversity supporters found the book contemptible, *Coloring the News* clearly resonated with many of their peers in the media. Indeed, in 2002 the National Press Club delivered the diversity community a stunning rebuke by awarding McGowan's book its Arthur Rowse Award for Press Criticism.

Nonwhites Only

When the ASNE board enacted the Goal 2000 parity program, it was responding, albeit ten years later, to the Kerner Commission's 1968 report on the news media's failure to represent race accurately in news coverage and to integrate their news staffs. For progressive ASNE leaders in the 1970s, racial civil rights—specifically civil rights for African Americans—was the great, unfinished task on the American social and political agenda. As a result, the ASNE made race the focus—the sole focus—of Goal 2000, a position that would taint the newsroom integration initiative and compromise the ASNE's moral authority on the issue of diversity. Because Goal 2000 was a racial remedy only, which by definition excluded gender, sexual orientation, and other identities from the hiring initiative, Goal 2000 was itself an instrument of discrimination and was, therefore, structurally flawed. Interestingly, most ASNE leaders seemed not to recognize the irony in asking others to embrace an exclusionary cause to end discrimination in newsroom hiring.

The point was not lost on editor Dorothy Jurney, who developed her own newsroom survey in 1979 to track women's advancement in newsrooms. Nor was the point lost on gay and lesbian journalists in 1998, when the ASNE would acquiesce to the demands of the nonwhite journalist organizations and jettison a proposal to add sexual orientation to the annual census. This inherent contradiction in the ASNE diversity effort also created tensions among marginalized journalists and pitted them against one another in the struggle over finite resources.[14] The racially exclusive model also foreclosed the possibility that all marginalized journalists would collaborate toward a common goal of inclusion for all—which would have been the logical and democratic objective of any project dedicated to diversifying newsrooms.

The exclusive focus on race reserved the resources of the ASNE's diversity programming, particularly the annual newsroom census, for nonwhites from 1978 until 1998, when the ASNE agreed to count women as well. Yet nonwhite journalists did not benefit from being privileged in this way. While the census produced data on the number of journalists in four racial categories, its ultimate effect was toxic. The annual census results, which were publicized each April, reduced nonwhite journalists to objects for counting. The census became an annual ritual through which newsroom managers were required to label individual journalists as not-white, as different and not representing the idealized professional norm, and in so doing perpetuated the racial hierarchy in daily newspaper journalism. Although it certainly does not excuse the hostile treatment many nonwhite journalists experienced, the dehumanizing effect of the annual quantification undoubtedly contributed to white backlash in daily newspaper newsrooms, where white journalists saw nonwhite colleagues as ASNE census numbers rather than as professionals making an important contribution to daily journalism.

A Proposition from the Heart

The decision to commit the ASNE's organizational resources to bringing nonwhite employment in daily newspaper newsrooms into parity with the U.S. nonwhite population was noble but naive and uninformed. The ASNE record from the late 1970s contains no evidence to suggest that anyone within the organization's leadership investigated whether Goal 2000 would be demographically achievable, given the number of nonwhite journalists in the labor pool or the number of college-educated nonwhites with writing and editing skills who might be persuaded to become journalists. There is, however, plenty of evidence that the founders of Goal 2000 believed the simple declaration that integrating newsrooms was the right thing to do, morally and financially, would make it so. Indeed, in adopting Goal 2000, members of the ASNE board proclaimed that parity would be achieved well before the turn of the century.[15] In the spirit of the moment, "Goal 2000" seemed like a catchy title for a shorter-term endeavor.

The members of Eugene Patterson's ASNE board can hardly be faulted for a making a heartfelt stand for social justice; seeing more clearly the difficulty of the task that lay before them would not have increased the project's chances for success. At the same time, this misjudgment, which was perpetuated by the ASNE boards that followed, did cause ASNE leaders to employ the self-destructive strategy of assuming that the wisdom of Goal 2000 was obvious to all and treating the hiring initiative as an edict. In so doing, the ASNE continuously underestimated the intransigence of racism's legacy within the daily newspaper industry, which had constructed institutionalized professional norms that made white journalists—as well as male and straight journalists—seem more qualified for newsroom work. As passionate believers in the promise of the civil rights movement, Patterson and his board missed the full significance of their place on the historical continuum of social progress. While they had arrived at a juncture where fundamental change in the newspaper industry finally could be discussed, they also were removed by just thirty years from Senator James Eastland's speech to the ASNE defending segregation, a little more than twenty years from editor Harry Ayers's racist tirade during an ASNE convention, and just ten years from the ASNE's silent response to the Kerner Commission's report on racism in the media. Achieving a paradigm shift on the magnitude of the one imagined in the Goal 2000 effort, and doing it in just twenty-two years, was hardly realistic.

The ASNE itself provides an example of the difficulty of dismantling institutionalized professional norms that have been structured around such an enduring notion of human value as race. Even as the ASNE expected the newspaper industry to achieve the demographic parity target, the organization itself remained predominately white. For example, by 2004, twenty-six years after the ASNE launched the newsroom integration project, the portion of ASNE members who were identified as nonwhite had risen to just 6.3 percent.[16] The discrepancy between that figure and the 12.95 percent nonwhite employment reported in the 2004 newsroom census reflected the enduring whiteness of top newsroom management, despite efforts to diversify newsrooms. Because ASNE membership had been reserved for those who had attained the highest levels in daily newspaper newsrooms, slow progress on nonwhite promotion to newsroom management registered distinctly in the demographic of the ASNE itself.

Interestingly, the ASNE did reward many of the nonwhites who joined the organization by electing them to the board of directors, which eventually gave the disproportionately white ASNE a leadership ladder that was disproportionately nonwhite, again offering concrete evidence of the disparity in commitment to diversity at the top of the ASNE and in the newsrooms where top editors remained predominantly white. The racial composition of the ASNE leadership ladder, the series of executive offices leading to the organization's presidency, in the first decade of the twenty-first century was the direct result of efforts, begun in the early years of Goal 2000, to diversify the ASNE board. During the 1980s, when nonwhite employment in newsrooms crept no higher than 7.86 percent, about one-quarter of the people who stood for election to the board were nonwhite or female. After 2000, nonwhites were so strongly represented in ASNE leadership that half the presidents were nonwhite. From 2001 to 2010, the presidency was held by three white men (one with a physical disability), an Asian American man, a black woman, two Hispanic men, a black man, and two white women. The ASNE presidency hardly reflected the racial composition of the organization or the daily newspaper industry's workforce.

The 1978 ASNE board asked the organization and its members' newspapers to right a societal wrong without dismantling the professional norm that defined the ideal journalist as a white, straight man and while leaving intact the institutional framework that perpetuated the ideal. In fact, the ASNE actually affirmed this framework by insisting that journalists be college graduates as well as graduates of accredited college journalism programs—which excluded many institutions that educated large numbers of nonwhites. The ASNE also made newsroom integration more difficult by continuing to advocate small-town newspapers as the best training ground for young journalists, even if this placed nonwhites in inhospitable communities, and by ignoring journalism's traditionally low compensation, which made other higher-paying occupations more attractive to talented nonwhites with writing and editing skills.

Finally, the ASNE's stewardship of the newsroom hiring initiative was crippled by a continuing vacuum in the organization's institutional memory. Because diversity advocates rotated into and out of ASNE, often remaining directly engaged in the effort for just a few years, most had little sense of the hiring initiative's historical arc, specifically what had been tried before, what had worked, and what had not. This is understandable, given fluidity in the diversity staff position and annual turnover in the Diversity Committee chairmanship, a key position in a decentralized organization that has not consistently maintained a repository of committee records. As a result, the hiring initiative did not benefit from cumulative experience and spun its wheels, continually revisiting a limited range of strategies and treating them each time as if they were new initiatives. The ASNE leadership repeatedly trumpeted information about newsroom diversity that had been in circulation for years and rolled out programming that was purported to be innovative, when previous renditions had produced negligible results.

When ASNE leaders proposed in 2001 that the organization conduct a survey to find out why retention of nonwhites was a problem, they were unaware that a number of surveys, dating back more than a decade, had already been conducted and that the information they sought was already available. Attrition had been eroding the hiring initiative's gains since the 1980s and researcher Lawrence McGill, who compiled existing data into a meta-analysis, was able to draw upon thirteen surveys relevant to nonwhite newsroom employment that had been completed between 1989 and 2000. Even so, the ASNE leadership treated McGill's meta-analysis as new information.

More astonishing is the ASNE leadership's continual return to the business imperative as a silver-bullet rationale for diversity. With indisputable consistency, from 1978 forward, many editors remained unpersuaded by dire warnings that their newspapers' profitability was linked to a diversified newsroom. Editors who had rejected the business imperative based on their understanding of their local newspaper marketplace were validated in

2002 by a household penetration analysis conducted by Bill Dedman. That study, which laid the groundwork for Dedman and Doig's 2005 finding that newsroom diversity had already peaked, "found zero correlation between diversity of staff and change in newspaper sales over the past decade."[17] This analysis was followed in 2006 by a study suggesting that increased nonwhite staffing did not increase trust or readership among nonwhite readers. Indeed, researchers reported, "The data show that as the number of minority staff at a newspaper increases, the *less likely* the Black population is to believe all or almost all of what they read in the paper with which it is most familiar."[18]

Yet as late as 2011, the ASNE announced that its most recent diversity conference, supported by an impressive list of underwriters, had "largely succeeded in its attempt to reframe the argument for diversity from a social good to a business imperative." In an email newsletter, the ASNE also indicated that the new effort was recycling the arguments, in circulation since the 1970s, that comprehensive coverage is impossible without a diverse staff and historically black colleges are the place to recruit nonwhite hires.[19] Following the initial implementation of Goal 2000 programming in the 1980s, those leading the ASNE diversity effort demonstrated a stunning lack of historical perspective by continually recommitting to ineffectual strategies already tested, even multiple times, by their predecessors.

The Denouement

Despite the slow rate of progress, the ASNE provided a nagging conscience as daily newspapers integrated their newsrooms from 1978 forward, as the percentage of nonwhite newsroom employees inched upward from the 3.95 percent reported in the first census. Even without the impetus of Goal 2000, newsrooms undoubtedly would have seen an increase in the number of nonwhite journalists, as nonwhites entered American professional culture in greater numbers following the civil rights movement of the 1960s. It stands to reason, however, that the hiring efforts by those newspapers and corporate owners who embraced the cause of newsroom diversity were more intense because of the pressure the ASNE brought to bear. At the same time, those who trace the history of Goal 2000 and the 2025 initiative must conclude that the newsroom diversity movement, when measured against its designated numerical targets, failed.

Even if the newspaper industry were to discover the formula for profitability in a post-newsprint world, this book has demonstrated that an exclusively race-focused, census-based model cannot disrupt the institutionalized and exclusionary professional norms that constructed segregated newsrooms to begin with. Though this analysis has been an accounting of past failure, it still holds out the possibility for future success for those who remain concerned with social justice in the media. Racial inequity, particularly as it is experienced in the multi-identity twenty-first century, in this increasingly globalized media culture, cannot be compartmentalized and addressed without considering the other signifiers that combine to produce whole persons. Perhaps the UNITY Journalists of Color alliance realized this when, in 2011, its board finally voted to admit the National Lesbian and Gay Journalists Association to the coalition on a trial basis and, in 2012, agreed to drop the reference to "color" from the organization's name.[20] Any project that seeks to advance social justice in the media must offer a model of true inclusion in which power is shared equitably, not reserved for the few based on discrete categories of identity, as it was in the ASNE and the hiring initiative. For all its good intent, the ASNE's newsroom diversity project is an anachronism of an era in which Jim Crow defined American race relations.

In 2012, the ASNE stopped counting the nonwhite employees in newsrooms. As a sign of the times, perhaps, the ASNE elected to outsource the annual census to the Center for Advanced Social Research at the University of Missouri.[21] The moment also may have passed for the ASNE itself. In 2009, members approved bylaws changes "to assure a robust future," according to 2008–9 ASNE President Charlotte Hall,[22] and bring the organization, which for several years had struggled to maintain its membership numbers, into line with the realities of twenty-first century media. Time will tell whether the organization's repositioning within the media marketplace will save it. Even as ASNE leaders canceled their 2009 convention, citing the economy, the organization dropped the reference to newsprint in its name and became the American Society of News Editors. Among other changes, editors voted to expand membership eligibility to include directors of online news sites and, most strikingly, to remove the requirement that members be affiliated with "daily" news organizations—the criterion that traditionally had served as a barrier to the ASNE membership of nonwhite editors. Had ASNE been as magnanimous five decades earlier, when Louis Martin of the *Chicago Defender* first applied for membership, the organization might have recorded a much different history.

APPENDIX A

Draft Statement on Newsroom Diversity

Newsroom diversity is essential to the newspaper's responsibility in a democratic society and success in the marketplace. To accurately and sensitively cover the community, newsroom staffs must reflect society as a whole. The newsroom should be a place in which all employees contribute their full potential, regardless of their race, ethnicity, color, age, gender, sexual orientation, physical disability or other defining characteristic.

To drive the quest for diversity and inclusion in the work place, the American Society of Newspaper Editors will:

- Commit a significant portion of the Society's energy and resources to fostering newsroom diversity.
- Advocate diversity in content as a journalistic core value.
- Encourage and assist all newspapers to have minority journalists [*sic*] representation, to increase representation of journalists of color to reach 20 percent industrywide by 2010, and to achieve parity with local communities as soon as possible.
- Monitor year by year the employment of Asian Americans, blacks, Native Americans, and Hispanics in the newsroom.
- Encourage collaboration on diversity among various groups.

ASNE Board of Directors Minutes, ASNE Archives, Reston, Va., March 31, 1998: 1416.

APPENDIX B

Mission Statement: Newsroom Diversity 2000

While American newsrooms have become more diverse in recent years, newspapers will fall short of achieving racial parity in newsrooms with the population by 2000.

ASNE reaffirms its commitment to racial parity in newsrooms and to full and accurate news coverage of our nation's diverse communities. The Society urges everyone in journalism—newsroom professionals, publishers, educators, journalism associations and others—to join the quest for greater newsroom diversity.

ASNE has adopted the following mission statement on newsroom diversity:

> To cover communities fully, to carry out their role in a democracy, and to succeed in the marketplace, the nation's newsrooms must reflect the racial diversity of American society by 2025 or sooner. At a minimum, all newspapers should employ journalists of color and every newspaper should reflect the diversity of its community.
>
> The newsroom must be a place in which all employees contribute their full potential, regardless of race, ethnicity, color, age, gender, sexual orientation, physical ability or other defining characteristic.

ASNE will pursue the following strategies, which may be expanded or amended periodically:

- Conduct an annual census of employment of Asian Americans, blacks, Native Americans, Hispanics and women in the newsroom.

- Encourage and assist editors in recruiting, hiring and managing diverse newsrooms.
- Expand ASNE efforts to foster newsroom diversity.
- Establish three-year benchmarks for measuring progress.

ASNE Board of Directors Minutes, ASNE Archives, Reston, Va., March 31, 1998: 1432.

Notes

Introduction: The Black and White of Newspapers

1. A 1955 Lincoln University study reported that twenty-one black journalists were employed at white-owned daily newspapers, while earlier studies placed the number at twelve in 1952 and fifteen in 1948. Armistead Scott Pride, "Low Man on the Totem Pole," *Nieman Reports,* April 1955, 21, quoted in David R. Davies, *An Industry in Transition: Major Trends in American Daily Newspapers, 1945–1965* (PhD diss., University of Alabama, 1997) chap. 6.

2. American Society of Newspaper Editors, *Problems of Journalism: Proceedings of the American Society of Newspaper Editors,* April 15–17, 1948: 99. Until 2004 the ASNE self-published bound transcriptions of each year's convention proceedings. Hereafter, references to volumes in this series will be abbreviated as *Proceedings.*

3. The American black press is usually dated to the publication of *Freedom's Journal* in 1827. For comprehensive histories of the black press, see Armistead A. Pride and Clint Wilson II, *A History of the Black Press* (Washington, DC: Howard University Press, 1997) and Roland E. Wolsley, *The Black Press, U.S.A.* (Ames: University of Iowa Press, 1990).

4. Campbell Gibson and Kay Jung, *Historical Census Statistics on Population Totals By Race, 1790 to 1990, and By Hispanic Origin, 1970 to 1990, For The United States, Regions, Divisions, and States,* U.S. Census Bureau, Population Division, Working Paper Series no. 56, Table 1, September 2002.

5. Edward Seaton, "Some Light on ASNE's Revised Diversity Goal," *American Editor* 791 (May 1998): 2, and Diversity Committee Report, *Proceedings,* April 8–11, 1997: 232.

6. Mary L. Dudziak argues that civil rights reform was, in part, a response to growing international concern that racial inequality robbed the United States of the moral

authority to lead the fight against Communism after World War II. She cites the foreign policy implications of Truman's initiatives and identifies them as the beginning of civil rights reform. *Cold War Civil Rights: Race and the Image of American Democracy* (Princeton University Press, 2000), chap. 3.

7. President Warren Harding, a newspaper publisher, was a member of the ASNE, although he died a year after its founding and there is no record that he spoke to the organization. Calvin Coolidge, who occupied the White House between Harding and Hoover, is not on record as addressing the ASNE.

8. Gunnar Myrdal, *An American Dilemma: The Negro Problem and Modern Democracy,* vol. 1 (New Brunswick, NJ: Transaction Publishing, 1996), 29.

9. Ibid., vol. 2, chap. 42.

10. Led by Robert Hutchins, the University of Chicago president, the commission emphasized the need for accuracy in news reporting and the constitutional obligation to provide forums for a broader diversity of information and opinion. Commission on Freedom of the Press, *A Free and Responsible Press* (Chicago: University of Chicago Press, 1947), 20–21.

The indignation in the ASNE's response to the report was noteworthy. Crafting its public rebuke of the commission's meddling in press affairs consumed a good portion of the organization's convention business that year. According to *Arkansas Gazette* editor Harry Ashmore, the Hutchins report caused defensive ASNE members to "huddle rumps together, horns out, in the immemorial manner, say of the National Association of Manufacturers faced by a threat of regulated prices." *Columbia Journalism Review* (Summer 1967), quoted in Paul A. Pratte, *Gods Within the Machine: A History of the American Society of Newspaper Editors, 1923–1993* (Westport, CT: Praeger, 1995) and James Aronson, *The Press and the Cold War* (Indianapolis: Bobbs-Merrill Co., 1970), 266. In addition, Norman Isaacs comments upon the editors' "visceral" reaction to the report. *Untended Gate: The Mismanaged Press* (New York: Columbia University Press, 1986), 103.

11. Theodore Peterson, "The Social Responsibility of the Press," in Fred S. Siebert, Theodore Peterson, and Wilbur Schramm, *Four Theories of the Press* (Urbana: University of Illinois Press, 1984), 74.

12. National Advisory Commission on Civil Disorders, *Report of the National Advisory Commission of Civil Disorders* (New York: New York Times Co., 1968), chap. 15.

13. *Proceedings,* April 25–26, 1924: 57.

14. See chapters 2 and 3.

15. *Proceedings,* April 25–26, 1924: 56.

16. In 1924, the ASNE board decided that newspapers in cities with populations greater than 100,000 each could have four ASNE members, papers in cities with populations of 75,000 to 100,000 could have two, and papers in cities with 50,000 to 75,000 in population were allotted one member each (ASNE board minutes, ASNE Archives, Reston, Va., April 24, 1924: 21). In response to industry changes and declining membership, the ASNE board has made piecemeal revisions through the

years, retaining for many years the daily newspaper requirement but broadening the definition of a directing editor. Eventually, as economic strain in the newspaper industry impacted ASNE membership, the ASNE board modified the restriction on the number of editors from a single paper or circulation category who could join and expanded membership to include news directors of wire services and online news enterprises and journalism educators (ASNE Bylaws, Article II).

17. The daily newspaper requirement had been invoked in other contexts to maintain racial barriers within journalism and to marginalize the black press. For example, the daily newspaper criterion was used to bar representatives of black newspapers from the White House press corps. Franklin Roosevelt relaxed the restriction in the 1940s. Patrick Washburn, *A Question of Sedition: The Federal Government's Investigation of the Black Press during World War II* (New York: Oxford University Press, 1986), 197–202.

18. As chapter 1 notes, the ASNE interpreted the status of the *Chicago Defender* and its editors' eligibility for membership differently in the 1960s than in the 1950s, when the ASNE leadership had not felt compelled to integrate the organization and had denied membership to Sengstacke's managing editor. Similarly, in 1946 the ASNE board had denied full membership to Julio Garzon, editor of *La Prenza,* a leading Spanish-language daily in New York, who met all membership criteria related to daily publication and professional stature. ASNE board minutes, April 17, 1946: 242; "Julio Garzon Elected," *ASNE Bulletin* 274 (May 1946): 2; and "About Our Spanish-Speaking 'americano,'" *ASNE Bulletin* 278 (October 1946): 3.

19. For example, when Eleanor Patterson, editor of the *Washington Times-Herald* was nominated for membership in 1936, William Allen White, editor of the *Emporia (Kans.) Gazette,* expressed concern about her induction. William Allen White, letter to M. V. Atwood, March 28, 1936, William Allen White Papers, Library of Congress, Series C, Box 244. See also Walter M. Harrison, letter to White, February 8, 1930, White Papers, Series C, Box 163. During the 1939 convention, when he was president of ASNE, White also made disparaging remarks about Doris Fleeson, Washington correspondent for the *New York Daily News,* and two other women journalists who appeared on a panel about women newspaper readers. "It seems to me that the Program Committee who picked these three lovely little hellcats was just inspired," White said, then added of Fleeson, "I only wish she were my own pet panther." *Proceedings,* April 20–22, 1939: 86.

20. Women were not admitted to the National Press Club until 1971. The ASNE elected to move the main portion of its meeting to a hotel in 1950, but occasionally held events in the NPC thereafter. "SDX Breakfast at 8, But Minus the Ladies," *ASNE Bulletin* 330 (April 1951): 4, and *Proceedings,* April 18–20, 1935: 14.

21. "Ladies of the ASNE," *ASNE Bulletin* 302 (October 1948): 3.

22. Within a year of its founding, the ASNE had a functioning Committee on Schools of Journalism, which collaborated with the Accrediting Council for Education in Journalism and Mass Communication and its precursors. ASNE supplied many of the accrediting council's chairs and retained permanent representation on its board.

23. *Proceedings,* April 17–19, 1930: 44–45.

24. Accreditation would remain closed to journalism programs at historically black colleges until 1982 when Florida A & M was accredited. When the ASNE launched its newsroom diversity initiative in 1978 and encouraged its members to hire nonwhite journalists, candidates from accredited programs were in short supply and representatives from historically black colleges and universities perceived the journalism accreditation structure as a barrier. Lee Stinnett, "Minorities in the Newsroom," *ASNE Bulletin* 640 (March 1981): 3.

25. Albert Fitzpatrick, telephone interview with author, November 9, 2004. Fitzpatrick was part of the small wave of African American journalists who secured reporting jobs in white newsrooms during the 1950s and were hired as each newspaper's only black. Pamela Newkirk, *Within the Veil: Black Journalists, White Media* (New York: New York University Press, 2000), 57–62.

26. For example, in 1972 the U.S. Court of Appeals, Fifth Circuit, ruled for the newspaper in Montgomery, Alabama, in a case brought by an African American man who had asked, to no avail, that his fiancée's photograph be published on the newspaper's society page, not its black page. *Cook et al. v. The Advertiser Co., Inc., et al.,* 458 F.2d 1119 (1972).

27. Richard Dyer, *White* (London: Routledge, 1997), 1.

28. This understanding of the concept of whiteness is synthesized from and most strongly influenced by scholarship that views whiteness both as a social construction and as an organizing force in social and political relationships and institutions. This work includes Ruth Frankenberg, *White Women, Race Matters: The Social Construction of Whiteness* (Minneapolis: University of Minnesota Press, 1993); David Roediger, *The Wages of Whiteness: Race and the Making of the American Working Class* (London: Verso, 1991); Howard Winant, "White Racial Projects," in *The Making and Unmaking of Whiteness,* ed. Birgit Brander Rasmussen et al. (Durham, NC: Duke University Press, 2001), 107; and George Lipsitz, *The Possessive Investment in Whiteness: How White People Profit from Identity Politics* (Philadelphia: Temple University Press, 1998).

The application of whiteness as an analytical tool follows from the historical and cultural analyses contained in the work of Roediger and others: Dyer, *White;* Theodore Allen, *The Invention of the White Race,* Vol. 1: *Racial Oppression and Social Control* (London: Verso, 1994); Matthew Frye Jacobson, *Whiteness of a Different Color: European Immigrants and the Alchemy of Race* (Cambridge, MA: Harvard University Press, 1998); Ian Haney Lopez, *White by Law: The Legal Construction of Race* (New York: New York University Press, 1996); and Tomas Almaguer, *Racial Fault Lines: The Historical Origins of White Supremacy in California* (Berkeley: University of California Press, 1994).

Since the 1990s, whiteness studies have generated a strong following in academia but also a fair amount of criticism. For a critical review of the literature on whiteness, see Eric Arnesen, "Whiteness and the Historian's Imagination," *International Labor and Working Class History* 60 (Fall 2001): 3–32.

29. A number of scholars—including Roediger, Frankenburg, Dyer, Lipsitz, Haney Lopez, and Winant—have demonstrated persuasively that whiteness historically has derived much of its power from its invisibility. In addition, Toni Morrison has noted that the invisibility of whiteness historically has been tied to subject position, that whiteness always has been a salient feature of life for nonwhites. Others have worked with this concept, including bell hooks, who located the power of whiteness in the oppositional gaze, and Stuart Hall, who defined it as "the 'absent' but imperializing 'white eye'; the unmarked position from which all these 'observations' are made and from which, alone, they make sense." For the white editors of ASNE, whiteness becomes visible when it is interrogated and challenged. When whiteness is allowed to resume its status as unquestioned and taken for granted, it again disappears from their view. Toni Morrison, *Playing in the Dark: Whiteness and the Literary Imagination* (New York: Vintage Books, 1993); bell hooks, *Black Looks: Race and Representation* (Boston: South End Press, 1992), 115–31; and Stuart Hall, "The Whites of Their Eyes," in *The Media Reader,* ed. Manuel Alvarado and John O. Thompson (London: British Film Institute, 1990), 14. See also David Roediger's work on the "white look" in *Colored White: Transcending the Racial Past* (Berkeley: University of California Press, 2002), 44–54, and Ruth Frankenberg's modification of her earlier argument in "The Mirage of an Unmarked Whiteness," in *The Making and Unmaking of Whiteness,* 73–74.

30. Jacobson, *Whiteness of a Different Color,* 10.

31. John Dorst, *Looking West* (Philadelphia: University of Pennsylvania Press, 1999), 31.

32. Michel Foucault, *The Archaeology of Knowledge* (New York: Pantheon Books, 1972), 49.

33. Michel Foucault, *The History of Sexuality, Vol. 1: An Introduction* (New York: Vintage Books, 1990), 27.

34. Lee Stinnett, telephone interview with author, March 10, 2005.

35. Maynard, who had been editorial page editor at the *Washington Post,* and Hicks Maynard, who had been a reporter at the *New York Times,* had made a career of newsroom integration activism and training nonwhite journalists to take jobs in daily newspaper newsrooms. Fitzpatrick was then at the *Akron Beacon Journal,* while Jay Harris was an associate director of the Gannett Urban Journalism Center at the Medill School of Journalism at Northwestern University.

36. Telephone interviews with author: Gilbert Bailon, October 20, 2004; Rick Rodriguez, July 20, 2005; Edward Seaton, November 17, 2004.

37. Seaton interview and Bobbi Bowman, "Newspapers Crippled by Lessons Unlearned after Forty Years," Maynard Institute for Journalism Education, February 21, 2008, available at http://mije.org/bobbibowman/newspapers_crippled (accessed February 27, 2012).

38. Self-published by the ASNE in 1974 and written by Alice Fox Pitts, a longtime ASNE staff member, *Read All About It! 50 Years of the ASNE* is a self-congratulatory institutional memoir that provides little critical insight into the organization's coming to terms with issues of race and gender. Pitts's book was followed twenty years later by *Gods Within the Machine: A History of the American Society of Newspaper Editors, 1923–1993.* Written by Paul A. Pratte, this history documents the organization's policies and key figures but makes only passing mention of issues related to newsroom diversity and no mention of the Goal 2000 initiative.

39. Newkirk, *Within the Veil;* Maurine Beasley and Sheila Gibbons, *Taking Their Place: A Documentary History of Women and Journalism,* 2nd ed. (State College, PA: Strata, 2002).

40. Michael Omi and Howard Winant, *Racial Formation in the United States: From the 1960s to the 1990s,* 2nd ed. (New York: Routledge, 1994), and Douglas S. Massey and Nancy A. Denton, *American Apartheid: Segregation and the Making of the Underclass* (Cambridge, MA: Harvard University Press, 1993).

41. See note 29.

42. Michael K. Brown et al., *White-Washing Race: The Myth of a Color-blind Society* (Berkeley: University of California Press, 2003) and Elizabeth Anderson, *The Imperative of Integration* (Princeton: Princeton University Press, 2010). See also Michelle Alexander, *The New Jim Crow: Mass Incarceration in the Age of Colorblindness* (New York: New Press, 2012), and Eduardo Bonilla-Silva, *Racism Without Racists: Color-blind Racism and the Persistence of Racial Inequality in the United States* (Lanham, MD: Rowman & Littlefield, 2003).

43. William Julius Wilson, *When Work Disappears: The World of the New Urban Poor* (New York: Knopf, 1997); Deidre Royster, *Race and the Invisible Hand: How White Networks Exclude Black Men from Blue-Collar Jobs* (Berkeley: University of California Press, 2003); Terry H. Anderson, *In Pursuit of Fairness: A History of Affirmative Action* (Oxford: Oxford University Press, 2004). See also, Philip F. Rubio, *A History of Affirmative Action, 1619–2000* (Oxford: University of Mississippi Press, 2001).

44. *Oliver Brown, et al. v. Board of Education of Topeka, et al.*, 347 U.S. 483 (1954).

45. Vron Ware and Les Back, *Out of Whiteness: Color, Politics, and Culture* (Chicago: University of Chicago Press, 2002), 9.

Chapter 1. Manning the Barricade

1. Virginius Dabney, "Dissension," *ASNE Bulletin* 400 (July 1957): 16.

2. Grover C. Hall Jr., "Defiance from the Southland," *ASNE Bulletin* 400 (July 1957): 16.

3. Michael J. Ogden, "North Team a Close Second," *ASNE Bulletin* 401 (September 1957): 15. The Civil War analogies continued. Two years later, Dabney wrote on behalf of himself and Hall, "As representatives of the two Confederate capitals, we

hurl our defi most specially at any dam-Yankees who are in the mood, but we also are amenable to challenges from Dixie racketeers. We may be heading for Appomattox on this one, but we're sticking our necks out anyway." Virginius Dabney, "Virginia Defi," *ASNE Bulletin* 417 (February 1959): 10.

4. Although the political joke lost its relevance, Dabney and others participated in the convention tennis tournament as late as 1968. Virginius Dabney, letter to William Snider, March 11, 1968, Virginius Dabney Papers, University of Virginia, MSS 7690-n, Box 1.

5. Relevant history of this period and of the press's role in reporting it is found in Taylor Branch, *Parting the Waters: America in the King Years, 1954–63* (New York: Touchstone, 1988) and Gene Roberts and Hank Klibanoff, *The Race Beat: The Press, The Civil Rights Struggle, and the Awakening of a Nation* (New York: Vintage, 2006).

6. National Advisory Commission on Civil Disorders, *Report of the National Advisory Commission of Civil Disorders* (New York: New York Times Co., 1968), chap. 15.

7. *Proceedings,* April 21–23, 1955: 93.

8. Ibid. Pope likely was referring to editor C. A. Scott of the *Atlanta Daily World,* which had published as a daily since 1934. The *Chicago Defender* did not publish a daily edition until 1956.

9. *Proceedings,* April 21–23, 1955: 89.

10. The black reporter in question appears to have been writing for the "Negro page" in the paper. Carroll said, "Our newspaper has a Negro reporter who is a regular member of the reportorial staff, who has a desk in our news room. [*sic*] He covers news on the same basis as any other reporter. This is in North Carolina. I don't know of any other newspaper any place in the country that has a Negro reporter. We try to give full coverage in our news. On Sunday we have a full page on which we principally print all sorts of news of the Negro community." *Proceedings,* April 21–23, 1955: 90.

11. *Proceedings,* April 19–21, 1956: 78–80, 84–85.

12. Ibid., 88.

13. Ibid., 89.

14. Ibid., 92–93. In addition to Scott of the *Atlanta Daily World*, MacDonald likely was referring to John Sengstacke, editor of the *Chicago Defender,* who transformed that paper into a daily in 1956.

15. For a comprehensive analysis of the evolution of Ayers's positions on race, see Kevin Stoker, "Liberal Journalism in the Deep South: Harry M. Ayers and the 'Bothersome' Race Question," *Journalism History* 27, no. 1 (Spring 2001): 22–33.

16. Following the 1955 convention, Carl Lindstrom, chair of the Bulletin Advisory Committee, wondered whether a follow-up article in the *Bulletin* might be necessary, because the subject of the panel discussion was to have been news coverage of the civil rights issue. He wrote, "There were those who thought the Washington discussions to a degree got off the track of newspaper technique and attitudes, and got lost in the race issue itself. Maybe there is a need to get it back on the beam of the

newspaper problem as suggested." However, he did not indicate that the members in question found the remarks themselves objectionable. Carl Lindstrom, letter to Virginius Dabney, July 16, 1955, Dabney Papers, 7690-g, Box 1.

17. Robert C. Albrook, "Editors Heatedly Debate Senate Probe of Press," *Washington Post and Times-Herald,* April 20, 1956: 1, 24. Ayers's widow would claim in 1994 that her husband's diatribe at the convention was a symptom of Alzheimer's disease. Stoker, "Liberal Journalism in the Deep South," 29. Even if his health was failing, Ayers maintained correspondence and continued to express variations of the racist views he shared at the 1956 convention. For example, he wrote Reed Sarratt, the editor from Winston-Salem, later in 1956 to criticize a speech in which Sarratt had advocated acceptance of the *Brown* ruling because it would have no impact on social patterns in the South. Ayers told Sarratt, "My criticism of your speech lies in the fact that you seem more interested in helping the Negro than in protecting the whites." Ayers went on to reference the portrayal of a black soldier in "Ginzberg's book," likely a reference to *The Negro Potential,* published by Columbia University scholar Eli Ginzberg in 1956. Ayers said of the book, "I think it shows the Negro up just about for what he is, an irresponsible and immoral individual, generally speaking." Harry Ayers, letter to Reed Sarratt, July 25, 1956, Reed Sarratt Papers, Southern Historical Collection, University of North Carolina–Chapel Hill, Box 6.

18. The editor who made the request is not identified by name in the convention proceedings; however, Alicia Patterson, editor and publisher of *Newsday,* wrote Sarratt a few months after the convention to say, "I have been meaning to write you for sometime [*sic*] on the courage you showed at the ASNE convention when that charmer from South Carolina spoke out of order. I wish there were more like you around." Although Ayers was from Alabama, not South Carolina, Patterson's reference is very likely to Ayers. The proceedings offer no indication that Sarratt spoke at any other point during the session in question. In addition, a *New York Post* editorial points in the direction of Sarratt in denouncing Ayers's speech. The *Post* said, "In fairness, it should be reported that Ayers' oration evoked visible pain among both Southern and Northern editors. Indeed, it was a young editor from North Carolina who finally leaped to his feet and reminded the chairman that the speaker was exceeding his time—a chivalrous way of saying that the man was out of bounds." Letter from Alicia Patterson to Reed Sarratt, August 3, 1956, Sarratt Papers, Box 6, and *New York Post,* " . . . The Unpleasant Sound," April 22, 1956.

19. Virginius Dabney, notes of telephone call to Jenkin L. Jones, March 9, 1956, Dabney Papers, MSS 7690-g, Box 1.

20. Virginius Dabney, letter to Kenneth MacDonald, May 7, 1956, Dabney Papers, MSS 7690-g, Box 1.

21. George Clapp, untitled letter to the editor, *ASNE Bulletin* 389 (August 1956): 19.

22. Quoted in Stoker, "Liberal Journalism in the Deep South," 28.

23. After being scolded by the moderator for making a joke in poor taste ("Recently, I got a communication from Albuquerque saying that the Women's Press

Association of New Mexico had voted me the editor of the year, the one with whom they would most like to put the paper to bed"), Mahaffey characterized himself as "kind of a middle-of-the-roader" on race and then offered a mocking reminiscence of his childhood mammy, "old Aunt Mary, who was as black as the Ace of Spades." A rambling commentary on race followed. *Proceedings,* April 19–21, 1956, 81–82.

24. Alice Fox Pitts, letter to Virginius Dabney, April 28, 1956, Dabney Papers, 7690-g, Box 1.

25. At Pitts's suggestion, the additional member comment was included with the explanatory note, apparently contrived, that these were comments for which time ran out during the convention. Alice Fox Pitts, letter to Kenneth MacDonald, April 24, 1956, Dabney Papers, 7690-g, Box 1.

26. Clapp, untitled letter to the editor, 19, and Pitts, *Read All About It!,* 282.

27. *Proceedings,* April 19–21, 1956: 94, and "Desegregation Coverage: A Further Look," *ASNE Bulletin* 387 (May 1956): 3.

28. "Desegregation Coverage: A Further Look," 3.

29. Clapp, untitled letter to the editor, 19.

30. Virginius Dabney, letter to Alice Fox Pitts, April 30, 1956, Dabney Papers, 7690-g, Box 1.

31. Alice Fox Pitts, letter to Virginius Dabney, May 2, 1956, Dabney Papers, 7690-g, Box 1.

32. Pitts, *Read All about It,* 283.

33. The convention transcript states, "President MacDonald later ruled that remarks once put on the record could not be expunged and that statements made during the panel discussion would stand." However, the ASNE's fifty-year history says the section of the transcript was "bowdlerized" to remove a potentially libelous statement Ayers made about a U.S. Army officer. *Proceedings,* April 19–21, 1956, 94, and Pitts, *Read All About It,* 282.

34. Kenneth MacDonald, letter to Virginius Dabney, May 9, 1956, Dabney Papers, 7690-g, Box 1.

35. ASNE board minutes, October 17–18, 1958: 167.

36. Wallace Lemoe, letter to ASNE board members, May 6, 1957, Dabney Papers, 7690-h, Box 3.

37. Ibid.

38. ASNE board minutes, October 17–18, 1958: 168, and October 31, 1959: 191.

39. In an article in the *Atlantic Monthly,* Dabney had warned at length that extremist black leaders and the black and white newspapers that sympathized with their criticism of segregation risked inciting race riots more devastating than those during World War I, a development that could aid the Axis powers. "Nearer and Nearer the Precipice," *Atlantic Monthly* 171 (January 1943): 94–100.

40. Inconsistencies in the application of the membership standards were noted by ASNE directors from time to time. See, for example, ASNE board minutes, November 12, 1939: 157, and December 13–14, 1946: 247–48.

41. ASNE board minutes, November 12, 1965: 304, and letter from Arthur Deck to Robert Henry Mason, September 20, 1965, Robert Henry Mason Papers, University of North Carolina–Chapel Hill, Southern Historical Collection, Folder 37.

42. Martin would go on to serve as a civil rights advisor to the Kennedy, Johnson, and Carter Administrations. He remained affiliated with the *Defender,* was granted ASNE membership in 1973, and remained on the rolls through 1977. Albert Fitzpatrick of the *Akron Beacon Journal* would be the first African American editor of a white-run newspaper to be elected to ASNE membership.

43. In his presidential message, Healy, a native Mississippian, drew distinctions between mere Southerners in the ASNE and those with greater authenticity. He said, "Reconstruction really was over the day a member from the Deep South became president of the American Society of Newspaper Editors." In this hierarchy, editors from such states as Virginia, Oklahoma, Kentucky, and Georgia did not make the cut. The Mississippi Legislature also saw Healy's election to the ASNE presidency as worthy of a resolution of commendation. "Presidential Message," *ASNE Bulletin* 409 (May 1958): 3–4, and 410 (June 1958): 16. In addition, a sense of Healy's politics on race emerges from a profile he wrote for the *Bulletin* featuring a new member from Mississippi. George Healy Jr., "A Crusader for State's Rights and the Free Enterprise System," *ASNE Bulletin* 417 (January 1959): 13.

44. W. J. Cash, *The Mind of the South* (New York: Vintage, 1941), 226. Cash's book, widely regarded as a classic on the history of Southern thought prior to World War II, has been supplemented by James C. Cobb, *Away Down South: A History of Southern Identity* (Oxford University Press, 2005). Also indispensible to an understanding of the South in the 1950s is John Egerton, *Speak Now Against the Day: The Generation before the Civil Rights Movement* (Chapel Hill: University of North Carolina Press, 1995).

45. For comprehensive discussions of the ambivalence about, and even aversion to, desegregation that afflicted progressive Southern editors, see Morton Sosna, *In Search of the Silent South: Southern Liberals and the Race Issue* (New York: Columbia University Press, 1977); John T. Kneebone, *Southern Liberal Journalists and the Issue of Race, 1920–1944* (Chapel Hill: University of North Carolina Press, 1985); Reed Sarratt, *The Ordeal of Desegregation: The First Decade* (New York: Harper and Row, 1966); Alex Leidholdt, "Virginius Dabney and Lenoir Chambers: Two Southern Liberal Newspaper Editors Face Virginia's Massive Resistance to Public School Integration," *American Journalism* (Fall 1998): 35–68; Ralph McGill, *No Place to Hide: The South and Human Rights,* ed. Calvin M. Logue (Mercer University Press, 1984), 1:xi–xlvi; and Ralph McGill, "Civil Rights for the Negro," *Atlantic Monthly* 184 (November 1949): 64–66.

46. Egerton, *Speak Now Against the Day,* 616.

47. Grover C. Hall Jr., "To: Northern Editors of ASNE," *ASNE Bulletin* 389 (August 1956): 5. For a detailed account of Hall's obsession with the hypocrisy of the Northern press, see Douglas Cumming, "How the Alabama Press Prepared the Ground

for *New York Times v. Sullivan,*" Association for Education in Journalism and Mass Communication, 2002.

48. Hall, "To: Northern Editors of ASNE," 5.

49. Prior to 1950, the only Southerners to hold the ASNE presidency were Walter M. Harrison, *Oklahoma City Oklahoman,* 1928–30, and Tom Wallace, *Louisville Times,* 1940–41.

Within ASNE operations, the power of the president registers primarily in the appointment of committee chairs. For example, owing to the small number of professional staff employed by ASNE at the time, the content in the *Bulletin* was greatly influenced by the chair of the Bulletin Advisory Committee. *Bulletin* chairmen during the 1950s included Jenkin Lloyd Jones, *Tulsa Tribune,* 1951–52 and Miles Wolff, *Greensboro Daily News,* 1957–61.

50. "People at the Convention," *ASNE Bulletin* (387) May 1956: 6.

51. Virginius Dabney, "Tennis Tidings," *ASNE Bulletin* 433 (June 1960): 11.

52. Hall, "To: Northern Editors of ASNE," 6.

53. Harry M. Ayers, "Criticism," *ASNE Bulletin* 409 (May 1958): 16.

54. John Harris, "Race Identification in Stories," ASNE *Bulletin* 355 (June 1953): 11.

55. John T. O'Rourke, "Race Identification," *ASNE Bulletin* 410 (June 1958): 13.

56. E. T. Stone, "We Went the Distance . . . and Eliminated Racial Distinction on Our Society Pages," *ASNE Bulletin* 378 (August 1955): 3.

57. *ASNE Bulletin* 444 (July 1961): 7. Delegations of ASNE members occasionally have made international trips to visit with government and media leaders in foreign countries, often in conjunction with freedom of press initiatives. It appears that the editors of the 1950s did not always display respect for the people they encountered. In addition to the mockery of the women photographed in Chad, another group also ridiculed women they met on a trip to the Soviet Union. The following description appeared in a detailed package of stories about the trip: "The average Russian woman is big, broad, stocky and plain looking. A corset manufacturer would have a field day. The younger women seem to be going in more for cosmetics (the way they smear on eye makeup is something—makes them look as if they are going to a masquerade party) but a good-looking, happy looking Soviet girl is a rarity. There are some beautiful women, however, and they stand out all the more by contrast." William Woestendiek, "Everything You Need to Know about Russian Women," *ASNE Bulletin* 456 (September 1962): 9.

58. See note 23.

59. John Q. Mahaffey, "The West Is Still Wild in Texarkana," *ASNE Bulletin* 410 (June 1958): 15.

60. John Q. Mahaffey, "The Night Texarkana 'Turned the Corner,'" *ASNE Bulletin* 507 (April 1967): 14–15.

61. In the *ASNE Bulletin,* see such profiles as Robert Mason, "Courtly Virginian," 426 (December 1959): 12; Creed Black, "The Disorganization Man," 435 (October 1960): 8–9; Harry Provenance, "Unscrambled Egghead," 448 (December 1961): 14–16;

James Walker, "Bill Loves Food, Children, Animals," 468 (October 1963): 8–9; Harry Ashmore, "Mr. J.N. at 91," 470 (December 1963): 13–15; and Edward C. Pierce, "Coming to Grips with Baggs," 494 (February 1966): 8–9.

62. John Q. Mahaffey, letter to Louis Harris, April 1965, Sylvan Meyer Papers, University of North Carolina–Chapel Hill, Southern Historical Collection, Box 5, Folder 1.

63. *Proceedings,* April 16–18, 1964: 68.

64. The possibility of placing African Americans on the convention program prior to 1964 apparently was discussed. Norman Isaacs, convention program committee chair, received a suggestion in 1959 to add to the 1960 convention lineup "a panel of four or five top Negro editors and/or reporters to tell us what sort of news and editorial the Negro press is talking." It is unclear why the Program Committee did not implement this suggestion. Letter from Sylvan Meyer to Norman Isaacs, June 2, 1959, Meyer Papers, Box 5, Folder 1.

65. *Proceedings,* April 16–18, 1964: 75.

66. Robert M. White II, "Whither Civil Rights?" *ASNE Bulletin* 475 (May 1964): 7.

67. *Proceedings,* April 16–18, 1964: 92–93.

68. Gene Giancarlo, letter to Robert Lasch, March 12, 1964, Robert Lasch Papers, Wisconsin Historical Society Library and Archives, Madison, Box 5.

69. Indeed, so many editors were leaving the hall that John C. Colburn of the *Wichita Eagle and Beacon*, who introduced the "Civil Rights Combatants" session, opened his remarks, saying, "Ladies and gentlemen, will those who are leaving this session please try to be as quiet as possible." Roy Wilkins, who was first on the panel to speak, then attempted what he described as "the miracle of trying to cram the civil rights question into five minutes." *Proceedings,* April 16–18, 1964: 75.

70. After the Lynchburg, Virginia, papers were criticized for not running black people's obituaries, the *ASNE Bulletin* surveyed thirty-seven Southern editors as to their practices. Three still segregated obituaries, and some had just recently begun to mix white and black death notices. Robert Mason, "How Does the Southern Press Treat Negro Death Notices?" *ASNE Bulletin* 510 (July 1967): 3–5, 8.

71. Donald K. Baldwin, "She Battles for Truth—and Survival," *ASNE Bulletin* 478 (September 1964): 15–16.

72. "Lady in a Lurch," *ASNE Bulletin* 489 (September 1965): 13.

73. Eugene C. Patterson, telephone interview, October 11, 2004.

74. John Seigenthaler Sr., telephone interview, November 17, 2004.

75. In the *ASNE Bulletin* 383 (January 1956), see "Where Are the Journalism School Graduates?" 3; Thomas Collins, "There Are Ladies Present," 4; Benjamin Carroll, "Woman Covers the Police Beat," 5–6; and Arthur Burrowes, "They're as Good as Men and Often Better," 6.

76. "Evaluation at Newsday," *ASNE Bulletin* 383 (January 1956): 2–3. In a profile story in 1960, Patterson would be characterized in stereotype, as managing by women's intuition, displaying piques of temper, and frequently changing her mind.

William Woestendiek, "Her Day at Newsday," *ASNE Bulletin* 435 (October 1960): 9–10.

77. Robert Atwood, "The Four-Stage Problem," *ASNE Bulletin* 494 (February 1966): 10–11.

78. Ken Tooill, "No Women, No Problems," *ASNE Bulletin* 494 (February 1966): 12.

79. "A Woman Speaks," *ASNE Bulletin* 468 (October 1963): 14.

80. Atwood, "The Four-Stage Problem," 10.

81. Vern Croop, "Reverse Discrimination," *ASNE Bulletin* 494 (February 1966): 12.

82. The ASNE had 562 members on April 1, 1955. ASNE board minutes, October 28, 1955: 107A. Oveta Culp Hobby of the *Houston Chronicle,* the first woman director, took inactive status from the ASNE in 1953, when she was appointed to the Eisenhower cabinet as the first secretary of health, education, and welfare.

Chapter 2. Seeking Justice in a Climate of Irony

1. Isaacs's passion for journalism ethics was not new. In 1955, he delivered the William Allen White Memorial Lecture at the University of Kansas on the topic "Conscience and the Editor." A decade later, he contributed a piece by the same title to an anthology on journalism issues: Gerald Gross, ed., *The Responsibility of the Press* (New York: Fleet Publishing Corp., 1966). Isaacs also wrote passionately of press irresponsibility in his book, *Untended Gates: The Mismanaged Press,* which critiqued the ethical performance of the press and laid out his case for the National News Council, which operated from 1973 to 1983. A detailed narrative on Isaacs's failed attempt to interest ASNE in a grievance procedure is found in Paul A. Pratte, *Gods Within the Machine: A History of the American Society of Newspaper Editors, 1923–1993,* 15–19. Isaacs's crusading spirit also was apparent in his leadership as editor of the *Louisville Courier-Journal,* which won the Pulitzer Prize for public service in 1967 for advocating reform of the Kentucky strip-mining industry.

2. *Proceedings,* April 19–21, 1972: 134.

3. In its 1974 report, the Minority Employment Committee said it had been unable to ascertain a census for nonwhite newsroom employees but that the figure probably had reached 1 percent. Information-gathering now was thwarted by editors' failure to respond to requests for information. *Proceedings,* April 19–21, 1972: 241.

4. The commission, chaired by Ohio governor Otto Kerner, had been specifically asked to test a pet theory of President Lyndon Johnson, who believed the media had indirectly fomented violence by providing black extremists with a public forum. The commission exonerated the press on that count, but found that "the media have thus far failed to report adequately on the causes and consequences of civil disorders and the underlying problems of race relations." *Report of the National Advisory Commission of Civil Disorders,* 363, 383.

5. Ibid., 366.

6. Ibid., 387.
7. Ibid., 384.
8. Tom Wicker, introduction to *Report of the National Advisory Commission on Civil Disorders*, ix. Wicker draws particular attention to the conservative membership of Herbert Jenkins, Atlanta's police chief; Charles B. Thornton, chairman and chief executive officer of Litton Industries; Katherine Graham Peden, Kentucky's commissioner of commerce; I. W. Abel, president of the United Steelworkers of America; and Senators William M. McCulloch of Ohio and Fred Harris of Oklahoma. The commission's membership also included New York mayor John Lindsay; Roy Wilkins, executive director of the National Association for the Advancement of Colored People; Senator Edward Brooke of Massachusetts; and Representative James Corman of California.
9. The Kerner report appeared on the *New York Times* bestseller list on April 7, 1968, then on May 5, 1968 rose to no. 1, where it remained almost four months. All told, the report was on the list for thirty-two weeks. *Bestseller Index* (Jefferson, NC: McFarland & Co., 1998).
10. Lori Demo, "The Shameful Delay: Newspapers' Recruitment of Minority Employees," Association for Education in Journalism and Mass Communication, 1999.
11. *Proceedings*, April 17–20, 1968: 32, 36–37, 45. In the *ASNE Bulletin* 519 (May 1968), see William Ringle, "Almost a Reprise of 'Firing Line,'" 18, and Tom Littlewood, "Are the Media Getting the Messages?" 19–20.
12. Ben W. Gilbert, "An Extraordinary Indictment of the Press," *ASNE Bulletin* 518 (April 1968): 14.
13. *Proceedings*, April 15–17, 1965: 78, and April 20–22, 1967: 35. In the *ASNE Bulletin* see Arthur Bertelson, "Mass Media and the Racial News Crisis," 493 (January 1966): 13–14; "Racial Disorders and the Role of Newsmen," 502 (November 1966): 3; Lawrence Newman Jr., "A Time to Play It Cool," 503 (December 1966): 15; Robert Mason, "How *Does* the Southern Press Treat Negro Death Notices?" 510 (July 1967): 3–5, 8; Frank L. Stanley Jr., "Race Poverty and the Press," 511 (September 1967): 1–2, 12; and Ben Gilbert, "Race Coverage," 515 (January 1968): 1–2, 13.
14. Carolyn Martindale, *The White Press and Black America* (New York: Greenwood Press, 1986), 2.
15. Edwin O. Guthman, "The Commission's Look at the News Media," in *The Media and the Cities* (Chicago: University of Chicago Press, 1968), 36.
16. The initial response of the Associated Press Managing Editors to the Kerner Commission, a 1968 report titled "In Black and White," was followed in 1969 by a second report, "Black Journalism: Obligation and Opportunity."
17. Norman Isaacs, "Agnew, the National Mood and the Media," *ASNE Bulletin* 537 (January 1970): 1–7, 13.
18. Philip Geyelin, "Regaining the Public's Trust," *ASNE Bulletin* 543 (July–August 1970): 3–4, 11.
19. "The Board Votes to Establish an Ethics Committee," *ASNE Bulletin* 549 (April 1970): 19.

20. In the *ASNE Bulletin* see, for example, Stanford Sesser, "Is There a Niche for Activism on the Altar of Objectivity?" 536 (December 1969): 14–15; William Hill, "Subjective Jottings on Objectivity," 537 (January 1970): 8–9; Derrick Daniels, "Separating Fact/Emotion—By Edict or By Example?" 538 (February 1970): 1–3; John Colburn, "Responsibility and Objectivity—The Debate Booms On," 538 (February 1970): 11–12; and Louis Gerdes, "Seeking Objectivity," 539 (March 1970): 17, 20.

21. Pete McKnight, "Where Are the Competent Newsmen Who Happen to be Negroes?" *ASNE Bulletin* 493 (January 1966): 6–8.

22. James Aronson, "Black Journalists: Why the Dearth?" *ASNE Bulletin* 558 (March 1972): 7.

23. ASNE board minutes April 12, 1971: 506, and April 16, 1971: 522.

24. "A Joint Report from the Committees on Minority Employment and Education for Journalism," April 20, 1972: 8.

25. Norman Isaacs, letter to John Troan, July 30, 1971, C. A. McKnight Papers, University of North Carolina–Charlotte, Box 4, Folder 18.

26. Norman Isaacs, letter to Ed Cony, July 7, 1971, McKnight Papers, Box 4, Folder 18.

27. The survey results released at the 1972 convention were based on answers to ten questions, which solicited a mix of numerical data and anecdotes from editors at newspapers with circulations of 75,000 and more. From the discussion of methodology in the joint report of the Committees on Minorities and Education, it is clear that the three-quarters of 1 percent is an estimate. Questionnaires, which were sent only to 252 daily newspapers with circulations of 75,000 or more (14.3 percent of the U.S. dailies publishing in 1972), were accompanied by a personal letter from an ASNE member and drew a 95.6 percent response rate. The survey's directors also factored an estimated number of unreported nonwhite employees into the data. The report said the survey confirmed "only 253 minority-group professionals on daily newspapers. Accepting the postulation that there may be another 50 such staffers on smaller newspapers not yet reached by the survey, the total professional figure nationally may reasonably be estimated at approximately 300—or three-fourths of one per cent of total writer-photographer-editor employment." "A Joint Report from the Committees on Minority Employment and Education for Journalism," 2.

28. For a useful examination of the role of biology in the conceptualization of race and racial difference, see David Theo Goldberg, *Racist Culture: Philosophy and the Politics of Meaning* (Oxford: Blackwell, 1993).

29. "A Joint Report from the Committees on Minority Employment and Education for Journalism," 3.

30. Norman Isaacs, letter to C. A. McKnight, August 16, 1971, McKnight Papers, Box 4, Folder 18. McKnight also cited supply as an issue in a letter to Harold Lappin, August 13, 1971, Box 4, Folder 18.

31. Aronson, "Black Journalists," 7.

32. "A Joint Report from the Committees on Minority Employment and Education for Journalism," 2.

33. Larry Jinks, letter to C. A. McKnight, July 9, 1971, McKnight Papers, Box 2, Folder 3.

34. Norman Isaacs, letter to Sylvan Meyer, September 13, 1971, Meyer Papers, ASNE-1971 Folder, Box 5.

35. Ibid.

36. Sylvan Meyer, memo to C. A. McKnight, "Encouraging More Minority Recruits to Journalism," December 27, 1971, ASNE archives.

37. "A Joint Report from the Committees on Minority Employment and Education for Journalism," 4.

38. Ibid.

39. Ibid., 3.

40. Untitled report of meeting, February 11–13, 1972, Columbia, Mo., Meyer Papers, ASNE 1972 Folder, Box 5.

41. For a detailed discussion of the complaint against the *Post,* see Newkirk, *Within the Veil: Black Journalists, White Media,* 110–14. A member of the Metro 7, as the plaintiffs came to be called, was LaBarbara Bowman, who would be hired in 1999 as diversity director for the ASNE.

42. "A Joint Report from the Committees on Minority Employment and Education for Journalism," 3–4.

43. Norman Isaacs, letter to C. A. McKnight, August 16, 1971, McKnight Papers, Box 4, Folder 18.

44. Norman Isaacs, letter to C. A. McKnight, March 30, 1972, McKnight Papers, Box 4, Folder 18.

45. Ibid., and *Proceedings,* April 19–21, 1972: 134.

46. Richard Cohen, "Convention Diary: How an Outsider Saw the April Meeting," *ASNE Bulletin* 560 (May–June 1972): 8.

47. *Proceedings,* April 19–21, 1972: 133–34.

48. Cohen, "Convention Diary," 8.

49. Concerns about the apparent emphasis placed on hiring blacks to the exclusion of other nonwhites also were raised during the question-and-answer session at the end of the panel. Armando Mantilla of the Latin-American News Service urged the panelists to improve the representation of all minorities. Isaacs responded that the survey conducted by his committee did include people of all groups. Later, an unidentified questioner asked whether there was a Chicano counterpart to the minority training programs that targeted blacks. Maynard said he had solicited candidates for his training program from other identity groups (*Proceedings,* April 19–21, 1972: 139–46). It is important to note that because the ASNE viewed race primarily as a black-white dichotomy, Latino, Asian American, and other journalists often were omitted from the conversation about inclusion. By this time the ASNE had admitted at least one active member from a Spanish-language paper—Padillo Vargas Badillo of *El Mundo* in San Juan, Puerto Rico, who joined in 1965—yet the

ASNE's focus was on the admission of John Sengstacke, the ASNE's first African American member, that same year. At this time, ASNE members seemed eager to categorize nonwhite people according to race but also uncertain what to do with nonblacks. Isaacs drew a distinction between Chicanos and Puerto Ricans, and Larry Jinks of the *Miami Herald,* in seeking survey data, asked editors to provide information about "Puerto Ricans, Cubans, Nisei, Chicanos, Chinese-Americans, and any others who genuinely fit the description" of nonwhite. ASNE board minutes, April 12, 1971: 506, and Larry Jinks, letter to C. A. McKnight, July 9, 1971, McKnight Papers, Box 2, Folder 3.

50. *Proceedings,* April 19–21, 1972: 134.

51. Ibid., 140–41.

52. Cohen, "Convention Diary," 8.

53. *Proceedings,* April 19–21, 1972: 137–38.

54. *Proceedings,* May 2–4, 1973: 18–19.

55. *Proceedings,* April 17–19, 1974: 241.

56. Leonard Lewin, "A Critic's View," *ASNE Bulletin* 569 (May–June 1973): 14.

57. Ibid., 15.

58. ASNE board minutes, April 19, 1974: 639. A year after this recommendation, the board discussed the phrasing of this directive as it appeared in the "Outline of ASNE Board Procedure on Membership Matters," a document designed to bring uniformity to the membership eligibility process. The minutes of the board meeting in 1975 show that John Sengstacke, the ASNE's first African American member and director, objected to the following language in the guidelines: "Directing editors of newspapers published by minority groups or editors of foreign language newspapers published in the United States should receive the same consideration for membership as is accorded applicants from other daily newspapers. It is the policy of the Society to encourage membership in such newspapers, so long as the newspapers meet the qualifications in other respects." The minutes state, "Mr. Sengstacke felt that singling out particular editors to 'receive the same consideration as' others was in itself objectionable, regardless of the Board's intent in choosing the language." The board voted to remove the language. ASNE board minutes, April 14, 1975: 679.

59. Pride and Wilson, *A History of the Black Press,* 204.

60. Cornelius Scott of the *Atlanta Daily World* would have been a likely addition to the ASNE, but in 1971 Sengstacke had been charged with the task of recruiting black members into ASNE and reported to the board and to McKnight that Scott was not interested. ASNE board minutes, April 12, 1971: 503, and letter from C. A. McKnight to Norman Isaacs, October 22, 1971, McKnight Papers, Box 4, Folder 18.

61. Martin took leaves of absence from the *Defender* during the 1960s to work on civil rights matters for the Kennedy and Johnson administrations, which interrupted his status as an editor. Interestingly, Martin's authorized biography omits any men-

tion of ASNE. Louis Poinsett, *Walking with Presidents: Louis Martin and the Rise of Black Political Power* (Lanham, MD: Madison Books, 1997).

62. Sengstacke's personal papers, which are housed at the Chicago Public Library, contain no ASNE-related correspondence or other materials prior to 1977.

63. See Dabney, "Nearer and Nearer the Precipice." Columnist Westbrook Pegler also was a vocal critic of the black press during the 1940s. Pegler's attacks on the *Chicago Defender* and the *Pittsburgh Courier* are described in Washburn, *A Question of Sedition: The Federal Government's Investigation of the Black Press during World War II,* 85–86.

64. Wolsely, *The Black Press, U.S.A.*, 324–26.

65. Mark Ethridge Jr., letter to the Nominating Committee, February 11, 1970, Mason Papers, Folder 37.

66. ASNE board minutes, April 18, 1969: 398.

67. C. A. McKnight, letter to Gene Giancarlo, March 30, 1971, McKnight Papers, Box 4, Folder 3.

68. ASNE board minutes, April 12, 1971: 503.

69. C. A. McKnight, letter to Norman Isaacs, October 22, 1971, McKnight Papers, Box 4, Folder 18, and ASNE board minutes, April 12, 1971: 503. McKnight at one point even suggested that he might be more effective than Sengstacke in recruiting the editor of the *Atlanta World*. "I've been worrying over the fact that we have only one black (Sengstacke) in ASNE," McKnight wrote. "He tells me he has talked to the editor of the *Atlanta World,* the only other black daily, about applying for membership but with no result. I may go after him." C. A. McKnight, letter to Norman Isaacs, October 22, 1971, McKnight Papers, Box 4, Folder 18.

70. Norman Isaacs, letter to C. A. McKnight, August 6, 1971, McKnight Papers, Box 4, Folder 18.

71. Hugh Morton, letter to Wilson Williams, November 4, 1970, and related correspondence, McKnight Papers, Box 3, Folder 12. Williams, the country club's president, responded with an undated, handwritten note across the bottom of Morton's letter: "It would be unrealistic for us to maintain a position that would cause you to pass up this opportunity. I would be most surprised if the board would not support your viewpoint and mine. Therefore, I suggest you go ahead and firm up your plans." On November 12, 1970, Morton sent McKnight a copy of the exchange. Six days later, McKnight received a letter from Morton, explaining that Williams was concerned that the frank discussion of the club's position on nonwhite guests should not have been copied to McKnight, because it might find its way into the press. On November 21, 1970, McKnight responded that the discussion of Sengstacke was "entirely confidential." He then assured Morton of Sengstacke's "professional accomplishments and his bearing as a gentleman."

72. Gene Giancarlo, letter to James Powell, August 9, 1977, James Powell Papers, University of Arkansas Library, Fayetteville, Box 2, File 12.

73. Nathan Pusey, letter to Louis Martin, January 16, 1970, Louis Martin Papers, Library of Congress, Box 1, Folder 3. Interestingly, Martin's papers in the LOC contain no archival correspondence regarding his membership and participation in ASNE. Similarly, Louis Poinsett's authorized biography of Martin (*Walking with Presidents: Louis Martin and the Rise of Black Political Power)* ignores Martin's involvement with the ASNE.

74. Wolseley, *The Black Press, U.S.A.*, 90–91.

75. C. A. McKnight, letter to Harold Lappin, August 13, 1971, McKnight Papers, Box 4, Folder 18.

76. "Proposed Amendments to the Society's Constitution," *ASNE Bulletin* 558 (March 1972): 26; "Amendments Ratified," *ASNE Bulletin* 560 (May–June 1972): 22.

77. "Outline of ASNE Board Procedure on Membership Matters," revised November 18, 1976, Powell Papers, Box 2, File 12.

78. Vincent Jones, "The Students View the Editors . . . and Vice Versa," *ASNE Bulletin* 542 (June 1970): 8–9. The title of the article is a reference to the editors' ogling of attractive women in short skirts.

79. Maggie Savoy, "Maggie Savoy: A Woman's Voice," *ASNE Bulletin* 546 (November–December 1970): 10.

80. Jean S. Taylor, "'Hell Hath . . . ' Just Ain't Good Enough," *ASNE Bulletin* 554 (October 1971): 3. A few months later, the *Bulletin* published a rebuttal of sorts, in which the author, a reporter for the *Kingsport* (Tenn.) *Times-News,* amid repeated references to "girl reporters," said she was seeking a middle ground on women's issues. Joan Roesgen, "How Much Relevance Can a Woman Take?" *ASNE Bulletin* 557 (February 1972): 4–5.

81. Taylor, "'Hell Hath . . .,'" 4.

82. J. Edward Murray, memo to members of the ASNE board, January 26, 1972, Meyer Papers, ASNE-1972 Folder, Box 5.

83. ASNE board minutes, April 17, 1972: 570–71, and "1972–73 Committees," *ASNE Bulletin* 560 (May 1972): 20.

84. bell hooks, *Ain't I a Woman: Black Women and Feminism* (Boston: South End Press, 1981), 7.

85. ASNE board minutes, November 20, 1972: 592.

86. Clayton Kirkpatrick and Judith W. Brown, "Women: Room at the Top?" *ASNE Bulletin* 567 (March 1973): 3.

87. ASNE board minutes, April 30, 1973: 598.

88. Kirkpatrick and Brown, "Women: Room at the Top?" 4.

89. Judith Brown, "Enlightened Program," *ASNE Bulletin* 569 (May–June 1973): 23. During her chairmanship of the Women's Rights Committee, Brown openly solicited information about women and increased the visibility of women in journalism through such *Bulletin* articles as Judith Brown and Richard Leonard, "Wanted: Info," 571 (September 1973): 15; Judith Brown, "Women in Newspaper Management," 573

(November-December 1973): 25; Richard Leonard, "Is There Equality for Women in Journalism?" 574 (January 1974): 24; and Marcia McQuern and Sally Jo Restivo, "The City Editor is a Woman," 575 (February 1974): 3–5.

90. "Wanted: More Women Members," *ASNE Bulletin* 578 (May–June 1974): 27.

91. "Amendment Ratified," *ASNE Bulletin* 587 (May–June 1975): 19, and ASNE board minutes, April 14, 1975: 662, 678, and October 23, 1975: 678.

92. Charles S. Rowe, letter to Howard Hays, May 15, 1975, and Charles S. Rowe, memo to the Membership Committee, May 23, 1975, ASNE archives.

93. Charles S. Rowe, letter to Howard Hays, May 15, 1975, ASNE archives.

94. Robert Chandler, letter to Charles Rowe, June 24, 1975, ASNE archives.

95. Loren Ghiglione, telephone interview with author, October 18, 2004.

96. Charles Rowe, letter to Loren Ghiglione, October 2, 1975, ASNE archives.

97. ASNE board minutes, October 23, 1975: 678, and "Two Amendments Voted," *ASNE Bulletin* 591 (November–December 1975): 23, and "Two Amendments Ratified," 596 (May–June 1976): 28.

98. Alicia Patterson, editor of *Newsday,* ran for the board in 1961 but lost. Until the 1970s, she and Hobby had been the only female board candidates.

99. "Read, Think and Vote," *ASNE Bulletin* 585 (March 1975): 14–17.

100. Christy C. Bulkeley, ". . . And About Women Members," *ASNE Bulletin* 598 (July–August 1976): 21. It is worth noting that John Sengstacke was elected to the board without a record of committee service.

101. "The Board Election Results," *ASNE Bulletin* 605 (May–June 1977): 19.

102. "Analysis of the Vote," *ASNE Bulletin* 615 (May–June 1978): 25.

103. Notably, the author of the article was a fashion writer. Blair Sabol, "Super Bowl Sportswriters Shatter a Fantasy," *ASNE Bulletin* 579 (July–August 1974): 24. Other pieces on women as sports writers include Jane Gross, "When a Woman Enters the Locker Room," *ASNE Bulletin* 586 (April 1975): 16–17.

104. Myra McPherson, "A Woman's View," *ASNE Bulletin* 569 (May–June 1973): 20–21. See also "When Was the Last Time You Hired a Homely Woman?" *ASNE Bulletin* 577 (April 1974): 20.

105. Tom Collins, "'We're Going to Have It All,'" *ASNE Bulletin* 588 (July–August 1975): 6.

106. Ibid., 7.

Chapter 3. "A Sensitive and Difficult Task"

1. The percentage of nonwhites in the United States in 1978 was assigned various numbers in the ASNE literature. For example, a 1977 *ASNE Bulletin* article gave the figure as 12 percent, while a year later another article cited 17 percent. Over the years, references to 11 percent and 15 percent also appeared. U.S. census data support the 17 percent figure. U.S. Department of Commerce, Bureau of the Census, "Population Profile of the United States: 1978," Series PO-20, No. 336, April 1979, and 1980 Census of Population, Vol. 1, Chap. B, United States Summary, Table 40.

2. The Minorities Committee made five recommendations to the board, which generally charted the direction of future newsroom integration work, without specifying how such goals should be implemented and achieved. The recommendations were these:

- The commitment to recruit, train, and hire minorities needs urgently to be rekindled. This is simply the right thing to do. It is also in the newspaper industry's economic self-interest.
- There should be at least an annual accounting by ASNE of minority employment, including not just total jobs but types of positions held.
- There should be special emphasis on increasing the number of minority newsroom executives.
- Smaller papers should be especially encouraged to add minority members to their staffs.
- Leaders among minority journalists have urged the industry to set a goal of minority employment by the year 2000 equivalent to the percentage of minority persons within the national population. The committee believes this is a fair and attainable goal.

Proceedings, April 9–12, 1978: 407.

3. Richard Smyser, telephone interview with author, October 4, 2004.

4. The ASNE board minutes indicate that John Quinn of Gannett Newspapers made the proposal to attach the addendum and Michael O'Neill of the *New York Daily News* drafted it. The diversity initiative appears to have had widespread support on the board, as Smyser's handwritten notes for remarks he made at an ASNE Minorities Dinner in Washington, D.C., in 1984 indicate that Bill Hornby of the *Denver Post* also spoke in favor of the addendum. In addition, the board minutes show that ASNE vice president John Hughes of the *Christian Science Monitor* made the motion to approve the Minorities Committee proposal, and Quinn and Robert Clark of the *Courier-Journal* and *Louisville Times* offered seconds. *Proceedings,* April 9–12, 1978: 308; ASNE board minutes, 757; and Richard Smyser, handwritten notes, February 15, 1984, Richard Smyser Papers, now housed at the Southern Historical Collection, University of North Carolina–Chapel Hill.

5. Smyser interview. By the time of the board's vote, the National Conference on Minorities and the News had been under way for two days; Smyser and some other ASNE members had been participants in the conference. However, many ASNE board members had not attended and Smyser also had to act as an emissary from the minorities conference to the board. The ASNE board minutes suggest that at least some of the directors may have remained wary of the conference and perceived the gathering as menacing on some level. Nancy Hicks Maynard, one of the conference organizers, recalled in 2005 that some members of the ASNE were afraid to come to the conference and were wary of the "protest" nature of it. ASNE board minutes, April 8, 1978: 756, and Nancy Hicks Maynard, telephone interview with author, May 9, 2005.

It should be noted that during the 1970s Nancy Hicks Maynard used her maiden name and only later began appending Maynard to her last name.

6. Hicks Maynard interview. The parity goal had been proposed to ASNE, but the Maynards and their allies with the Institute for Journalism Education were publicly pushing the goal even before the ASNE board convened. A month before the 1978 convention, the *Bulletin* quoted Hicks Maynard as saying that the goal of the National Conference on Minorities and the News was the "commitment of the newspaper industry to full participation by minorities in all aspects of news production by the year 2000. It is meant to provide a new rallying point for the news business to aggressively recruit and promote minority journalists and to support their training." "Preconvention Seminar," *ASNE Bulletin* 613 (March 1978): 10.

7. Nancy Hicks, letter to Richard Smyser, September 30, 1977, Smyser Papers.

8. In the 2004 interview, Smyser characterized that early work of the Associated Press Managing Editors General News Committee as "terribly quaint" and "terribly primitive." Although the report contained a section called "Blackening the Newsroom," its primary thrust was not newsroom integration. Rather, the report made an accounting of what newspapers had been doing to include African Americans in coverage and offered story ideas for newspapers wanting to increase their "black news." A follow-up report prepared by Smyser's APME committee in 1969, titled "Black Journalism: Obligation and Opportunity," pursued the same themes, but included references to "blackening up journalism" and "blackening up news values," unfortunate puns on blackface minstrelsy's practice of applying burnt cork or charcoal to the face to create an African American caricature.

9. Smyser asked George Chaplin of the *Honolulu Advertiser,* the 1976–77 ASNE president, to allow him to form an ad hoc committee for the examination of non-white newsroom employment and integrated news coverage a decade after the Kerner report. Chaplin gave Smyser's proposal a polite but cool response and forwarded it to a committee that already had another assignment, and there the matter died. Richard Smyser, letter to George Chaplin, February 9, 1976; George Chaplin, letter to Richard Smyser, March 4, 1976; and Richard Smyser, letter to Eugene Patterson, February 3, 1977; all in Smyser Papers.

10. John Quinn, telephone interview with author, March 3, 2005.

11. Minorities Committee report, *Proceedings,* April 9–12, 1978: 403.

12. Hicks Maynard interview.

13. Editorial autonomy, always a hot-button issue, had been at the top of editors' thinking during the 1970s as a case involving the *Miami Herald* made its way through the appeals process to the U.S. Supreme Court, which ultimately affirmed the editor's First Amendment right to determine content in his or her newspaper. *Miami Herald Publishing Co. v. Tornillo*, 418 U.S. 241 (1974).

14. Smyser interview.

15. Gene Giancarlo, "A Pre-Convention Suggestion," memo to ASNE members, February 13, 1978, Smyser Papers. The memo from Giancarlo, the executive director

of ASNE, stemmed from a vote of the board in October. The minutes of that meeting state that "a proposal that ASNE cooperate with the Institute for Journalistic [*sic*] Education of Berkeley in promoting a conference on minority problems in journalism in conjunction with the next ASNE convention in Washington drew considerable interest. The conclusion was that ASNE should cooperate, but not to the extent of formal sponsorship or of commitments which would make it appear that ASNE was responsible for the degree of attendance at the conference." ASNE board minutes, October 22, 1977: 747.

In planning the National Conference on Minorities and the News, Nancy Hicks intentionally set the gathering for the days immediately before the ASNE convention and encouraged editors to participate before their own meeting began. Nancy Hicks, letter to Richard Smyser, October 17, 1977, Smyser Papers.

16. Anderson, *The Pursuit of Fairness: A History of Affirmative Action*, 148–58.

17. Roy Peter Clark, "A Journalist's View," in *The Changing South of Gene Patterson: Journalism and Civil Rights, 1960–1968*, ed. Roy Peter Clark and Raymond Arsenault (Gainesville: University of Florida Press, 2002), 4. Clark emphasizes that Patterson remained sensitive to his readers' investment in their social traditions and sought to persuade them to take the moral high road. Even after leaving Atlanta, Patterson remained conscious of the South's role in perpetuating and exacerbating racial apartheid in the United States. For that reason, Patterson believed it was important for a Southerner to be at the forefront of the newsroom integration effort. Patterson interview, and email to author, September 23, 2004.

18. Clark, "A Journalist's View," 9.

19. Clark, a journalism scholar who also is Patterson's friend and biographer, wrote, "Friends and foes alike tended to comment on Patterson's physical presence, which reinforced his image as courageous leader or tough opponent. He was compared to Jimmy Cagney. His hair was as red as a stump on fire; his eyes blue and piercing; his jaw jutting; his chest a barrel; his strut determined. Then there was the matter of his height, which Georgian Joe Parham described as 'sawed off, standing five feet, seven inches, with all hackles raised.'" Clark, "A Journalist's View," 8. The Joe Parham referenced in the quotation was editor of the *Macon (Ga.) News*.

20. Patterson interview.

21. Ibid.

22. Quinn interview. Quinn and his wife, Loie, remained committed to the cause of newsroom integration through the establishment of the Chips Quinn Scholars program, a memorial to their son, a newspaper editor who was killed in an automobile accident. The program helped place more than 1,100 nonwhite journalism students in newspaper newsrooms. http://www.chipsquinn.org (accessed June 6, 2011).

23. Seigenthaler had taken a leave of absence from the *Tennessean* to work for Attorney General Robert F. Kennedy. In spring 1961 he was dispatched by the U.S. Department of Justice to Alabama, where the mob assault occurred as the Freedom

Riders arrived in Montgomery. Seigenthaler's work for the government and his near-fatal injuries are chronicled in Taylor Branch, *Parting the Waters: America in the King Years, 1954–63*, chap. 11.

24. Smyser interview.

25. For a detailed account of the work of the initiatives of the Summer Program for Minorities and the Institute for Journalism Education, see Alice Carol Bonner, *Changing the Color of the News: Robert Maynard and the Desegregation of Daily Newspapers* (PhD diss., University of North Carolina–Chapel Hill, 1999), especially chap. 6.

26. Robert Maynard, "This Far by Fear," *Kerner Plus 10: Minorities and the Media, A Conference Report,* University of Michigan, Howard R. Marsh Center for the Study of Journalistic Performance, April 22, 1977, 2.

27. Fitzpatrick was admitted in 1978, Maynard in 1979, and Harris in 1985. Hicks Maynard was never a member of ASNE.

28. Hicks Maynard interview. She credited John Quinn and other Gannett executives with this concept.

29. Quinn interview.

30. Fitzpatrick interview.

31. The first mailing produced a response rate of just 25 percent, which was deemed to be not a representative sample. After the second mailing, the census results were calculated from a 43 percent response rate. Christy Bulkeley, "Finding Journalists from Minority Groups," *ASNE Bulletin* 631 (March 1980): 4.

32. *Proceedings,* April 7–10, 1980: 328. The reference to "fear of legal reprisals" refers to the concern that the federal government might mandate the hiring of nonwhites by newspapers. During the "Kerner Plus Ten" discussion at the 1978 convention, Rolfe Neill of the *Charlotte Observer* said, "My own hunch is if you don't do it it will soon be done for you." *Proceedings*, April 9–12, 1978: 302. This echoes a concern Neill had raised privately: "You must decide at your newspaper whether you wish your staff to approximate the racial balance of the community. If you don't, the government may some day do it for you. Meanwhile, it makes sense either pragmatically or morally to do so yourself." Rolfe Neill, letter to Richard Smyser, September 28, 1977, Smyser Papers. Compulsory newsroom integration also is raised as a possibility by David Lawrence, "Good Will and Good Intentions Don't Add Up to Solutions," *ASNE Bulletin* 645 (October 1981): 8.

33. Tom Winship, "Our Failure in Minority Hiring," *ASNE Bulletin* 642 (May–June 1981): 38. Winship is a contradictory figure within the ASNE diversity movement. While he was one of the most outspoken supporters of the hiring initiative, he became embroiled in a controversy after he served as an expert witness for the *New York Daily News* in a lawsuit brought by four black reporters and editors who sued over promotions in the newsroom. In the *ASNE Bulletin,* see Daniel Alterman, "The Daily News Case: Is it a Useful Stick?" and Thomas C. Morrison, "'Inaccurate Statements and Innuendos,'" 707 (September–October 1988): 26–27.

34. *Proceedings,* May 9–12, 1983: 399. Seigenthaler's report also recommended that the ASNE hire a full-time minority affairs director to coordinate the initiative. This was a significant step, as it concretely imbricated the newsroom integration effort into the organization's infrastructure and reinforced the notion that ASNE had a long-term commitment to the cause. Carl Morris was hired later that year to serve in that position, the first in a series of African American journalists who would direct the ASNE's programmatic efforts on diversity.

35. Creed Black, letter to Donald Sodewald, June 10, 1983, Creed Black Papers, Wisconsin Historical Society, Library and Archives, Madison, Box 2.

36. Fitzpatrick authored the report, although Jay Harris, still at Northwestern University, and his wife Christine Harris, who directed the Consortium for the Advancement of Minorities in Journalism Education, also based at Northwestern, contributed extensively to the document. Excerpts from the report were published in Jay and Christine Harris, "Editors [*sic*] Attitudes Reveal Wide Diversity on Employing Minorities," *ASNE Bulletin* 645 (October 1981): 10–14, and in *Proceedings,* May 4–7, 1982: 246–54.

37. ASNE Minorities Committee, "Minorities and Newspapers," May 1982: 6.

38. Ibid., 1. The "Tensions in Newsroom" section is found on pages 12–14 of the report.

39. Ibid., 33–36.

40. Ibid., 36.

41. Ibid., 35 and 36.

42. Fitzpatrick interview.

43. Smyser interview.

44. Smyser was particularly concerned that editors of smaller papers become comfortable interacting with nonwhite journalists as smaller papers typically served as a training ground for the profession. "This is where the paucity of minority staffers has been most apparent," Smyser said. Without smaller papers supplying the pipeline, larger papers would be unable to hire experienced nonwhite journalists into high-profile positions, as was the pattern for young white journalists. Richard Smyser, letter to Joseph Shoquist, June 30, 1980, Joseph William Shoquist Papers, Wisconsin Historical Society Library and Archives, Madison, Box 4, Folder 2.

45. Smyser interview.

46. Ibid.

47. Ibid.

48. Hicks Maynard interview.

49. Richard Smyser, letter to Eugene Patterson, February 3, 1977, Smyser Papers.

50. ASNE board minutes, April 8, 1978: 756.

51. Reg Murphy, "Minorities: A Five-Year Plan," *ASNE Bulletin* 618 (October 1978): 15. The article still offers substantial support for the moral imperative. In fact, Murphy, the Minorities Committee chair, goes to great lengths to make that argument

when he writes, "In this most human undertaking many hope that the editors would somehow redress the wrongs of segregation and exclusion in the spirit of Tennyson's lines: *Oh yet we trust that somehow good / Will be the final goal of ill*" (14). Interestingly, the committee's recommendation that newspapers formulate a five-year plan was discussed at the midyear board meeting in September. In that discussion the plan's goal was defined as "affirmative action hiring," terminology that generally is not used in the ASNE publications and convention sessions. ASNE board minutes, September 6, 1978: 781.

52. Winship, "Our Failure in Minority Hiring," 38.

53. Ibid., 39. This may have signaled a slight modification in Winship's position and indicated that the business imperative argument gained wider acceptance among diversity advocates in the early years of the initiative and as the census results failed to show significant integration in newsrooms. In 1978, during the convention discussion of the diversity initiative's founding, Winship then called the low number of nonwhite journalists "journalism's greatest failing—something far more vital to our conscience than circulation or advertising increases or decreases." *Proceedings,* April 9–12, 1978: 292.

54. Fitzpatrick interview.

55. Jay Harris, telephone interview with author, October 13, 2004. "Penetration," which is the newspaper industry's concept for gauging market saturation, refers to the percentage of addresses within a circulation area that receive a newspaper, as opposed to basic circulation figures, which report the number of copies sold. In an interview, Hicks Maynard acknowledged that she had subscribed to the business imperative argument as well.

56. David Lawrence, "We Must Discard the 'Excuses for Failure,' Insist on Progress," *ASNE Bulletin* 684 (February 1986): 8.

57. *Proceedings,* April 12–15, 1988: 10.

58. *Proceedings,* April 11–14, 1989: 356.

59. Bill Ketter, "Business, Demographic Trends Indicate Minority Recruiting is More Crucial Than Ever Before," *ASNE Bulletin* 713 (April 1989): 11.

60. Newspaper ad revenues, which had grown steadily and approached $32.37 billion in 1989, dropped to $32.28 billion in 1990, $30.35 billion in 1991; $30.64 billion in 1992; and $31.87 billion in 1993; and then resumed a steady climb until the next economic downturn in 2001. In 2004 total newspaper advertising revenues were $46.7 billion. "Annual Advertising Expenditures," Newspaper Association of America, http://tinyurl.com/6zzkjvb (accessed March 6, 2012).

61. *Proceedings,* April 11–14, 1989: 358. The 1989 Minorities Committee report indicated that 59 percent of daily papers with all-white staffs had circulations of less than 10,000.

62. Newspaper Association of America, "Daily Newspaper Readership Trends—Race/Ethnicity (1970–1997)," http://tinyurl.com/785ymvo (accessed March 6, 2012)

and Virginia Dodge Fielder and Leonard Tipton, "Minorities and Newspapers: A Survey of Readership Research" (American Society of Newspaper Editors, 1986): 27.

63. Mervin Aubespin, "Newspapers' Survival Depends on Serving a Changing Constituency, and Minority Journalists Are Essential to that Effort," *ASNE Bulletin* 721 (April 1990): 51–52.

64. Patterson interview.

65. Harris interview.

66. A stirring exception to this general omission was provided by Arnold Rosenfeld, the 1988 Minorities Committee chair, who made this report to the convention: "The industry needs to remind itself constantly that racial parity is more than a headcount. Fairness in recruiting is only meaningful when it means fairness in coverage—coverage that is more inclusive, more reflective of the issues, trends, and diversity that characterizes American life at its fullest." *Proceedings,* April 12–15, 1988: 337.

67. Patterson interview.

68. Ibid.

69. Smyser interview.

70. *Regents of the University of California v. Bakke,* 438 U.S. 265 (1978).

71. See Newkirk, *Within the Veil: Black Journalists, White Media*, chap. 4.

72. Fitzpatrick interview.

73. Census results were reported by racial category in 1978, 1982, and from 1985 forward. In 1978, the survey reported five categories, owing to numbers for both Chicano and Latino journalists. These categories were not defined, however.

74. William Ketter, "Business, Demographic Trends Indicate Minority Recruiting is More Crucial Than Ever Before," *ASNE Bulletin* 713 (April 1989): 11.

75. ASNE board minutes, April 20, 1981: 866.

76. Deborah Howell, "Best Way to Find Minority Journalists Is to Get Them While They're Young," *ASNE Bulletin* 688 (July–August 1986): 27. It should be noted that the title did not reflect the informative, straightforward tone of the story.

77. Lee Stinnett, "Minorities in the Newsroom," *ASNE Bulletin* 640 (March 1981): 33.

78. The name of the organization was changed in 1980 to add "and Mass Communication."

79. Stinnett, "Minorities in the Newsroom," 32. Kearney appears to be ignoring the "substantial newspaper experience" of journalists who worked for the African American press and redefining "newspaper experience" as employment on white-controlled dailies.

80. ASNE board minutes, November 14, 1980: 849. A Tallahassee meeting in January 1981 was thought to be the first time that white editors and black educators had sat down together. Stinnett, "Minorities in the Newsroom," 32.

81. James Hawkins, "Why Not Recruit from Historically Minority Schools?" *ASNE Bulletin* 673 (November–December 1984): 22.

82. ASNE board minutes, April 6, 1980: 825.

83. Mireille Grangenois Gates, "Minorities Effort Focuses on Historically Black Colleges," *ASNE Bulletin* 707 (September–October 1988): 25.

84. ASNE board minutes, April 7, 1990: 1218–19.

85. ASNE board minutes, April 7, 1987: 1090. Six months later, Education Committee chair Bill Hilliard, who would be elected the first African American ASNE president in 1993, reported that the Accrediting Council for Education in Journalism and Mass Communication was enforcing the liberal arts standard (ASNE board minutes, October 8, 1987: 1103). In 1998, the Education for Journalism chairman "noted," the minutes stated, "that ASNE had recently encountered several tough years of confrontation with journalism schools" over the liberal arts issue (ASNE board minutes, April 16, 1988: 1135).

86. ASNE was an active supporter of the Standard 12 initiative prior to its implementation and also monitored its enforcement. In the *ASNE Bulletin,* see Robert Ruggles, "Accrediting Council Is Pressing Minority Standards at J-Schools and Editors Should Help," 698 (September–October 1987): 23–25; "ASNE Urges Newspapers, Educators to Focus on Minorities at Journalism Schools," 701 (January 1988): 12; Bill Hilliard, "Editors Urge J-Schools to Focus on Hiring More Minorities, Women," 704 (April 1988): 24–25; and John F. Greenman, "J-Schools Are Taking Many Approaches to Increase the Pool of Minority Journalists," 708 (November 1988): 24–28. See also ASNE board minutes, October 9, 1987: 1103; April 12, 1988: 1124; and October 7, 1988: 1147.

87. *Editors' Exchange* 8, no. 6 (August 1985).

88. *Editors' Exchange* 10, no. 1 (January 1987).

89. "We Are Changing the Way We Distribute the Editors' Exchange," *Editors' Exchange* 9, no. 5 (June 1986).

90. Hicks Maynard interview.

91. Linda Grist Cunningham, telephone interview with author, October 22, 2004.

92. Because the ASNE did not include women in the annual newsroom census, year-to-year numbers of women employees are not available to compare to the totals for nonwhites. In reporting on diversity to the board in 1980, Richard Smyser, who then was the Membership Committee chair, said the ASNE had sixteen Canadian members, thirty-six women, and seven blacks. This report was typical of the view at the time of race, which tended to define it solely in terms of African Americans. Allowing for a handful of members who might self-identify as Hispanic or as other nonwhites, the ASNE probably had a dozen nonwhite members at the time. ASNE board minutes, April 6, 1980: 818.

93. Women accounted for 61.5 percent of journalism graduates in 1981–82. Maurine H. Beasley and Kathryn T. Theus, *The New Majority: A Look at What the Preponderance of Women in Journalism Education Means to the Schools and to the Professions* (Lanham, MD: University Press of America, 1988), 43. In October 1980, 34 women

were among the ASNE's 860 members. The *Bulletin* reported that the number of women had risen by 50 percent in the previous three years. "Women on the ASNE Rolls," *ASNE Bulletin* 636 (October 1980): 40.

94. ASNE board minutes, April 11, 1980: 836.

95. *Proceedings,* May 9–12, 1983: 335. In an interview in 2004, Linda Grist Cunningham mentioned Seigenthaler as an editor within the Gannett chain who actively mentored women during the 1980s and encouraged them to aspire to editorships.

96. "Biographical Sketch," Dorothy Misener Jurney Papers, 1920–92, Western Historical Manuscript Collection, University of Missouri (C3904), http://tinyurl.com/7y4jd3j (accessed March 6, 2012). Jurney, who was born in 1909, died in 2002.

97. Dorothy Jurney, "Women Are Creeping into Policymaking Jobs on U.S. Newspapers," *ASNE Bulletin* 629 (December 1979–January 1980): 14–16, and Lois Wolfe, "Women Made up 16.2 Percent of Top Editors in 1989," *ASNE Bulletin* 723 (May–June 1990): 48.

98. Some years the reports' critique of the exclusivity of ASNE membership was extremely clear. For example, in 1988, the report took pains to note that women accounted for 13 percent of directing editors at daily newspapers but just 7 percent of ASNE members. The report also noted that ASNE membership either was not attractive to many eligible women or their bosses did not feel it was a priority. The 65 women ASNE members in 1988 represented just 15 percent of those who were eligible to join. By comparison, 26 percent of the 2,923 men who were eligible had joined. The report also noted that five of the twenty ASNE directors were now women. Even so, the math was not heartening. "Yet at the current rate of attracting new women members, ASNE parity membership for women will be reached in 2115, 60 years after women become more than half of the directing editors," the report said. Jean Gaddy Wilson, "Women Make Up 13 Percent of Directing Editors at Dailies," *ASNE Bulletin* 701 (January 1988): 14–17.

99. In 1987 the National Federation of Press Women took over Jurney's annual survey.

100. Clayton Kirkpatrick and Judith W. Brown, "Women: Room at the Top?" *ASNE Bulletin* 567 (March 1973): 3.

101. Dorothy Jurney interview, Women in Journalism Oral History Project, National Press Club Library, Session 1, January 16, 1990: 43.

102. Thomas Winship, "Kay Fanning: ASNE's 57th President Is First Woman on the Job," *ASNE Bulletin* 695 (April 1987): 41.

103. Ibid., 40.

104. Ghiglione interview.

105. ASNE board minutes, May 12, 1984: 995, and Loren Ghiglione, "Minorities Effort 'Won't Succeed if Editors Don't Push Now,'" *ASNE Bulletin* 669 (June–July 1984): 22.

106. Ghiglione, "Minorities Effort," 22. Within a year Ghiglione would expand the

size of the Minorities Committee to more than fifty members. ASNE board minutes, April 8–9, 1985: 1020.

107. The *ASNE Bulletin* highlighted for the first time the activities of the organizations for nonwhite journalists. In the September 1985 issue (680), see Mervin Aubespin, "National Association of Black Journalists: 1,000 Members and Growing," 5; Gerald Garcia, "National Association of Hispanic Journalists sets April Meeting in Tucson," 6; William Dulaney, "Native American Press Association Plans First Convention in March," 8; and Bill Sing, "Asian American Journalists Association Enlarging Focus to National Scope," 10. In addition, during Ghiglione's presidency in 1989–90, representatives of the minority journalist organizations made reports to the board of directors. ASNE board minutes, April 15, 1989: 1176–77.

108. ASNE board minutes, October 10, 1985: 1045. The effort would focus on smaller newspapers that had no nonwhite employees. Because smaller papers have traditionally been regarded as training grounds for larger publications, smaller papers were considered indispensable to the "pipeline" for nonwhite journalists.

109. Loren Ghiglione, "The Year 2000 Is Now," *ASNE Bulletin* 675 (February 1985): 3.

110. Ibid.

111. By 1985, for example, diversity became a meaningful part of the convention program, with sessions on "The Black Experience and How We Cover It" and "How to (and How Not to) Recruit Minorities." *Proceedings,* April 9–12, 1985: 55–68, 195–202. In the *ASNE Bulletin,* information about diversity, including women's issues, appeared on 142 pages in 1984, 1985, and 1986, compared to 126 pages for the six years from 1978 through 1983.

112. ASNE board minutes, April 8–9, 1985: 1020.

113. Loren Ghiglione, "Minority Employment in Newsrooms Remains Stuck at 5.7 Percent," *ASNE Bulletin* 677 (May 1985): 31, and Ghiglione interview.

114. Planning for the ASNE minority scholarship program began in 1985. Twenty-two college students received $500 each in the 1986–87 competition. Forty scholarships were awarded in 1987–88, sixty in 1988–89 (when the award was increased to $750), and sixty were awarded in 1989–90. At the end of the decade, the competition was receiving 321 applicants. In the *ASNE Bulletin,* see Loren Ghiglione, "Scholarships, Task Force, Job Fairs, Visits—We've Done A Lot, But It Will Take More to Achieve Diversity in the Press," 684 (February 1986): 3; Sanders LaMont, "ASNE's First Minority Scholarships: 'We Had 44 Great Applicants, and Money for 22,'" 693 (February 1987): 34–36; Sanders LaMont, "40 Minority Students from 20 States Win ASNE Journalism Scholarships," 701 (January 1988): 26–28; Mireille Grangenois Gates, "Minorities Effort Focuses on Historically Black Colleges," 707 (September–October 1988): 25; David Corcoran, "This Year's 164 Scholarship Winners Reveal Commitment to Journalism," 710 (January 1989): 26–29; and Larry Allison, "1989–90 Minority Scholarship Winners Led 'Impressive' Field," 720 (January 1990): 36–39.

115. Rolfe Neill, "Good Intentions Can't Replace 'Grunt Work' in 'Blending' All-White Staffs," *ASNE Bulletin* 684 (February 1986): 4.

116. ASNE board minutes, April 7, 1986: 1058.

117. *Proceedings,* April 7–10, 1987: 292.

118. ASNE board minutes, October 8, 1988: 1150.

119. *Proceedings,* April 11–14, 1989: 281.

120. Mervin Aubespin, "Newspaper Industry Leaders Continue to Press for a Diversified Work Force, but 'The Excuses Continue,'" *ASNE Bulletin* 721 (April 1990): 50.

121. *Proceedings,* April 11–14, 1989: 302.

122. Ibid., 305.

123. Ibid.

124. Aubespin, "Newspaper Industry Leaders Continue to Press," 49.

Chapter 4. The Gay Nineties

1. This book's theoretical approach to gay identity and the closet as it functioned within the ASNE is informed by Eve Kosofsky Sedgwick, *Epistemology of the Closet* (Berkeley: University of California Press, 1990); Michael Warner, *The Trouble with Normal: Sex Politics and the Ethics of Queer Life* (Cambridge: Harvard University Press, 1999); Judith Butler, *Excitable Speech: A Politics of the Performative* (New York: Routledge, 1997); Edward Alwood, *Straight News: Gays, Lesbians, and the News Media* (New York: Columbia University Press, 1996); and Larry Gross, *Up from Invisibility: Lesbians, Gay Men, and the Media in America* (New York: Columbia University Press, 2001).

2. Lee Stinnett, telephone interview with author, March 11, 2008. Membership figures are from the ASNE secretary's annual report: *Proceedings,* April 3–6, 1990: 344.

3. Steve Friess, "NLGJA Mourns Roy Aarons, Founder and Pioneering Journalist," Pride Source, Dec. 9, 2004, http://tinyurl.com/7720f29 (accessed March 7, 2012).

4. "The 1990s: A Time for Frontline Fighters," *Proceedings,* April 3–6, 1990: 12–14.

5. Alex S. Jones, "Menu for Newspaper Editors: Criticism and '60s Headlines," *New York Times,* April 5, 1990, A15, and Ellis Cose, "Newsroom Homophobia," *Time,* April 16, 1990, http://tinyurl.com/61qfo9t (accessed March 7, 2012).

6. Leroy F. Aarons, "Membership Is Approaching 500 in New Association for Gay and Lesbian Journalists," *ASNE Bulletin* 738 (January–February 1992): 20–22; Joe Holley, "Leroy Aarons: Started Gay Journalist's Group," *Washington Post,* November 30, 2004, B6.

7. Stinnett interview, 2008; Leroy Aarons and Sheila Murphy, *Lesbians and Gays in the Newsroom: 10 Years Later* (Annenberg School for Communication, University of Southern California, and National Lesbian and Gay Journalists Association, 2001).

8. ASNE board minutes, October 18, 1996. The proposal had come before the board in November 1991 as well, when it adopted a recommendation from the Minorities

Committee to retain the name. Wanda Lloyd, "And the Winner is—'Minorities Committee'!" *ASNE Bulletin* 737 (December 1991): 25–26.

9. Chris Barker, *Cultural Studies: Theory and Practice* (London: Sage, 2000), 360. For a comprehensive history of multiculturalism, see Christopher Newfield and Avery F. Gordon, "Multiculturalism's Unfinished Business," in Avery F. Gordon and Christopher Newfield, ed., *Mapping Multiculturalism* (Minneapolis: University of Minnesota Press, 1996), 76–115.

10. Angela Y. Davis, "Gender, Class, and Multiculturalism," in Gordon and Newfield, *Mapping Multiculturalism,* 44.

11. Dinesh D'Souza, *The End of Racism* (New York: The Free Press, 1995) and Stephan Thernstrom and Abigail Thernstrom, *America in Black & White: One Nation, Indivisible* (New York: Touchstone, 1997). Other critiques of affirmative action published during the 1990s included Frederick Lynch, *Invisible Victims: White Males and the Crisis of Affirmative Action* (New York: Praeger, 1991).

12. For comprehensive analyses of the racial dimensions of the Rodney King and O. J. Simpson cases, see Robert Gooding-Williams, ed., *Reading Rodney King, Reading Urban Uprising* (New York: Routledge, 1993) and Darnell Hunt, *O.J. Simpson Facts and Fictions: News Ritual in the Construction of Reality* (Cambridge University Press, 1999).

13. Stinnett interview, 2008.

14. John Seigenthaler Sr., telephone interview, January 30, 2006.

15. The only mention of Stinnett's sexuality to appear in the ASNE board minutes was triggered by Stinnett when he thanked the board for its support: "Not a thing had been said about it to that point in the board meeting, and I said, 'I just want to thank the officers and dear John Seigenthaler about the care and thought and support they gave me as I came out as a gay man.' So when I was saying this, it was such an emotional experience my voice started quivering, and I didn't know whether I was going to cry or what was going to happen, but . . . I was trying to speak and my voice was like the waves in the ocean. It was really quivery" (Stinnett interview, 2008). Stinnett's remarks to the board of directors at its meeting the following year received brief mention: "He thanked the officers and staff in Reston for their support during a year in which he made public that he is a gay man" (ASNE board minutes, April 11, 1989: 1161).

16. Stinnett interview, 2008, and Cal Thomas, "Editors' Survey on Gays is Ridiculous," *News and Courier,* November 20, 1989; http://tinyurl.com/7u3vwz9 (accessed March 7, 2012).

17. American Society of Newspaper Editors, "Tribute to Lee Stinnett," October 28, 1999, http://tinyurl.com/70wufwm (accessed March 7, 2012). Stinnett's partner also was acknowledged in ASNE press releases announcing Stinnett's intention to retire and following his death in 2009. American Society of Newspaper Editors, "Stinnett to Retire from ASNE," undated, http://tinyurl.com/7n6wjya (accessed March 7, 2012), and "Lee Stinnett dies," November 9, 2009, http://tinyurl.com/6qtvphs (accessed March 7, 2012).

18. Stinnett interview, 2008.

19. Lee Stinnett, letter to Leroy Aarons, October 3, 1993, Leroy Aarons Papers, National Lesbian and Gay Journalists Association, Washington, D.C., ASNE Folder.

20. Stinnett interview, 2008.

21. Pamela Strother, telephone interview with author, March 10, 2008.

22. Pamela Fine, interview with author, December 17, 2008. Within the newspaper industry, the visibility of gay journalists has at times raised questions about their ability to remain objective and the credibility of the news organization that employed them. At the *Washington Post,* for example, executive editor Leonard Downie Jr. underscored this concern in 1993 by barring newsroom employees from participating in a gay rights march that April. William Glaberson, "Gay Journalists Leading a Revolution," *New York Times,* September 10, 1993, http://tinyurl.com/783bfxm (accessed March 7, 2012).

23. "Minorities Committee Report," *Proceedings,* April 3–6, 1990: 365.

24. Mireille Grangenois, "With Minorities Now 7.86 Percent of U.S. Newsroom Staffs, ASNE's 'Year 2000' Goal is Slipping Farther Away," *ASNE Bulletin* 722 (April 1990): 51.

25. Ibid., 52.

26. Tom Pellgrine, "Women, Minorities Are Most Likely to Leave Newspapers in their First Year on the Job," *ASNE Bulletin* 736 (November 1991): 18–19.

27. Walterene Swanston, telephone interview with author, November 4, 2009. The official name of the coalition is UNITY Journalists of Color Inc., however it often appeared as Unity in ASNE publications and documents, which are quoted here verbatim.

28. Elizabeth Grieco, "The White Population: 2000," U.S. Census Bureau, August 2001: 4, available at http://tinyurl.com/4dcqxjm (accessed March 7, 2012).

29. John Greenman, "Staying the Course Despite Tough Times," *ASNE Bulletin* 731 (April 1991): 20.

30. David Lawrence, "Newsroom Managers Must Take the Lead in Promoting Diversity," *ASNE Bulletin* 732 (May–June 1991): 2.

31. Researchers analyzed the *Rockford Register Star*'s diversity performance against papers in the 50,000 to 100,000 daily circulation category. When Cunningham was hired in 1991, 11.8 percent of newsroom employees were nonwhite. That percentage peaked in 2000 at 22.2. In 2005, when the research was completed, the *Register Star*'s news staff was 19 percent nonwhite, compared to a community nonwhite demographic of 19.7 percent. Bill Dedman and Stephen K. Doig, "Newsroom Diversity Has Passed Its Peak at Most Newspapers, 1990–2005 Study Shows," John S. and James L. Knight Foundation, June 1, 2005, http://powerreporting.com/knight/ (accessed March 7, 2012).

32. Grist Cunningham interview.

33. Judson Randall, "ASNE's Next President is Known for Pushing Quiet—but Persistent—Change," *ASNE Bulletin* 748 (March 1993): 22–26.

34. William Hilliard, telephone interview with author, November 19, 2004.

35. Ibid.

36. Brian Cooper, "How Do We Attract Minorities to a Town Notorious for Burning Crosses?" *ASNE Bulletin* 739 (March 1992): 22.

37. From its founding in 1922, the ASNE's membership bylaws reserved the greatest power within the organization for newspapers with the largest circulations "so that there might not be upset that balance of metropolitan spirit and direction which the members of the Board believe the Society should retain" (*Proceedings,* April 25–26, 1924: 66). This was achieved by allowing individual newspapers in the largest circulation categories to have more ASNE members than smaller newspapers. In addition, the number of total members admitted from all smaller newspapers in a given year was limited. Although the membership structure was modified several times over the years, this historical and deliberate imbalance of power within the organization persisted and sometimes generated resentment among editors from smaller papers.

38. The percentage of newspapers in other lower-circulation categories that employed nonwhites in 1990 were these: 50,001 to 100,000, 89 percent; 25,001 to 50,000, 68 percent; and 10,001 to 25,000, 43 percent. Aubespin, "Newspaper Industry Leaders Continue to Press for a Diversified Work Force, but 'the Excuses Continue,'" 50.

39. Elise Burroughs, "How Small Newspapers Attract Minority Journalists," *ASNE Bulletin* 721 (April 1990): 4–5. Burroughs also noted that papers with circulations of less than 50,000 employed 41 percent of white journalists and 23 percent of nonwhite journalists.

40. Stinnett interview, 2005.

41. Seymour Topping, "Diversity Audits Examine Newspaper Content," *ASNE Bulletin* 747 (January–February 1993): 2.

42. Gregory Favre, telephone interview with author, October 15, 2004.

43. Christopher P. Campbell, "Beyond Employment Diversity: Rethinking Contemporary Racist News Representations," in Yahya R. Kamalipour and Theresa Carilli, ed., *Cultural Diversity and the U.S. Media* (Albany: State University of New York Press, 1998), 53–54.

44. Topping, "Diversity Audits Examine Newspaper Content," 2.

45. "Race: The Conversation You're Not Having in Your Newsroom," *Proceedings,* April 19, 1996: 248.

46. Ibid., 252.

47. The sixteen-page guide, which was inserted into the March 1992 issue of the *ASNE Bulletin,* included advice on managing employees within a demographic that was becoming more racially diverse. "By the year 2000, only 15 percent of new entrants into the work force will be U.S.-born white males; here is a guide on how to deal with workers who are not 'just like you,'" the cover said. The guide was part of a larger package on managing diversity. "Your Work Force is Changing; Are You Ready?" *ASNE Bulletin* 739 (March 1992): 1–12, 22–25.

48. William Hilliard, "Multiculturalism is More than a Numbers Game," *ASNE Bulletin* 752 (September 1993): 2.

49. "Why Isn't There More Progress in Minority Hiring?" *Proceedings,* April 9–12, 1991: 93.

50. Philip Terzian, "Painful Obsessions," *ASNE Bulletin* 735 (October 1991): 26.

51. Ibid., 27.

52. Gilbert Bailon, "Gulf between Minority, White Journalists Wide," *American Editor* 779 (October 1996): 16.

53. Ruth Shalit, "Race in the Newsroom: The Washington Post in Black and White," *New Republic* 213 (October 2, 1995): 14. Accessed on EBSCOhost, March 3, 2005.

54. Howard Kurtz, "A Diversity of Opinions; New Republic Story on Race in the Newsroom Stirs Up the Post," *Washington Post,* September 21, 1995, C1.

55. Jonathan Alter, "Black and White and Mad All Over," *Newsweek,* October 2, 1995: 75.

56. Jill Nelson, *Volunteer Slavery: My Authentic Negro Experience* (Chicago: Noble Press, 1993).

57. Quoted in Alter, "Black and White and Mad All Over," 75.

58. Quoted in Kurtz, "A Diversity of Opinions," C1.

59. Betty Winston Baye, "A Shot across the Masthead," *ASNE Bulletin* 726 (October 1990): 38.

60. Walker Lundy, "Is it Possible that Minorities and Whites Fundamentally Disagree about Whether the Playing Field is Tilted—and that this Difference in Perception Fuels our Lack of Communication?" *ASNE Bulletin* 742 (July–August 1992): 11.

61. Ibid.

62. National Association of Black Journalists Print Task Force, "Muted Voices: Frustration and Fear in the Newsroom," 1993, 5. The survey's findings applied not only to newspaper newsrooms but also to those in broadcasting.

63. Ibid.

64. Hilliard, "Multiculturalism is More than a Numbers Game," 2.

65. Ibid.

66. The other 49 percent broke down this way: Five years or fewer, 24 percent; Don't know, 23 percent; and No answer, 2 percent. NABJ, "Muted Voices," 22.

67. Jim Clark, "White Managers Were Dismayed by the Views of Their Black Employees," *ASNE Bulletin* 752 (September 1993): 29.

68. Laurence O'Donnell, "Unfinished Business," *ASNE Bulletin* 755 (December 1993): 25.

69. Hilliard interview.

70. William Hilliard, "Values Deserving of Our Attention," *Proceedings,* April 12–15, 1994: 23.

71. William Hilliard, "ASNE's Employment Survey Continues to Evoke Heat as Well as Light on Diversity," *ASNE Bulletin* 757 (March 1994): 2.

72. Hilliard, "Values Deserving of Our Attention," 24.

73. Gilbert Bailon, "About my First ASNE Convention . . .," *ASNE Bulletin* 759 (June–July 1994): 12.

74. Kenneth Bunting, "Too Much Diversity on the Convention Program?" *American Editor* 768 (May–June 1995): 52.

75. For a more complete discussion of this episode, see chapter 1.

76. Harris interview; Fitzpatrick interview.

77. Wanda Lloyd, telephone interview with author, October 19, 2004.

78. "Race in America Near the End of the Anglo Century," *Proceedings,* April 4–7, 1995: 34.

79. Bunting, "Too Much Emphasis on Diversity . . . ?" 52.

80. Lloyd interview.

81. Gilbert Bailon, "A Poor Showing: Why So Few to See Franklin?" *American Editor* 791 (May 1998): 19.

82. Rick Rodriguez, telephone interview with author, July 20, 2005.

83. "UNITY's History," UNITY Journalists of Color Inc., http://tinyurl.com/7fua677 (accessed March 7, 2012).

84. Lloyd interview.

85. Ibid.

86. Stephanie Wong, "NLGJA Proposes Change in Alliance via 8-Point Plan," UNITY Journalists of Color Inc., 1999, http://tinyurl.com/6vg3drz (accessed December 5, 2005).

87. For a history of the National Lesbian and Gay Journalists Association's relationship with UNITY, which continued to be strained throughout the 1990s and into the 2000s, see ibid.; David Carr, "Media Talk: Race Remains the Focus of Journalism Groups," *New York Times,* August 9, 2004, http://tinyurl.com/73qzf94 (accessed March 7, 2012); and Rebecca Perlow, "Unity Partnership Elusive," NLGJA Convention Online, August 31, 2007, http://tinyurl.com/7tqphcu (accessed March 7, 2012).

88. Favre interview.

89. Those presidents were Tim McGuire, *Minneapolis Tribune,* 2001–2; Diane McFarlin, *Sarasota Herald Tribune,* 2002–3; Karla Garrett Harshaw, *Springfield News-Sun,* 2004–5; Rick Rodriguez, *Sacramento Bee,* 2005–6; and Gilbert Bailon, *Al Dia,* 2007–8.

90. By allowing individual newspapers to have more members than they were allowed under the bylaws, as long as the new members were women, ASNE leaders hoped to increase the number of women members. ASNE board minutes, November 20, 1972: 592.

91. "The Newsroom Workforce: A '90s Kind of Place," *Proceedings,* April 8–11, 1997: 100–101. Voakes also reported that nonwhite journalists tended to be younger. For example, half of all African Americans working in newsrooms were under thirty. Voakes's study also was published in April 1997 in a sixty-page ASNE report titled "The Newspaper Journalists of the '90s."

92. Janet Weaver and David Zeeck, "For Presidency, Rowe Has Come to Work," *American Editor* 783 (March–May 1997): 18–22, and Thomas Winship, "Kay Fanning: ASNE's 57th President Is First Woman on the Job," 40–41.

93. President's Address, *Proceedings,* April 8–11, 1997: 46.

94. Diversity Committee Report, *Proceedings,* April 8–11, 1997: 232.

95. Ibid.

96. President's Address 1997, 46.

97. Lloyd interview.

98. Joan Shorenstein Center for Press, Politics and Public Policy, *Implementation of Racial and Ethnic Diversity in the American Press: Objectives, Obstacles, and Incentives* (Harvard University, 1996): 7.

99. Ibid., 26–34.

100. Ibid., 25.

Chapter 5. Diversity in Crisis

1. Among those who viewed Ghiglione as an impassioned and unrelenting champion of diversity was Walterene Swanston, who became executive director of the National Association of Black Journalists in 1993 and was one of the organizers of UNITY's first convention in 1994. "He was very, very passionate," Swanston said of Ghiglione. "He was a crusader." Swanston interview.

2. A decade later, the 1999 ASNE census, which covers the year in which Seaton became president, indicated that 12.5 percent of the *Manhattan Mercury*'s newsroom staff was nonwhite. ASNE, "Percentage of Minorities at Participating Newspapers," April 4, 1999, http://tinyurl.com/7zndykw (accessed March 7, 2012).

3. Seaton could have avoided the controversy entailed in that snarl of issues, but he believed the future of Goal 2000, a project that had to a large extent defined the ASNE within the newspaper industry and to the American public for the previous twenty years, deserved a public discussion and an unhurried and thoughtful approach. Time was running out, Seaton said. "Could have left it, I suppose, for 1999, but then the person who took over in '99 was going to be president at the 2000 convention, and I thought that was really too late, that we needed more time on it, so I decided to take it on." Edward Seaton, telephone interview with author, November 17, 2004.

4. Loren Ghiglione, "Pondering Diversity as 2000 Approaches," *American Editor* 785 (July–August 1997): 16.

5. Loren Ghiglione, "'Beyond 2000' Goal Prompts Deliberation," *American Editor* 787 (October 1997): 13.

6. This recurring concern was forcefully articulated by Sanders LaMont, ombudsman of the *Sacramento Bee,* "Demographically Challenged, Editors Tiptoe as They Talk," *American Editor* 800 (May–June 1999): 11.

7. Minorities Committee Report, *Proceedings,* April 8–11, 1986: 353–54.

8. ASNE board minutes, April 15, 1989: 1176–79, and Loren Ghiglione, telephone interview.

9. During the 1930s, the ASNE was embroiled in a monumental controversy over whether and how to enforce standards in the organization's code of ethics against a transgressing member. For a summary of this episode in ASNE history, see Pratte, *Gods Within the Machine: A History of the American Society of Newspaper Editors, 1923–1993*, chap. 1.

10. Anderson, *In Pursuit of Fairness: A History of Affirmative Action*, 264.

11. Michael Lind, *The Next American Nation: The New Nationalism and the Fourth American Revolution* (New York: Free Press, 1995), cited in ibid.

12. Paul DeMain, letter to Sandra Mims Rowe, February 6, 1998, ASNE archives.

13. Rick Rodriguez, "A Meeting of the Minds on Diversity," *American Editor* 789 (March 1998): 10; 1998 Diversity Committee Report, *Proceedings*, March 31–April 3, 1998: 266–67; and Rodriguez interview.

14. 1998 Diversity Committee Report, 266.

15. Rodriguez interview.

16. Beverly Kees, "Advice to ASNE: Stick to Diversity Goals," The Freedom Forum, February 4, 1998, http://tinyurl.com/7zutga4 (accessed March 7, 2012).

17. Rodriguez, "A Meeting of the Minds on Diversity," 10.

18. Swanston interview.

19. Keith Woods telephone interview with author, July 17, 2009.

20. 1998 Diversity Committee Report, 266.

21. Sharon Rosenhause, telephone interview with author, July 30, 2009.

22. Edward Seaton, "Some Light on ASNE's Revised Diversity Goal," 2.

23. Seaton interview.

24. Rodriguez, "A Meeting of the Minds on Diversity," 10.

25. Mark Fitzgerald, "ASNE, Minority Journalists Wrestle over Year 2000 Goal," *Editor & Publisher* 131, no. 13 (March 28, 1998): 14.

26. Rodriguez, "A Meeting of the Minds on Diversity," 10.

27. Steven Gray and Carolyn Salazar, "New Definition to Cover Gays, Women, Disabled," *ASNE Reporter,* April 1, 1998, http://tinyurl.com/6qc9aor (accessed December 17, 2001).

28. Fitzgerald, "ASNE, Minority Journalists Wrestle over Year 2000 Goal," 14.

29. Rodriguez, "A Meeting of the Minds on Diversity," 10.

30. Woods interview.

31. Ibid.

32. Loren Ghiglione, "Goals for the New Century: Diversity/Unity 2000+5," report presented to the ASNE board of directors, March 13, 1998, 13, ASNE archives.

33. Ghiglione, "Goals for the New Century," 13.

34. Kees, "Advice to ASNE"; ASNE board minutes, April 3, 1998: 1421.

35. Ghiglione, "Goals for the New Century," 15. In addition to these two recommendations, Ghiglione asked the ASNE board to push harder on job fairs, internships, school programs, small-paper training, and other mechanisms for increasing entry into newsrooms; make retention a top priority; devote as much attention to news coverage—what gets reported and how it gets reported—as to newsroom inclusiveness; encourage dialogue and collaborative work across fault lines; expand the diversity initiatives at smaller newspapers; target middle school as well as high school and college students; undertake or support research designed to transform newspapers; begin to think about diversity as a global, not a domestic, issue; pursue greater cooperation with other organizations devoted to diversity; and be clear as to the paradigms being pursued in the diversity effort.

36. ASNE board minutes, March 31, 1998: 1416.

37. Diversity was added to the ASNE's mission statement in 1994, but remains apart from the ASNE Statement of Principles, which was crafted in 1922 and revised in 1975.

38. ASNE board minutes, March 31, 1998: 1416.

39. Edward Seaton, email to Tony Pederson, January 29, 2002.

40. ASNE board minutes, April 3, 1998: 1421.

41. Edward Seaton, email to Tony Pederson; Seaton interview.

42. Kelvin Childs, "ASNE Pulls Back from Diversity Goal," *Editor & Publisher* 131, no. 16 (April 18, 1998): 83.

43. Rodriguez interview.

44. Greg Moore telephone interview with author, July 20, 2005.

45. Franklin described his disappointment in his reception by the ASNE, which might have provided him "an opportunity for a dialogue with the media" on the Clinton intiative.

"And, indeed," he recalled,

> I could hardly make my way to the ballroom where the session was to be held because of the enormous crowds in the hallways. Alas, when I arrived, only the chairman who had invited me and a few others awaited me. We delayed my address for a few minutes, during which time a few more drifted in. However, when the chairman of the session called the meeting to order, there were fewer than a hundred people out of several thousand attending the annual meeting who came to hear a discussion on "One America: The President's Initiative on Race." . . . The chair of the committee was obviously disappointed that so few editors and reporters had attended the session, later writing me a letter of apology for taking time out of my busy schedule to talk about a matter that was obviously of quite limited interest to the members of America's fourth estate.

Mirror to America: The Autobiography of John Hope Franklin (New York: Farrar, Strauss & Giroux, 2005), 358.

46. Richard Prince, "John Hope Franklin: No Soft Spot for Media," Maynard Institute for Journalism Education, March 25, 2009, http://tinyurl.com/82ychqg (accessed March 7, 2012).

47. Mark Fitzgerald, "ASNE Gets Earful from Hispanic Journalists," *Editor & Publisher* 131, no. 28 (July 11, 1998): 20.

48. Gilbert Bailon, "The Mission: Reflect America," *American Editor* 796 (December 1998): 6.

49. Seaton, "Some Light on ASNE's Revised Diversity Goal," 2.

50. ASNE board minutes, October 20, 1998: 1432.

51. In 1998, the Journalism & Women Symposium board of directors approved resolutions encouraging members to phone and email ASNE directors. "Herstory," Journalism & Women Symposium, http://tinyurl.com/6n67c2q (accessed March 7, 2012), and Rosenhause interview.

52. ASNE board minutes, October 20, 1998: 1432.

53. ASNE, "1998 ASNE Newsroom Census: Minority Employment Inches up in Daily Newspapers," April 10, 1998, http://tinyurl.com/7kf67k7 (accessed March 7, 2012).

54. Gilbert Bailon telephone interview with author, October 20, 2004.

55. Edward Seaton, letter to Paul DeMain, February 16, 1998, ASNE archives.

56. ASNE, "U.S. Newsroom Employment Declines," April 16, 2009, http://tinyurl.com/7vsps4n (accessed March 7, 2012); Newspaper Association of America, "Total Paid Circulation," http://tinyurl.com/6gfw8v3 (accessed March 7, 2012). Total paid circulation of daily and Sunday newspapers, which peaked at 62,566,000 in 1993, dropped from 59,894,000 in 1999 to 49,115,000 in 2008.

57. Woods interview.

58. Vanessa Williams, "Aren't We Beyond Seeing Diversity as a Burden?" *American Editor* 796 (December 1998): 9.

59. Charlotte Hall, telephone interview with author, August 15, 2005.

60. Bailon, "The Mission: Reflect America," 6–7.

61. The highest one-year increase, 0.86 percent, was recorded in the newsroom census of 1991. *Proceedings,* April 9–12, 1991: 304; Bailon, "The Mission: Reflect America," 7.

62. Seaton interview.

63. Ibid.

64. Richard Oppel, "The Long Haul to Diversity," *American Editor* 812 (September 2000): 2.

65. Seaton interview.

66. ASNE Foundation board minutes, April 9, 2002, ASNE archives.

67. Diane McFarlin, "A New Effort to Fill the Diversity Glass," *American Editor* 829 (April 2003): 2.

68. ASNE Foundation board minutes, April 20, 2004.

69. "Diversity Action Plan Adopted," *American Editor* 800 (May–June 1999): 29; McFarlin, "A New Effort to Fill the Diversity Glass," 2.

70. ASNE, "1999 ASNE Newsroom Census: Minority Employment Inches Up at Daily Newspapers," March 22, 1999, http://204.8.120.192/index.cfm?ID=1455, and "U.S. Newsroom Employment Declines," April 16, 1999, http://tinyurl.com/886m7uy (accessed March 7, 2012). The percentage, which peaked at 13.73 percent in 2006, dropped from the previous year in 2001, 2007, 2009, and 2010. ASNE, "Newsroom Census, Table A," http://tinyurl.com/7mtzdwp (accessed March 7, 2012).

71. For the first decade of Goal 2000, the percentage of nonwhite newsroom employees rose 2.61 percent in the annual census. From 1988 to 1997, nonwhite newsroom employment rose 4.33 percent. For the decade that ended in 2007, the ten-year difference was just under 2 percent. ASNE, "Newsroom Census, Table A."

72. The five benchmarks and their 2003 targets compared with 2000 levels were these: percentage of nonwhite newsroom employees, 15.5 percent versus 12.55 percent; percentage of nonwhite interns, 34.1 percent versus 31.85 percent; percentage of nonwhite supervisors, 13 percent versus 10 percent; number of papers employing no nonwhites, 320 versus 380; and number of papers at parity with their communities, 174. Data had previously not been collected for this final category. ASNE board minutes, September 30, 1999.

73. The 2003 performance levels on other benchmarks were these: nonwhite supervisors, 9.9 percent versus a target of 13 percent; nonwhite interns, 30.6 percent versus a target of 34.1 percent; number of newspapers with no nonwhite employees, 373 versus a target of 320; and number of newspapers at parity with their communities, 134 versus a target of 174. ASNE, "Minority Newsroom Employment Inches up in 2003," April 2, 2003, http://tinyurl.com/79stlkw (accessed March 7, 2012).

74. The 2009 performance levels on the remaining four benchmarks and their targets were these: percentage of nonwhite supervisors, 11.2 percent versus a target of 19 percent; percentage of nonwhite interns, 26.4 percent versus a target of 38.6 percent; number of newspapers with no nonwhites on staff, 458 versus a target of 230; and number of newspapers achieving local parity, 111 versus a target of 522. ASNE, "U.S. Newsroom Employment Declines."

75. Rosenhause interview. Ironically, race provided one rationale for including gender in the census. Sharon Rosenhause, who had helped organize the Diversity Dialogue in January 1998, said, "This was also a time when a lot of black women were moving up in newsrooms—much more so, I think, than black men—and that was another thing that I think people wanted to get a handle on."

76. Leroy Aarons and Sheila Murphy, "Lesbians and Gays in the Newsroom: 10 Years Later," Annenberg School of Communication, University of Southern California, 13, 25.

77. Ibid., 24.

78. Loren Ghiglione, "Ten Years Later, Survey Finds Progress, Failings," *American Editor* 813 (October 2000): 14.

79. Jose Alfredo Flores and Saba Bireda, "Minorities Make Small Gains in Daily

Newspapers," *ASNE Reporter,* April 12, 2000, http://tinyurl.com/8ayrnol (accessed March 7, 2012).

80. LaBarbara Bowman, "Retention in Focus after Diversity Drops," *American Editor* 818 (May–June 2001): 10.

81. Ibid.

82. Ibid.

83. "Advice on Keeping the Best and Brightest in Newsrooms," *Proceedings,* April 3–6, 2001: 134–44.

84. Ibid., 142.

85. National Association of Black Journalists, "Voices of Anger, Cries of Concern," April 2001, http://members.nabj.org/voices (accessed June 3, 2012).

86. Ibid.

87. Freedom Forum, "Newsroom Diversity: Meeting the Challenge," April 2000, quoted in Bowman, "Retention in Focus after Diversity Drops," 10.

88. Amy Leang, "Newsrooms Must Walk the 'Diversity' Walk, Not Just Talk the Talk," *ASNE Reporter,* April 6, 2001, http://tinyurl.com/6quqso6 (accessed December 17, 2001).

89. ASNE President Tim McGuire later wrote that complaints about his handling of the Capitol Steps incident, "for not apologizing for allowing the skit and for not walking out during the performance," came from the presidents of the Asian American Journalists Association and UNITY, a representative of the U.S. Civil Rights Commission, and a group of Asian journalists who were alumni of the *ASNE Reporter,* the convention newspaper. Tim J. McGuire, "Lessons in Sensitivity and Courage," *American Editor* 818 (May–June 2001): 2.

90. Lloyd Grove, "The Reliable Source," *Washington Post,* April 13, 2001, C3.

91. Marsha Ginsberg, "Crisis Inflames Bias Against Asians; Ethnic Stereotypes in Broadcast, Print Media Prompt Protests," *San Francisco Chronicle,* April 14, 2001, A1.

92. Ibid.

93. Bailon interview.

94. McGuire, "Lessons in Sensitivity and Courage," 2.

95. Tim McGuire, telephone interview with author, October 25, 2004.

96. Terry Greenberg, "Walking the Walk," *American Editor* 818 (May–June 2001): 13.

97. William Woo, "The Lessons to Learn from the Capitol Steps Skit," *American Editor* 818 (May–June 2001): 12.

98. Swanston interview.

99. Ernie Suggs, "Sidmel Estes-Sumpter, 1991–1993," National Association of Black Journalists, updated December 24, 2007, http://tinyurl.com/7pxlur4 (accessed March 7, 2012).

100. Tim McGuire, "Out of Adversity, Diversity Progresses," *American Editor* 823 (January–February 2002): 2.

101. Ibid.

102. Lawrence T. McGill, "Newsroom Diversity: Meeting the Challenge," Freedom Forum, 2001, 4.

103. Ibid., 6.

104. Ibid., 5.

105. Ibid., 2.

106. ASNE board minutes, November 9, 2001.

107. McGuire interview.

108. McGuire, "Out of Adversity, Diversity Progresses," 30.

109. Swanston interview; Dan Shelley, "Doing More for Diversity in the Newsroom," *Communicator* (July–August 2005): 16.

Afterword: Closing a Chapter of Newspaper History

1. Greg Moore, telephone interviews with author, July 20, 2005, and July 20, 2010.

2. In 2000, paid circulation for daily and Sunday newspapers was 59,421,000. In 2005, it would drop to 55,270,000 and by 2008, the number would decline to 49,115,000. Print ad expenditures, which were $48.7 billion in 2000, dropped to about $47.4 billion in 2005 and $24.8 billion in 2009. From 2005 to 2009, online advertising revenues increased from about $2.03 billion to $2.7 billion. Newspaper Association of America, "Trends and Numbers," Advertising Expenditures and Total Paid Circulation, http://tinyurl.com/6zzkjvb and http://tinyurl.com/79ywmbx (accessed March 9, 2012).

3. The Magazine Publishers of America also eliminated its diversity director's position in 2009. Richard Prince, "Diversity's Greatest Hits, 2009," Maynard Institute, December 30, 2009, http://tinyurl.com/828eqpv (accessed March 9, 2012).

4. Richard Prince, "ASNE Losing Diversity Director," Maynard Institute, May 18, 2009, http://tinyurl.com/7beh22t (accessed March 9, 2012).

5. Seaton interview, 2005.

6. Bill Dedman and Stephen K. Doig, "Newsroom Diversity Has Passed Its Peak at Most Newspapers, 1990–2005 Study Shows."

7. ASNE, "Decline in Newsroom Jobs Slows," April 11, 2010, http://tinyurl.com/882gsaa (accessed March 9, 2012).

8. Stinnett interview.

9. See, for example, ASNE board minutes, April 12, 1988: 1121.

10. Patterson interview.

11. "Analysis of the Vote," *ASNE Bulletin* 615 (May–June 1978): 25.

12. Tim McGuire, telephone interview with author, October 25, 2004.

13. McGowan specifically acknowledges the Bradley, John M. Olin, and Earhart Foundations as well as individuals affiliated with the Manhattan Institute, where McGowan was a senior fellow, and the Social Philosophy and Policy Center. William McGowan, *Coloring the News: How Crusading for Diversity Has Corrupted American Journalism* (San Francisco: Encounter Books, 2001), 250.

14. We are reminded here of George Lipsitz's assessment that "the power of whiteness depend(s) not only on white hegemony over separate racialized groups, but also on manipulating racial outsiders to fight against one another. . . ." *The Possessive Investment in Whiteness: How White People Profit from Identity Politics*, 3.

15. ASNE board minutes, April 8, 1978: 757.

16. Christine Schmitt, memo to author, January 9, 2004.

17. Bill Dedman, "Newspapers Fall Short of Diversity Goal," *Boston Globe*, April 11, 2002, http://boston.com/asne/ (accessed September 18, 2002).

18. Terry Adams and Johanna Cleary, "The Parity Paradox: Reader Response to Minority Newsroom Staffing," *Mass Communication & Society* 1, no. 9 (2006): 52.

19. "ASNE Conference Reframes Diversity Discussion," *This Week @ ASNE* (email newsletter), September 21, 2011. The conference, the second in a series, was hosted by the *New York Times* and underwritten by the *Times*, the Ford, Gannett, and McCormick Foundations, and the Philip L. Graham Fund.

20. UNITY Journalists of Color Inc., "NLGJA Enters UNITY Journalists' Alliance," September 19, 2011, http://tinyurl.com/3rqcgzl (accessed March 9, 2012), and Richard Price, "Unity Drops 'Journalists of Color,'" Maynard Institute for Journalism Education, April 17, 2012, http://tinyurl.com/d3rmcmb (accessed June 4, 2012). It should be noted that shortly before UNITY's decision to admit the NLGJA, the NABJ left the coalition because of a dispute over its business model. Tanzina Vega, "Black Journalists Group Leaves Minority Coalition," *New York Times*, April 11, 2011, http://tinyurl.com/ccevv28 (accessed June 4, 2012).

21. "ASNE Partners with RJI Research Organization on Newsroom Employment Census," *This Week @ ASNE* (email newsletter), October 19, 2011.

22. Charlotte Hall, email to ASNE members, December 16, 2008.

Index

Note: Illustrations are found following page 106 and are represented in *italics* as *106.1, 106.2,* etc.

GWYNETH MELLINGER is a professor and chair of the Department of Mass Media and Visual Arts at Baker University.

THE HISTORY OF COMMUNICATION

Selling Free Enterprise: The Business Assault on Labor and Liberalism, 1945–60 *Elizabeth A. Fones-Wolf*

Last Rights: Revisiting *Four Theories of the Press* *Edited by John C. Nerone*

"We Called Each Other Comrade": Charles H. Kerr & Company, Radical Publishers *Allen Ruff*

WCFL, Chicago's Voice of Labor, 1926–78 *Nathan Godfried*

Taking the Risk Out of Democracy: Corporate Propaganda versus Freedom and Liberty *Alex Carey; edited by Andrew Lohrey*

Media, Market, and Democracy in China: Between the Party Line and the Bottom Line *Yuezhi Zhao*

Print Culture in a Diverse America *Edited by James P. Danky and Wayne A. Wiegand*

The Newspaper Indian: Native American Identity in the Press, 1820–90 *John M. Coward*

E. W. Scripps and the Business of Newspapers *Gerald J. Baldasty*

Picturing the Past: Media, History, and Photography *Edited by Bonnie Brennen and Hanno Hardt*

Rich Media, Poor Democracy: Communication Politics in Dubious Times *Robert W. McChesney*

Silencing the Opposition: Antinuclear Movements and the Media in the Cold War *Andrew Rojecki*

Citizen Critics: Literary Public Spheres *Rosa A. Eberly*

Communities of Journalism: A History of American Newspapers and Their Readers *David Paul Nord*

From Yahweh to Yahoo!: The Religious Roots of the Secular Press *Doug Underwood*

The Struggle for Control of Global Communication: The Formative Century *Jill Hills*

Fanatics and Fire-eaters: Newspapers and the Coming of the Civil War *Lorman A. Ratner and Dwight L. Teeter Jr.*

Media Power in Central America *Rick Rockwell and Noreene Janus*

The Consumer Trap: Big Business Marketing in American Life *Michael Dawson*

How Free Can the Press Be? *Randall P. Bezanson*

Cultural Politics and the Mass Media: Alaska Native Voices *Patrick J. Daley and Beverly A. James*

Journalism in the Movies *Matthew C. Ehrlich*

Democracy, Inc.: The Press and Law in the Corporate Rationalization of the Public Sphere *David S. Allen*

Investigated Reporting: Muckrakers, Regulators, and the Struggle over Television Documentary *Chad Raphael*

Women Making News: Gender and the Women's Periodical Press in Britain *Michelle Tusan*

Advertising on Trial: Consumer Activism and Corporate Public Relations in the 1930s *Inger Stole*

Speech Rights in America: The First Amendment, Democracy, and the Media
Laura Stein
Freedom from Advertising: E. W. Scripps's Chicago Experiment *Duane C. S. Stoltzfus*
Waves of Opposition: The Struggle for Democratic Radio, 1933–58
Elizabeth Fones-Wolf
Prologue to a Farce: Democracy and Communication in America *Mark Lloyd*
Outside the Box: Corporate Media, Globalization, and the UPS Strike *Deepa Kumar*
The Scripps Newspapers Go to War, 1914–1918 *Dale Zacher*
Telecommunications and Empire *Jill Hills*
Everything Was Better in America: Print Culture in the Great Depression
David Welky
Normative Theories of the Media *Clifford G. Christians, Theodore L. Glasser, Denis McQuail, Kaarle Nordenstreng, Robert A. White*
Radio's Hidden Voice: The Origins of Public Broadcasting in the United States
Hugh Richard Slotten
Muting Israeli Democracy: How Media and Cultural Policy Undermine Free Expression *Amit M. Schejter*
Key Concepts in Critical Cultural Studies *Edited by Linda Steiner and Clifford Christians*
Refiguring Mass Communication: A History *Peter Simonson*
Radio Utopia: Postwar Audio Documentary in the Public Interest *Matthew C. Ehrlich*
Chronicling Trauma: Journalists and Writers on Violence and Loss *Doug Underwood*
Saving the World: A Brief History of Communication for Development and Social Change *Emile G. McAnany*
The Rise and Fall of Early American Magazine Culture *Jared Gardner*
Equal Time: Television and the Civil Rights Movement *Aniko Bodroghkozy*
Advertising at War: Business, Consumers, and Government in the 1940s
Inger L. Stole
Media Capital: Architecture and Communications in New York City *Aurora Wallace*
Chasing Newsroom Diversity: From Jim Crow to Affirmative Action
Gwyneth Mellinger

The University of Illinois Press
is a founding member of the
Association of American University Presses.

Composed in 10.5/13 Minion Pro
with Meta display
by Celia Shapland
at the University of Illinois Press
Manufactured by Thomson-Shore, Inc.
University of Illinois Press

1325 South Oak Street
Champaign, IL 61820-6903
www.press.uillinois.edu